Creating

Wealth

Through
Probate

Creating Wealth Through Probate

The Best-Kept Secret in Real Estate Investing

James G. Banks

Dearborn™
Trade Publishing
A **Kaplan Professional** Company

This publication is designed to provide accurate and authoritative information in regard to the subject matter covered. It is sold with the understanding that the publisher is not engaged in rendering legal, accounting, or other professional service. If legal advice or other expert assistance is required, the services of a competent professional should be sought.

Vice President and Publisher: Cynthia A. Zigmund
Acquisitions Editor: Mary B. Good
Senior Project Editor: Trey Thoelcke
Interior Design: Lucy Jenkins
Cover Design: DePinto Design
Typesetting: Elizabeth Pitts

Published by Dearborn Trade Publishing
A Kaplan Professional Company

Printed in the United States of America

05 06 07 10 9 8 7 6 5 4 3 2 1

Library of Congress Cataloging-in-Publication Data

Banks, James G. (James Garfield), 1946–
    Creating wealth through probate : the best-kept secret in real estate investing / James G. Banks.
        p. cm.
    Includes index.
    ISBN 1-4195-0514-9
1. Real estate investment—United States. 2. Real property—United States—Purchasing. 3. Probate law and practice—United States. I. Title.
    HD255.B36 2005
    332.63'24—dc22

                                                          2004029801

Contents

INTRODUCTION TO PROBATE 101

Probate is the legal process by which, when someone dies, his or her assets are distributed. These assets are comprised of real property—homes, commercial buildings, agricultural land, raw land, apartments—and personal property, which includes vehicles, furniture, jewelry, clothing, and knick-knacks down to the World's Fair paperweight that sat on Uncle Ed's desk.

Probate real estate investors, what few there are, move in a world unlike any other. Essentially, they buy assets and help settle estates, and they make a healthy profit doing it. But aside from the obvious profit potential of buying a house or other piece of real estate for 30 percent or more off market value and reselling it at fair market value, these investors also invest in the buying and selling of personal property, where treasures lie waiting to be discovered.

Occasionally, a story arising from probate makes the newspaper. You've seen them. An unsuspecting art lover buys a watercolor painting for $10 because she likes the frame, and discovers a priceless masterpiece hiding underneath. A home purchaser climbing through the attic of his new acquisition opens a chest and finds a sheaf of letters from Abraham Lincoln. The news article never mentions the word *probate*, but it will likely tell you these "finds" were purchased at an estate sale, which is part of the probate process.

Let me tell you the ultimate estate sale story. Around 400 BC, Chinese philosopher Lao Tzu had his nephew implant a small amulet depicting the faces of Buddha, Confucius, and himself into a clam. The clam formed a pearl and the philosopher's descendents reimplanted it over and over into bigger clams, creating an ever larger pearl containing the images. During the Ming Dynasty (1368-1644), while being transported through a storm, the pearl was lost in a shipwreck.

In 1934, the giant pearl was found in the mud of a Philippine river and brought to a tribal chief. Five years later, the chief presented it to archaeologist Wilburn Cobb as a gift for curing the chief's son of malaria. When Dr. Cobb died in 1980, a Beverly Hills investor bought the pearl from the Cobb estate *during the probate process* for $200,000. In 1990, the 14-pound, football-sized pearl was valued at $42 million by the San Francisco Gem Institute. Hoffman reportedly sold it in 1999 for $25 million, 125 times what he paid for it.

Would you be happy with that kind of return on investment? If your answer is no, then return this book for a refund. It's not for you.

There is more opportunity for achieving wealth in probate than in any other type of investment. Why? Because, among other reasons, there are more than 5.7 million unsettled probate cases every hour of every day. That amounts to over $3 *trillion* in probated assets available every hour of every day—assets that people want to get rid of! All other investment vehicles combined don't add up to that volume of opportunities! Savvy probate investors, what few there are, have virtually no competition in finding and buying real property and personal property out of probate to turn around and sell for enormous profit.

Almost anybody who has ever even dabbled in real estate as an investment has pursued a foreclosure property. An article in the May 11, 2003, issue of the *Los Angeles Times* Real Estate Section discussed foreclosures in California. In that state alone there are over 44 times more probates than there are foreclosures. Bidding on a foreclosure is a great way to meet people, but not a way to make money, because of too much competition. Look at these two properties for sale.

PROPERTY A

PROPERTY B
8229 James Drive

Which property is the easier to locate? Which is going to be found by virtually any real estate investor? Which will get more exposure in the real estate market? Which will sell for close to its fair market value?

And which would you buy below fair market value?

Of all the investment properties I've purchased over the past 34 years, none had a published or listed address. Not one had an address in print that could be tracked down by a conventional real estate investor. I had no competition, and I bought every property for at least 30 percent below fair market value.

Do *you* want to compete with every Tom, Dick, or Mary, or do you want to compete against nobody?

If you buy probate properties correctly, you will buy real estate with no competition, because it has never been exposed to the public. For real estate investors today, there's nothing, *nothing* better than probate!

It's never too soon to start. My youngest student was a 19-year-old boy from San Antonio who made $14,000 on a probate real estate deal. *Anybody* can do this if they know how!

I'm the only national speaker on probate. There's no book in bookstores you can buy on how to buy real estate out of probate and build your wealth. Nothing in any library. Nothing in any law school or even real estate course that can walk you step by step through buying real and personal property through probate. No wonder it's a wide-open field.

For years, every time I've visited the county assessor's office to check out leads and do my probate homework, I've always been alone! I used to wonder, where are all the other real estate investors? Then I realized they were standing in crowds with other investors trying to buy properties everybody else wanted. Or they were out driving all over town looking for For Sale by Owner signs. Or scanning the classifieds for "motivated" sellers everyone else was calling too.

I told you about the giant pearl. Sure, not every house has a treasure hiding in the attic—usually just cobwebs and musty remnants of a long life. But finding and buying personal property in probate can be a real adventure—a *profitable* adventure. Just like my student from Evanston, Illinois.

We'll call her "Dolly," because she bought 25 antique dolls for $500 out of probate. Then she sold them wholesale to an antique dealer for $65,000 cash! Hey, whether it's real or personal property, one probate deal can equal a year's salary! Everything in an antique store comes out of probate.

Probate investing is the perfect business. You need no employees, pay no payroll taxes or workers comp, and work when and as often as you want.

I urge you to read this book carefully. In this one book, I've packed more than 30 years of information, tips, forms, and secrets about buying assets out of probate and reselling it for profit. My three-day workshop is endorsed by the state of California, and in most states, if you're a real estate agent or broker, you get 15 hours of continuing education credit on your real estate license.

The following examples illustrate the good, the bad, and the ugly in the world of probate.

- *A Million in* Magnolia Blossoms. Carl Rice was about to lose his job, but he still went to an estate sale in Tucson at the home of a Martha Nelson who had just died at age 94, and bought two floral paintings for $60. It had been his hobby to buy estate art in the hope the next one he bought would be a "lost master" worth big money. In view of their dire financial condition, however, his wife Anne thought he must be crazy. Six months later, Carl and Anne learned that the paintings were originals by the 19th-century artist Martin Johnson Heade. One of the paintings, *Magnolia Blossoms,* subsequently sold at a New York auction house for $937,500.
- *The Secret of the Cast Iron Stove.* It was Bob's bad luck he didn't buy the home of Mary McGinnis. Mary, of Philadelphia, lived alone for years, wore cheap clothes, and lived in a run-down house with no heat, TV, or even a radio. Even at age 87, she rode the bus every day to get free meals at a local senior center. At her death she left $1.4 million to her parish church for a scholarship fund. Then her pastor, visiting her home, happened into the kitchen and discovered $500,000 in bonds and cash stuffed in a tin box inside her old-fashioned cast-iron stove.
- *Early American Table Makes This American Rich!* Claire Weigand, a retired schoolteacher, came across a small rickety table at a garage sale, shelled out $25, and took it home. When she examined it more closely, she discovered a delicate pattern of inlaid ribbons and flowers, and other fine touches that made her curious. Finally, she took the table to PBS's *Antique Roadshow* for a free appraisal. The unassuming table turned out to be an original work by John Seymour, a wood craftsman in post-Revolutionary Boston. It was appraised to have a value of between $200,000 and $300,000. She took

the table to New York, to Sotheby's Americana auction, and sold it for $490,000, a record for Boston furniture from the Federal period.

- *A Judge of Poor Character . . . and His Wife.* In Tulsa a few years ago, a former district judge and his wife were charged with 23 counts of felony for embezzling more than $100,000 from a 90-year-old widow. Prior to becoming a judge, this servant of the people had been an attorney for the City of Tulsa and a probate attorney. He had prepared the will of an associate, another judge, and after the associate died in 1994, he prepared a trust for the widow's estate, amending it later to make himself and his wife trustees. Dipping into the widow's funds, the judge and his wife bought themselves season hockey tickets, clothing, and other personal items, and paid the private school tuition for their children. Like others who are familiar with the labyrinth of probate, the judge used his knowledge to create a complex paper cover for the couple's theft. A next-door neighbor blew the whistle on the judge when she saw furniture being removed from the widow's house and became concerned enough to notify police.

- *Crooked Lawyer Goes Straight . . . to Jail–Three Times!* Several years ago in Detroit, a certain probate lawyer named Douglas Elliard made it his practice to defraud clients of probate property, taking more than $225,000 from six probate clients over a period of years. He was apprehended, arrested, tried, and convicted. In addition to paying back others, was ordered to repay $5,000 to the estate of Connie Sabbath and surrender a deed to a seven-acre lakeside vacation home. Elliard refused, was arrested and booked into jail. He then promised to repay the estate and was released. He still did not make restitution, keeping the $5,000. The following week he was arrested and jailed again. Once more he promised to repay the $5,000 but didn't, so it was back to jail for Elliard for a third time. All the while, his primary concern was that his conviction for embezzlement might ruin his reputation and get him disbarred in Michigan. We never learned whether the estate got its $5,000 and Elliard his freedom.

- *Bookkeeper Embezzles $750,000 from 23 Estates. At Least.* You don't have to be a lawyer to be an embezzler in Riverside, California. Bonnie Cambalik, a court-appointed conservator, was charged with the embezzlement of more than $750,000 from the estates of 23 people who were too old or infirm to handle their own financial affairs. Also charged was Cambalik's lawyer, Mike Molloy, who had attested to the accuracy of her estate management. Since her appointment as a conservator, she had managed the estates of some 300 mentally incompetent individuals, but the statute of limitations had elapsed for prosecuting most of Cambalik's theft.

As you can already see, probate is filled with spellbinding tales and colorful characters. You'll meet more of them in Chapter 7. Right now, let me further introduce you to probate real estate investing and the potential it holds for earning you comfortable wealth.

CreatingWealthThroughProbate.com
jamesgbanks@creatingwealththroughprobate.com

This book is the compilation of more than 30 years of my personal experience in probate real estate. To list all the people who contributed to that wealth of experience would be impossible. Just as I've learned from my own successes and failures, I've tried to learn from the experiences of others, including my own students, who often went out and did things wrong before they did things right. I thank them for that.

In fact, I would be amiss not to acknowledge all those students over the years, seminar attendees whose sharp minds and sometimes insightful questions forced me to keep my skills and techniques honed and current in the probate real estate industry.

We who invest in real estate, stocks, or options are many times drawn into the seminar business, training thousands of others in the arts of making money much the same way we have. Over the years, several of those associates in the seminar business stand out as having contributed to my platform marketing skills. They include real estate gurus Robert Allen and Russ Whitney, men who have become real estate investing legends and, thanks to the magic of TV infomercials, are household synonyms for "no money down." In addition, Howard Ruff taught me a great deal about marketing and the selling strategies that reveal to audiences their need to get into personal investing.

More immediately, I want to thank Mary Good, acquisitions editor at Dearborn Trade Publishing, who worked patiently with me through the book birthing process. Finally, special thanks go to Florida freelance writer Jim Bullard, who took several pounds and decades of dog-eared clippings and almost legible notes, and organized them into what would become this book.

No one goes to college to learn how to invest. Sure, you can get a wealth of theoretical business and financial knowledge. You can learn all about the Federal Reserve and interest rates and the nature of stocks and bonds. But try to find in any college catalog a course called "Building Your Wealth," or "How to Invest to Retire a Millionaire." Imagine a three-hour course called "Fixer-Uppers—The Road to Early Retirement." Such courses would be virtual heresy to academicians for whom theory is the only reality, professors whose business experience in the trenches of free enterprise—if any—may have ended years ago.

Those courses would also be filled to the walls.

Like virtually all Americans, my formal education had nothing to do with real estate. At the time, to my knowledge, no courses on real estate even existed. I graduated with a major in math and a teaching credential from Indiana University. I immediately moved to California and did some MBA work at the University of Southern California. I worked five years in the computer industry when there was no money in it at NCR. Then I manufactured brass, gold-plated Christmas ornaments for a while. Finally, I entered law school, and while studying to become a lawyer I got my real estate license and became a real estate broker.

By 1978, still in law school, I was all set to make my fortune as a real estate investor.

That was before the age of TV infomercials and national workshop weekends that cost thousands and drew tens of thousands of wannabe millionaires. Even then, "flipping" houses was, as it is today, considered by many a great way to build wealth. Including me. After all, conventional thinking says that owning real estate drives your net worth sky high!

But when you own ten houses with an average fair market value of $100,000, does that make you a millionaire? No! You only own a million dollars worth of houses. At least you may have ten times the equity you had when you just owned one house. Hopefully!

Before you launch into this book on real estate investing through probate, let me make it absolutely clear that thousands of Americans have made comfortable livings for themselves buying real estate below fair market value. They all do it about the same way. They prowl the streets, the classifieds, and title listings to find homes to buy in foreclosure, through real estate agents, from "motivated sellers," or through tax sales. They chase down For Sale by Owner (FSBO) signs, put "Will Buy Your House for Cash" signs on utility poles—whatever it takes to buy a house below fair market value.

I was ready to join the hunt when a friend of mine suggested I look for real estate properties tied up in probate. "Probate? What's probate?" I asked.

"Look," my friend said, "People die every day. They leave houses their grown kids don't want. They leave personal property the kids don't have room for or give a hoot about, the stuff of estate sales and garage sales. Whether or not there's a will, all that property is what they call an *estate*. And it goes into probate."

My friend, who was already a real estate broker, prompted me and two other friends to purchase a house out of probate. He would simply act as broker on the deal. He graciously led us through one purchase, and then another. On my second deal, though, I discovered that, serving as our broker, he was making more money than I was.

I figured out quickly that I wanted to be my own broker, concentrating on probate properties, so I took the broker's course and got my license. Quicker than I could have imagined I was the proud owner of a dismal 50-foot-by-50-foot cracker box that I had bought for $35,000—an incredible 68 percent below fair market value! I took a picture of it, and to this day I show my audiences the sad, humble house that was the beginning of a fascinating and lucrative career.

If there was ever a fixer-upper—or *fixer*—that little house was it. Being new to all this, I decided to go over one Saturday, take up the kitchen linoleum myself and put in a nice tile. I discovered that linoleum doesn't like to come up, nor does tile fit neatly against every wall and into every corner. I never did the labor on a fixer-upper again.

After a few coats of paint and some more cosmetic touches, I sold that starter bungalow for $95,000. My check at closing, for about $57,500, was an epiphany for me. The clouds parted and the message seemed to come from on high: "Jim, probate real estate investing is your life's calling."

I've never regretted that decision. Every deal excites me because every deal is different. Because of the enormity of probate cases stuck in the probate process across the country, there are enough properties for everyone. In fact, there are close to 6 million unsettled probates available every minute of every day, year after year. I tell my workshop students that they will never have competition from anyone, including me, because 99 percent of all real estate investors do not even know about probate real estate. They buy their properties the traditional ways—foreclosures, tax sales, FSBOs, motivated sellers.

A purpose of this book, then, is to answer your questions, the same questions I once asked: "What is probate?" "How can I purchase real estate and personal property sitting in probate—and at well below fair market value? How does it beat traditional real estate purchases hands down?"

My larger aim is to open your eyes, to expand your investing horizon, and to get you excited about the best-kept secret in investing. There is no better investment vehicle than probate. Over

$3 trillion (nine zeroes) in assets are out there all the time. I know for a fact—and I've built my own personal wealth on this knowledge—that probate real estate is a gold mine of wealth-building opportunities. Sometimes I think I'm the only prospector who knows about it! Sure, foreclosure buying can sometimes be a gold mine too, but that mine is so crowded with frantic prospectors fresh from a three-day real estate seminar that you're likely to get bonked on the head by some other guy's pick.

Here's some sad news. Just since you began reading this book, several more people in your community have passed away. Some new probates are about to begin, and the recipients will shortly be asking themselves, "What the heck are we gonna do with Daddy's old house? It's gonna be in probate for years, and we still have to make the payments! What about all that old furniture? Aw, man...."

Here's the good news. That's a cry for help. So get busy!

Below are two examples of probate properties I have done. They illustrate the limitless profit potential in probate. Both of these were single-family residences, but there are all types of real estate in probate: apartments, commercial, industrial, raw land, farmland, ranch land, and condos.

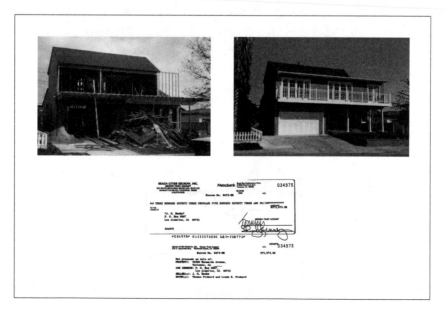

FREE OFFER

Occasionally, I publish a newsletter discussing probate and real estate trends and patterns. If you wish to receive the next one FREE, just e-mail me at the address below and provide a postal or e-mail address so I can send it to you.

CreatingWealthThroughProbate.com
jamesgbanks@creatingwealththroughprobate.com

1

PROBATE

The Lawyer's Gold Mine

Let's start this first chapter by answering the first question I had, and probably your first question. What is probate?

Probate is the term for the legal process of disposing of the estate of a deceased individual or *decedent*. Specifically, probate does the following:

- Proves in court that a decedent's will is valid
- Pays debts and taxes incurred by the decedent in his or her lifetime, including monthly mortgage payments on the old homestead
- Distributes the remaining property among people as the will directs—or among surviving members of the family and other claimants according to the judgment of the court

A WILL DOESN'T AVOID PROBATE—IT *INITIATES* IT

It doesn't matter whether the late owner has a will, estates must go through the probate process. Most states allow a certain amount of property to pass free of, or be exempted from, probate, or at least through a simplified probate procedure. In some states, you can exempt up to $100,000 of property from the probate process. These are called *small estates* or *summary estates*. (See the Glossary in this book for definitions of probate-related terms.) There's also a simple procedure for transferring any property left to a surviving spouse. In addition, property provided for outside the deceased's will, through a living trust or joint tenancy for example, is not subject to probate or IRS taxes. (See your estate planner for specifics.)

> *"A person who leaves a will ought to come*
> *back and see what a mess they left."*
> WILL ROGERS

Real life is not *Judge Judy* or *Court TV.* Because of the enormous volume—almost two million each year—and the enormous backlog of cases handled by the judicial system, probate cases usually take on average about three years to settle. Too long for loving but eager heirs.

THE TRUTH ABOUT PROBATE

Beyond simply knowing the definition of probate, you must truly understand probate. Over my two-plus decades of buying real estate through probate, and dealing with attorneys and probate judges, I have long since come to the realization that the judicial system exists for two reasons—to make lawyers money and to set up a statute of limitations. There is no third!

Probate is the poster child for that statement.

You may be thinking I have a prejudice against lawyers. Well, the term *prejudice* means, literally, "prejudged." I haven't prejudged anybody. My antipathy for probate lawyers comes from countless true-life experiences.

In fact, let me tell you about one gentlemen, age 92 at this writing, who in my opinion should be the poster boy for Probate Lawyers Under No Duty of Ethics or Responsibility (PLUNDER). His name is J. Love, a retired cattleman living in Texas. Here are excerpts from the text of a letter he wrote me several years ago, the handwritten original of which I keep to read to my workshops.

Jim Banks:

Please excuse my shorthand. I am writing on my knee in a big easy chair . . . I am a victim, past 81, but going strong and aim to live to age 107, at which time I want a jealous lover to shoot me dead.

For some 9 years, I have been in probate court. We had a million in cash in the bank when my dear wife of some 46 years went away because of Alzheimer's. The probate court cost us about $800,000 of that $1 million . . . . I am writing a book telling about my fate: how they came to my office—two lawyers, two mail clerks, and a bank trust officer—and advised they were gathering up things that made up the estate.

Ignorantly, I said help yourself. My lawyer was there too, but he said, "Let's try to get along with them as this is their first move." They took or seized what turned out to be 1,176 files . . . They periodically returned them to me over a period of about one year. They absolutely refused to give me a receipt or make a list at the time they took them. . . . Well, about the first week upon going through the files, one was found with a certificate for 125,000 shares of stock, so they put that on the inventory quickly. I contested and told them to keep looking and they would find a file showing I had borrowed every cent to pay for the stock long after [my wife's] date of death. A long tussle ended in them admitting the stock was no part of the estate. However, I was told that I just might be in debt to the estate, so they would hold the stock as security. (They already had half a million in cash, declared by their lawyer to be my personal property, and a log of tax-free bonds, etc.) They took the stock out of my name, placed it in the name of Bank of America, and it was held away from me for more than four years.

[It took] nine years for a short two-page will costing me $800,000 to probate. [I'd been] working, saving, sweating out there on horseback for years . . . then to see it go to people I didn't even know—lawyers and CPAs. I'm just an ordinary cattleman, businessman too. Been on two bank boards when banks were banks. Been a guest in the Governor's Mansion and the White House, and now I am a victim.

While they were holding my stock, it went down $179,000 and while they were holding half a million dollars cash, I lost $4.5 million in real estate as I could not meet some notes.

Well, I hope you can get the message over to someone to keep them out of trouble. Good luck.

J. Love

I have visited Mr. Love twice. He now lives in a modest, middle-class home in a nondescript neighborhood. A weathered, rusted out 1960 Lincoln Continental sits out front. Oh, what happened to his $800,000? It turns out that it was split among the bank's attorney, the probate attorney, and the probate judge. In 2003, Jack's housekeeper for 15 years told me she ran into the bank attorney out in town. He laughed when he told her that they all "referred to the Love estate as the 'Love Boat,' because everybody took a ride."

In 1975, wealthy philanthropist Beryl Buck died and left a clearly stated will leaving her entire estate to the Buck Foundation, an organization that cared for the needy of Marin County, California. If you're at all familiar with Marin County, your first reaction is, "They have needy in Marin County?" Lazing fashionably in the hills north of San Francisco, it's probably among the top five wealthiest counties in the country.

That's what subsequent Foundation trustees thought as well, and they were supported by neighboring counties, especially in blue-collar Oakland, who shared the belief that the late Beryl Buck was too shortsighted in her generosity. Meanwhile, others on the Foundation board wanted to honor Beryl's will to the letter, keeping all the funds in Marin County.

In 1984, as is the custom when millions of dollars are at stake, everyone hired high-priced attorneys. To complicate matters further, four years after Beryl's death, Shell Oil had bought Belridge Oil reserves, of which she had owned 7 percent. Her millions came to a total, in 1970s dollars, of $260 million. Greed escalated exponentially.

This epic legal struggle became known at the "Super Bowl of Probate." To make a long story mercifully short, this case was finally settled in the fall of 1989, some 14 years after Beryl's passing. The Foundation lost its case, and its mandate to distribute the Buck estate funds according to the clearly expressed wishes of Beryl Buck. Management of the estate was turned over to a community-based foundation in Marin County. Three different law firms were awarded a total of $8.8 million. In addition, the Buck Foundation had to pay $3 million in "transition fees" for lawyers to move the funds to the new foundation. In fact, the law firm that lost the case for the Foundation was awarded $3.3 million for its trouble.

By way of perspective, if every law firm worked 24 hours a day, 7 days a week for the five years between initial filings and court settlement—1984 through 1989—that would add up to 43,800 nonstop hours. Or $200.91 per hour, totaling $8.8 million. You can bet there were some lavish law firm Christmas parties that December!

The rich and famous, of course, are larger, brighter targets of opportunity. When Elvis Presley died in 1977, he left an estate valued at $10.2 million. He left a wife and small daughter, a father, a small sycophantic brigade of Tennessee "good ole boys," and dozens of claims of varying credence against his estate. As a result, probate took several years and $7.4 million of the Presley estate, or approximately 72.5 percent. Elvis needn't have worried, however. The Elvis industry that grew up around his Graceland home in Memphis, hundreds of rereleases, and assorted franchise rights have left Elvis worth more than 20 times what he was when he was alive.

When John D. Rockefeller, Sr., the old man, died in 1937, he left a personal fortune of almost $30 million, which he bequeathed to the Rockefeller Foundation, and to one granddaughter among many. As a result, probate attorneys eventually cost his estate $17.2 million, or 64 percent of the Rockefeller estate.

A more contemporary probate case involved the estate of singer Rick Nelson, who died in 1986. He left a modest estate of $744,400, yet it took 11 years to settle. By 1997, the estate had been milked of $238,200, or a little over 32 percent of the original value.

Adlai Stevenson was a distinguished statesman, U.S. ambassador to the United Nations, and twice the Democratic presidential nominee. He died leaving a gross estate valued at $1,398,236. His will went to probate, which ate up $615,670. When the legal smoke cleared, the value of his estate amounted to only $765,341—a 44 percent shrinkage of that estate.

Marilyn Monroe died in 1962, leaving an estate of $819,176. She left that entire estate to her longtime friend, director Lee Strasburg. Yet it took a record 18 years for her will to clear probate. Taxes and other settlement costs took $448,750 and lawyers got about $270,000, so her net estate was reduced to about $101,000, or 12.3 percent of the original estate.

Meanwhile, Strasburg himself died, leaving everything in his estate to his second wife. Over the years, Marilyn's estate has profited from her legend—products, photos, use of her name—to the tune of about $4 million a year. The final irony is that Marilyn's multi-million-dollar legacy is going to a woman she never knew!

Even the estates of those with less fame and fewer assets have suffered. Remember Fred Mertz in *I Love Lucy*? That was actor

William Frawley. During his retirement years—Frawley lived to almost 80—his career earnings dwindled so that when he died in 1966 his estate was valued at just $92,446. Even adjusting for inflation, that's probably less than many of us will leave. Nevertheless, the cost of probate took almost $46,000, or approximately 49 percent of his modest estate.

For your further enlightenment, Appendix J is a surprising list of other notables whose estates have left probate attorneys holding the bag . . . of cash.

In reality, of course, most of us are not Beryl Buck or any of the Rockefellers. In a cosmetic attempt to regulate more down-to-earth probate work, most states have established fee guidelines for legal costs of probate. At first glance, these fee structures, pegged at around 4 to 5 percent of probate assets, seem fair and reasonable. Some states have established the minimum cost of probate for various asset levels—not the maximum. That means you must be charged at least that much, so you don't take advantage of your poor probate lawyer. The following is an excerpt from that probate fee schedule:

Probate Assets	Minimum Probate Fees
$ 100,000	$ 8,000
200,000	14,000
400,000	22,000
700,000	34,000
800,000	38,000
1,000,000	46,000
2,000,000	66,000
4,000,000	106,000

As is true in every state, the above chart does not include "extraordinary fees" granted by the court during probate. Some examples of such fees are for handling sales of assets, preparation of death tax return (Form 706), and especially litigation expenses in the event some portion of the will is contested. Now, we may be talking fees ranging from 6 to 10 percent, or more, of probate assets. (For a state-by-state breakdown of statutory limitations on probate fees and administrator/executor commissions, see Appendix C.)

Then add to that the possibility that the decedent owned property in one or more other states. Now we're talking multiple probates!

When eccentric billionaire Howard Hughes died in 1976, he left an estate estimated at more than $2 billion. Because Hughes had died in a private jet somewhere in the air between Mexico and Texas, and there was no true residence, Texas, California, and Nevada began a long legal battle to determine which state was his legal domicile, and therefore able to collect hundreds of millions in inheritance taxes. By 1983, seven years later, Texas and California had spent $4 million in legal fees preparing their cases. In addition, 22 various cousins and 386 other potential heirs paid lawyers additional millions trying to get their slice of the Hughes pie. The case was settled the next year, with the inheritance being divided among the 22 cousins and the Howard Hughes Medical Center.

Then there's Hughes's Summa Corporation, the holding company that owned five Nevada casinos; real estate in California, Texas, Nevada, and other states; and Hughes Helicopter. Even now, well into the next century after Hughes died, Summa Corporation is still tangled in litigation that stems from his in-the-air death more than 20 years ago!

No wonder lawyers like to stand close to the Howard Hughes case. They get money all over them! I highly recommend you get a copy of *The Money: The Battle for Howard Hughes's Billions,* by James Phelan and Lewis Chester. If you like a good story about naked, nail-clawing greed, you'll love this one!

According to Maria Bezaire, an attorney who specializes in probate avoidance, the biggest issue is "cold, hard cash." She cites a prototype example that illustrates how lawyers can use the probate process to undermine the best intentions expressed in the wills of two parents.

Let's say they want to leave that home to their children, and let's say that the home has an $80,000 mortgage on it. In order to leave that home to the children, the children are going to have to pay probate fees based on the full $100,000 value of the house. They're going to have to pay at least $6,700 in probate fees. If the kids can't reach in their own pockets and come up with that $6,700, then the property will have to be sold in order to pay the probate costs.

The kids may want to keep the house and even live in it, but they have no choice. They must sell, and they also have to pay about 8 percent of the selling price in closing costs.

Bottom line? The family loses the house and the lawyer walks away with almost $7,000, not including fees based on the value of other personal property and other obscure fees. Not a bad day's work, especially when the lawyer's paralegal staff probably did all the research and prepared all the documents.

Of course, the opportunity for white-collar crime always shadows the legal profession. A few years ago, a county chief probate judge ordered an investigation into cases handled by a local law firm whose senior partner had prepared numerous wills for elderly residents of Leisure World, a large, upscale retirement community. It seems that the partner, James D. Gunderson, was making himself the recipient of millions of dollars in cash, stock, and real estate. In November 1992, a Superior Court judge ordered an investigation in numerous cases where Gunderson had served as an attorney for elderly clients. One case of special interest focused on $3.5 million Gunderson had paid himself out of the estate of Merrill Miller, a 98-year-old Leisure World resident.

In another case, Gunderson had persuaded a judge to name him legal guardian of a Canadian woman suffering from senile dementia and incapable of managing her financial affairs. After becoming her conservator, he drafted a new will that gave him the majority of her estate—$250,000 in AT&T stock! The same lawyer also received $3.5 million in stock from one estate and a 315-acre Fresno farm from another.

The wheels of justice turn slowly in the world of probate, and it wasn't until April 1998, almost six years later, that an Appeals Court judge upheld a lower court order for Gunderson to pay back the $3.5 million to Miller's estate, plus $500,000 in interest.

The point is that there is no limit to the unconscionable greed exhibited by many lawyers who know how to navigate through probate. It is complex beyond the comprehension of virtually all Americans and most attorneys, and filled with a vast potential for wealth that tempts too many of those who practice law to break it.

Though much of the cost of probate is initiated by lawyers, family members and others who feel they've gotten the short end of a "legal and binding" can also get in on the act. In years past, sons or daughters might disagree with Dad's apportionment of his estate, but grumbling disappointment was the extent of their reaction.

In more recent years, cohesion of the family has been watered down, particularly as younger generations move away to other parts of the country. A result of that is that the "sacred memory" of Dad or Grandma fades in the glare of the assets he or she left behind. There is far less respect for the dead, and especially what "Dad would have wanted if he were alive." The more prevailing attitude seems to be, "Dad's gone, and we're still here, so give me what I think is rightfully mine or else."

Women, particularly, are more likely to contest a will during probate. In the past, the family business was left to the son or sons to manage, and the daughter or daughters were bequeathed other, less valuable assets. No more. Women want the half or third of the estate they feel they're due by means of an equitable split, and they're more likely than ever to call an attorney to get it.

It has been said that lawyers win every probate case—and take their winnings to the bank. How has probate been such an unbridled gold mine for lawyers for so many years? There are several reasons.

First, of course, the probate judges who adjudicate probate cases are lawyers themselves. Probate court is the most unsupervised bench in the court system. Judges looking toward retirement are often rewarded with a probate judgeship. The fringe benefits to having your buddies present you with probate petitions relating to the disposal of millions so you can rule sympathetically are formidable.

Second, the sheer volume. There are almost two million probates every year, and the number is growing. There is no way the judge and/or court clerk can do a detailed analysis of each probate case, even if they wanted to.

Third, all probate work is handled, not at the federal or state level, but at the county level. There is no recourse to a higher court. You can forget writing the State Attorney General, who doesn't care what goes on in your county probate court. There's simply no one to protect the estate, which becomes an unsupervised slush fund.

Fourth, anybody can contest a will in probate. Anybody—a relative, a friend, a business associate, an employee—can hire a lawyer and bring the progress of probate to a screeching and expensive halt.

Fifth, sometimes deceased individuals, by their own actions and decisions during life, precipitate enormous probate expenses and litigious warfare after they are resting in peace. Doris Duke, legendary heir to the American Tobacco fortune, left a $1.2 billion estate when she died in 1993, but she had named her butler, Irish immigrant Bernard Lafferty, as chief executor.

Lafferty may have laid the charm on 80-year-old Doris, but he was "basically illiterate" according to the New York judge who removed him from that position. In addition to being an admitted alcoholic, the pony-tailed Lafferty spread Doris's wealth around with total irresponsibility, usually around himself. He crashed her Cadillac, for example, and then used estate funds to buy himself a new one, complete with chauffeur.

The co-executor was U.S. Trust Corporation of New York, a bank that acted irresponsibly as well, and was also removed from its position by the same New York judge. One reason was that it approved an exorbitant $8 million fee requested by—you guessed it—lawyers handling the affairs of the Duke estate. The law firm, Katten Muchin and Doyle, responded with a straight face that their fee was "reasonable compensation" and "wasn't excessive compared to New York standards." Translation: every law firm in New York robs estates—why shouldn't we?

When the Duke probate case was finally settled, Lafferty relinquished any role in the enormous Duke Foundation, and in return was awarded $4.5 million, plus an annual bequest of $500,000. He may be a grade school dropout, but he can buy some mighty fine wine with that kind of allowance.

Closer to home, a writer we know of had a 93-year-old childless aunt. We'll call her "Aunt Sara." She was married once upon a time to a man who already had three children by a previous marriage. After an ugly divorce just before World War II, Aunt Sara and the three stepchildren were permanently alienated from one another.

Aunt Sara reached her ninth decade in good health, with an estate in excess of $1 million, and with a will that clearly stipulated how all that wealth would be distributed—or in the case of her three former step kids, denied. Her nephew was advised by a friend to look into the advantages of a living trust for Aunt Sara, rather than one day having to drag her wishes through months or years of probate and squander much of her estate to enrich attorneys.

The dutiful nephew read up on living wills and the draining costs of probate, and then presented his case to Aunt Sara. She would hear none of it. She had a proper will, thank you, and besides, the lawyer who was "helping" her was, praise be, the little Cooper boy who grew up in their church and was so sweet and his parents had always been so dear. Case closed.

Inevitably, time ran out on Aunt Sara and she gently passed on to her reserved pew in the sky. The will went into probate of course, and took 15 months and vast mounds of paperwork for the court to resolve what Aunt Sara had known all along. The three grown step children, ornery as ever, made some overtures about contesting the will, but in the end did not. Nonetheless, that sweet Cooper boy billed the estate for just under $100,000— after all, it was a large estate—while a living trust would have run about $1,200 max and distributed the estate within days of Aunt Sara's demise.

AVOIDING PROBATE

As a real estate investor you benefit from probate in that you can locate some excellent investment properties and buy them for substantially below fair market value. But as an individual beginning to acquire wealth through probate real estate, you need to take immediate steps to avoid your own estate going into the shark's den of probate. Always, of course, check with your accountant or tax advisor.

The best way, according to every legal and accounting expert, is to open a living trust. I can't overemphasize this, especially for single persons and surviving spouses with an estate of $1.5 million or more. These days, that's a modest house and furnishings, a car, a few stocks and a small savings account. Once again, talk to your tax advisor about what's best in your particular circumstances.

Living trusts enable you to avoid probate completely, and cost much, much less than probate to initiate. When you set up a living trust, that trust is considered a separate entity apart from you. Think of it as a corporation—a separate legal entity. If you fund a trust, that trust owns your property, which means it can continue even when you pass away.

Probate courts have no jurisdiction over property owned by a living trust. After your death, property in the trust can be distributed, privately and easily, to your family or friends with no interference by probate. One caveat: When your property changes, when you sell one home and purchase another one—or several as a real estate investor—make sure that your living trust is updated to reflect your changing circumstances. I have purchased houses from the estates of deceased persons who died with an outdated, inapplicable living trust.

In order for the deceased's estate to avoid probate, all assets that require title, such as checking accounts, a safe deposit box, stocks, bonds, cars, planes, or real estate, must be in the living trust. If they are not, a probate must be initiated. In fact, if even one of these items is not included in the living trust, probate is required. I'll say it again. Always check with your tax advisor.

Another means of avoiding probate is joint tenancy, whether a joint tenancy of two, three, or more individuals. Joint tenancy is often thought of as applicable exclusively for couples, but any group of people can participate. All assets requiring title must be in joint tenancy. Again, check with your tax advisor.

As another option, you can also name your heirs as beneficiaries on certain retirement accounts, life insurance, and annuities. When you pass on, the proceeds from these accounts are distributed immediately to the designated individuals. The courts have no jurisdiction over these types of distributions.

Now that you know something of the nature of probate, and the scurrilous deeds that greed can spawn in otherwise normal men and women, it's time for you to hitch up your knickers and enter the world of probate. Prepare to enter that vast, barely tapped gold mine and wrest from its walls and crevices the wealth that is lies undiscovered by the vast majority of your peers in real estate investing.

2

REAL ESTATE

The Big Nuggets of Investment

This weekend, in large hotel ballrooms in several cities around the country, teams of nationally known real estate investing gurus are going to enchant roomfuls of average Americans who have paid $3,000 or more to learn how to make "thousands, even tens of thousands of dollars each month, working part-time" by investing in real estate. I should know. I'm likely to be one of those seminar speakers.

Many of the speakers at these two or three-day seminars have made a good living in real estate investing. I must acknowledge at the outset that the wealth they promise through real estate investing is very achievable. Thousands of people of all ages and backgrounds are building enormous net worth and enjoying a comfortable lifestyle beyond their wildest dreams because they've learned how to buy and sell real estate. These seminars are successful, and will always be successful because of one fact: There is a fortune to be made in real estate investing—if you know how to buy, sell, and rent the right kind of real estate. In all fairness, these workshops are motivational, instructive, and filled with strategies you can use to make a bundle.

The downside is that it is work—demanding work, requiring more than three or four hours a week to become successful. Learning this business, much like any business, requires patience, diligence, finesse, an orderly and somewhat methodical mind, advanced interpersonal and communication skills, and persistence.

Unlike the vast majority of real estate investors, I began by getting my real estate brokers license. I had a head start on all the information and tips others pay thousands for. And, guess what, I made some good money buying, holding, and selling residential and commercial real estate, using a nontraditional strategy—probate real estate, which I teach in my seminars.

REAL ESTATE INVESTING: GOLD FOR THE MULTITUDES

Before we even look at the tactics and techniques of probate real estate investing, let's spend some time talking about generic real estate investing. The first question you might ask is, "Why real estate?" Why not gold or currency trading or some other investment vehicle? Why not the stock market, especially now that it seems to be crawling back up after the dot-com crash.

Mark Cuban is no fan of the stock market. Cuban, star of ABC's TV program *The Benefactor,* owns the Dallas Maverick's basketball team and has an estimated worth of $1.3 billion. In September 2004, Cuban had this advice for investors in *USA Today,* "Don't buy stocks. The only people making money are brokers and company insiders. Put your savings in a bank."

Well, maybe not all of your savings in the bank. In fact, there are several good reasons why so many of us invest virtually everything in real estate. For starters, real estate has created more millionaires and billionaires—over 70 percent of them in the United

States—than all other wealth generators in history combined. I don't mean just the big guys like Donald Trump. I'm talking about people in your community who are quietly buying properties, holding them, renting them, selling them, and making substantial profits. The lady ahead of you in the checkout line, the couple down the street, the guy that sits behind you in church—these are today's real estate millionaires. How many millionaires are there in the United States today? According to *USA Today*, one out of every 125 Americans is a millionaire. Based on a population of 293 million Americans, that's about 2.34 million millionaires.

But don't get hung up on the word *millionaire*. What's more important day to day is how you can make $30,000 when you sell a property days, weeks, or months after you bought it, and how you rent it out for *more* than your monthly mortgage payment to create positive cash flow and let your tenants pay that monthly payment—not you.

This has little to do with that worn cliché by Will Rogers about "Invest in land because they ain't makin' any more of the stuff." Unlike stocks, the value of real estate rarely plummets through the basement. Sure, there are dips in the market as supply and demand varies, but real estate is the most stable of investment vehicles.

Real estate, as a rule, protects your principal. Once again, in a temporarily depressed market, you might lose a little of your original investment if you're forced to sell during that market, but you'll never wake up one morning to read that the value of your real estate is suddenly a fraction of what you've invested. Even if your investment property accidentally burns to the ground, insurance will reimburse you.

What About Diversifying Your Investments?

Conventional wisdom tells you to diversify your investments, so that if one market goes south, you've still got some money safe in other types of investments. "When stocks go down, bonds go up." "When T-bills go down, mutual funds go up." "Always hedge your bets by keeping your eggs in several baskets."

The classic model for diversifying your savings and investments is: 30 to 35 percent in real estate, 30 to 35 percent in stocks and bonds, 10 to 15 percent in precious metals, and about 10 to 15 percent in cash in the bank.

That's horsefeathers. Since the day I began investing in real estate, I've never given diversifying a second thought. Why diversify? Real estate investing gives you the luxury and the peace of mind of knowing you don't have to balance your investments against the possibility of a crash, a recession, a bank failure, or any other economic calamity. When the smoke clears from any economic disaster, your real estate will still be sitting there.

Real Estate: The Most Dynamic Market of All

Every market is dynamic in its own way. While the stock market, interest rates, and the price of gold move up and down, real estate is driven up or down by people moving around! Why? One reason is because homeowners are always moving either in or out, as they continuously experience changes and crises in their lives that force them to sell their homes.

Look in the paper. Drive around town. Are there fewer Home for Sale classifieds? Fewer yard signs? No. There are more, because we're a more mobile society than ever. Right now, particularly, a number of forces and factors are converging to make real estate an even more promising investment vehicle.

One of them is that we're experiencing the lowest interest rates we've seen in 40 years. When I started, interest rates were in the double digits. Today you can get a 30-year fixed-rate loan for under 6 percent Adjustable rate mortgages range from 2 to 3.5 percent. When I started, there was no such thing as an adjustable rate mortgage.

WHY REAL ESTATE? FIVE GREAT REASONS

In addition to the above factors, there are five overriding reasons why so many people are investing in real estate.

Leverage

This is the number one reason to invest in real estate. Here's why. In real estate, it's not so much what you own as it is what you control. The trick is to control and profit from property with as small an investment as you can. You want to put as little of your money as possible at risk. In many instances, in fact, you can borrow the entire amount and still control the property. Here are several examples of how leverage works.

Suppose you have $100,000 and you invest it in gold, silver, or precious stones, and your investment grows by 10 percent. You've made $10,000. If you decide to invest your $100,000 in stock options, you can control twice as much as you've bought. So when your stock goes up 10 percent, you realize a 20 percent return, and make $20,000.

In real estate investing, you can buy a $100,000 property for $1,000 down. That means you're controlling $100,000 with that $1,000. When that property increases in value by 10 percent, your return on investment is $10,000, and you've still only invested $1,000. You've made $10 on every dollar you've invested.

Here's another demonstration of leverage. You want to buy a $100,000 property, and, acting impetuously and against all investing wisdom, you pay $100,000 cash for it. In one year, it appreciates in value by 10 percent to $110,000. You've made 10 percent on your investment. That beats a certificate of deposit (CD), but not much else.

What if you put $20,000 down to secure a $200,000 property, and it appreciates by the same percentage, or $20,000. You've made 100 percent on your investment! What if you put only $2,000 down? What's your return on investment (ROI)? An incredible 1,000 percent. See if your stockbroker can match that ROI! No wonder real estate accounts for over 70 percent of all this country's millionaires!

Income

When you purchase an investment property—a house, a fourplex apartment, or a commercial building—you can earn income in many ways, depending on your financial strategy. Here are just three:

1. *Rental income.* You can rent your property. If you bought the property under terms that keep your monthly mortgage low, you can create a positive cash flow, covering that mortgage each month and generating some income as well. All the while, your investment is appreciating in value at anywhere from 5 to 8 percent per year, depending on your local real estate market. You can also increase the income. If your property is a rental property, raise the rent once a year, and every time a new tenant signs a lease. Put some of your income back into improving the property as well. A clean, tidy, attractive property will not only demand higher rent now, but if you put it on the market, it'll support a higher selling price.

2. *Cash lump sum.* You can generate immediate cash on your investment by making a few simple, cosmetic improvements to the house, such as a new coat of paint, basic repairs, and attractive landscaping. This is called *sweat equity.* Then sell the house for more than you paid for it. These are *fixer-uppers.* Suppose I needed $20,000. I'd buy a house, fix it, and sell it, probably over a period of no more than 90 days.

3. *Note income.* If you decide to sell your investment property and hold the note yourself, your buyers send you their mortgage payment every month instead of sending it to the bank. There's little risk involved, because should the buyers default on their note, you repossess the property, put it back on the market, and sell it to someone else.

Equity

The equity in your home is the difference between its fair market value and the balance of your mortgage principal. If your investment property is determined to have a sale value of $100,000, and the principal you owe on your mortgage is $40,000, your equity is $60,000.

Equity can be increased in several ways. The easiest way is to just sit on it and let your monthly payments reduce the principal while appreciation slowly and surely drives up the value. The quickest way is to buy your investment substantially below fair market value.

Tax Deductions

Your friends in Congress try to ensure as many Americans as possible own their own home—and invest in real estate. So the federal government is very tax-friendly to real estate investors. But there's a more fundamental reason that real estate owners and investors enjoy unusually generous tax relief. Virtually all Congressmen are also real estate owners or investors. They will never tax themselves. Instead, they will enact tax breaks from which they, and all of us, can benefit.

That's why you, as a property owner and self-employed entrepreneur, enjoy a number of tax benefits. The interest on your mortgage is, of course, tax deductible, as are all repairs and improvements to the property. Any commissions you pay are also tax-deductible. Deduct your telephone, computer, fax, office furniture, and office supplies. In addition, because this is a business enterprise, your house insurance, real estate advertising, and mileage to and from your property are all deductible expenses, as well as the closing costs you pay when you buy or sell real estate.

Appreciation

Real estate appreciates in two ways: in value and as income. Value increases in a real estate market in which a population or economic growth increases the demand for property. Often an area of a city or even a neighborhood will experience a surge in popularity that creates a real estate boom. In recent years in cities across America, rejuvenated areas near downtown or even in the inner city have substantially increased the value of properties in formerly depressed communities. In outlying suburbs, new schools, improved traffic arteries, or new mass transit systems add value to surrounding neighborhoods and subdivisions. Of course, market values rise most years, so that long-term returns at sale can be quite substantial. Property in these areas sells for more—and rents for more. Take your choice of benefit.

GET YOURSELF AN INVESTING PARTNER

If you want to prosper in real estate, but your credit is not yet established, or even damaged from past difficulties—or you're just short of cash—you'll need to partner with an investor. If you can't get approved to purchase an investment property because of your own credit limitations, there are investors out there who will put up the money you need. Because of the uncertain performance of the stock market in recent years, there's more money, available through more investors, than ever before.

You see, at one time senior citizens and baby boomers had their money in CDs getting 12 and 14 percent. Today, interest rates have plummeted, and they're hardly getting 2 percent interest from the bank. The cost of living and inflation is higher than that. So they pulled their money out and put it in the stock market. They didn't know a thing about the stock market, but at the time it didn't matter. It was a bull market and everybody made money for ten years.

Then, in the late 1990s, they lost everything they'd made. Their inflated 401(k) plans became essentially "101(k)s." That's when they figured it out—the stock market is legalized gambling. So they yanked what little money they had left and began to shop around. Guess what they discovered. Real estate!

That's when the real estate investing seminars began to reappear and flourish again around the country.

THE 15 PERCENT RULE FOR REAL ESTATE INVESTORS

Before we look at how to purchase properties, you need to know about the *15 percent rule*. This rule is often overlooked at real estate investment seminars. The rule says that the costs of buying and selling investment real estate are, as a rule-of-thumb, 15 percent of the purchase price. If, for example, you buy a

$200,000 property, you'll pay about $30,000 over the course of buying and selling that property. Five elements comprise that 15 percent:

1. Closing costs going in (2 percent of purchase price)
2. Closing costs going out (2 percent of sales price)
3. Fix-up expenses
4. Holding costs (e.g., the mortgage loan payments you make before you can sell it)
5. Sales costs

That means you must buy your property for at least 16 percent below market value to make a penny.

HOW DO YOU BUY REAL ESTATE?

With the 15 percent rule in mind, how do you buy real estate? Where do you shop? Remember the classic advice on buying anything for the purpose of making money: buy low and sell high. That's true in real estate as well, except that you may not want to wait years for your investment property to appreciate, when you can sell it immediately and make a profit.

Below are the five standard ways to buy real estate.

The Multiple Listing Service

You find a broker who scours the multiple listing service (MLS) to find a nice property that meets your requirements. The problem here is that every other broker has access to that property. Other buyers are looking at it as well, competing with you on price and terms. So how many properties in the MLS have ever sold below fair market value? Precious few. How many have sold for 16 percent or more below fair market value? None that I know of.

Properties that are good deals and listed with a broker don't even find their way to the MLS. These are called *pocket listings* because the broker keeps them in his or her pocket. This practice is common, even though the bylaws of the Board of Realtors state they are to be turned in within 24 hours of contract.

Foreclosures

Properties in foreclosure are published by name and location. The local paper and title companies list them. The foreclosing financial institution tells every investor it knows. Go to a foreclosure sale. It's a great place to meet people, because there will be lots of them there. But don't look to buy a property much below fair market value. Too much competition. Also, forget 16 percent or more below fair market value.

Tax Sales

Your county recorder lists every property on which property tax is delinquent. Go to the courthouse and get the book. Track down the property and see if you want to buy it. Sales are quarterly or semiannually and free to the public. The problem is that anybody who can read, every real estate investor in town, is your competition. The same property you like is the one they will like for all the same reasons. Think you'll get a bargain there? Forget it.

Real Estate Owned

Real estate owned (REO) properties are lender-owned properties that were in foreclosure, but didn't sell for the amount required to cover the loan. Foreclosure investors didn't want them, so the lender is stuck selling those properties themselves. Do you think any of those REOs will sell below fair market value? To receive a list of REO properties, all you have to do is call the lender and get on the mailing list with everybody else. Again, too many people know about them for anybody to take home much of a bargain.

Probate Real Estate

Here's the gold mine. Here's where you can find and purchase properties with addresses that have never been published in print or listed for access to the general public! For decades I've had no competition! For decades I've bought real properties for 30 percent, 45 percent, even 60 percent and more below fair market value. Not to mention personal property for pennies on the dollar. Hey, if you buy a $200,000 home out of probate for 60 percent below fair market value ($80,000) and sell it for 40 percent below fair market value ($120,000), subtract 15 percent of $200,000 in costs ($30,000) you still clear $90,000—as I did in a hot market in Redondo Beach. Not a bad day's work! More on how you do that in the next chapter.

For now—and I'll say this over and over—*never* pay fair market value! In fact, I don't buy any property at less than 30 percent of fair market value. Neither should you. Like every retailer in the world, expect 100 percent return on investment. Because your cost is 15 percent, you have to buy 30 percent below market to get that keystone (100 percent) profit.

REAL ESTATE INVESTING THE SEMINAR WAY

Here's a quick lesson in real estate investing as it's taught at seminars all over the country—and for my money, it's the *hard* way to do it.

The whole methodology is based on the premise of "motivated sellers." A motivated seller is a homeowner who must sell a house as quickly as possible, for reasons including:

- Loss of job
- Divorce
- Serious illness
- Bankruptcy
- Foreclosure
- Advanced age
- Settling an estate (probate)

Now I ask you, are any of these circumstances particularly happy ones? Of course not. The truth is that these property owners are over a barrel, and at a financial disadvantage that you as a trained real estate investor can turn to your advantage. I personally do not pursue "motivated"—read *desperate*—sellers. I just don't have the heart for it. More important, all of these strategies except probate remove someone from their home. The owners of the probate properties I buy have never complained—because they were all dead.

Conventional investing wisdom says that you must pay motivated sellers 25 percent off the fair market value of their property. Otherwise, should you decide to rent, the monthly rental you charge will not cover the mortgage payment and you'll be into negative cash flow. Sure, you'll be building equity in that property, but in the meantime you'll lose money every month on the mortgage payment.

As a real estate investor fresh out of a three-day seminar, you begin combing the newspaper classifieds for ads that read "Must Sell," "Make an Offer," "Relocating," "Distressed Property," even "Motivated Owner." Just like every other enthusiastic investor in town, you check the legal section for foreclosure notices. You drive around hunting for For Sale by Owner yard signs, just like everybody else who attended your seminar. Good luck!

OTHER SOURCES OF LEADS ON REAL ESTATE INVESTMENTS

In addition to the above suggestions, here are some other ways to locate investment real estate.

For Rent Ads in the Daily Newspaper

A lot of people renting properties they own would just as soon sell them and get out of the landlord business, which is the worst part of real estate. Many times, owner-landlords suffer a negative cash flow. They're "feeding the alligator" because rent doesn't cover the monthly house payment, and they're ready to unload the house. For a lot of reasons, after a period of being a landlord, many owners are ready to sell. Your call may be just the trigger they need to do it.

Your Own Eye-Catching Classified Ads

Place small ads in the classifieds on Saturdays and Sundays. Target them to reasons why a homeowner might be motivated to sell. Here are a few examples:

The above ad attracts homeowners who need cash in hand immediately. It plays on the urgency they're experiencing and moves them to call.

No one likes to lose his or her home. Nothing destroys personal pride so much as giving up a home. So the possibility of being able to keep that most precious treasure and its home equity—and save one's credit—makes this a powerful ad.

Foreclosures

Foreclosure is an unfortunate fact of life. Homeowners lose jobs or suffer other financial setbacks and begin to miss making monthly payments. Finally, the mortgage holder gets nervous and decides to foreclose to protect its investment. The foreclosure process begins with a Notice of Default (NOD). This is the first indication of a distressed property, months before the foreclosure sale on the courthouse steps. Again, foreclosure investors stand on the courthouse steps to bid for a property. They don't mind the crowd and don't avoid the competition.

Where do you get information about NOD's? They are printed in the legal section of the newspaper three times. That's a legal requirement in order to be a legitimate notice, and that's why there is so much competition.

You can also call a title company. If they're aware of the notice, they'll furnish you with addresses, owners' names, and phone numbers—all at no charge. That's because the title company wants your business. A lot of them will even send you a computer disk of current NODs. How easy is that?

Real Estate Agents

As we previously pointed out, real estate agents/brokers have access to the MLS. But more important, as investors themselves, many of them no doubt have an established network of contacts you can tap into, such as bankers, title companies, attorneys, insurance companies, even good reliable carpenters and painters to handle fixer-uppers.

Attorneys

Add to your network a few attorneys who specialize in handling the transitions of life—bankruptcy, divorce, and especially probate. Attorneys deal every day with people who are trying to manage a disaster of some sort and escape without financial harm. Whether it's money to pay off a lawsuit, pay for a criminal defense, or restart their lives with an infusion of cash, if there's a property that needs to sold quickly, you can help.

Tax (Delinquency/Lien) Sales

Check with your county recorder or tax assessor's office. Quite often you can pick up properties by simply paying off the back taxes, and get the property free of liens. Tax delinquencies and liens are a matter of public record, so call your title company and ask for a list. As with Notices of Default, they'll probably send you a free disk

Rundown Properties

Some leads arise when you just keep your eyes open. When you're a real estate investor, you begin to see houses in a different light, even the ones you happen to drive by. You notice a house with an overgrown yard, peeling paint, and that's just sort of ragged in appearance, so you write down the address and call your title company representative or use your own database source of real estate owners. Some title companies have a Web site that can tell you in 30 seconds who the owner is, when they bought it, and for how much. All for free! In addition, there are Web sites that list real estate owner and property information. Then call the owner and see if he or she might like to sell.

Out-of-Town Owners

Homeowners who no longer live in the same community as their property sooner or later get tired of the hassle of being an absentee landlord. They'd just as soon sell that house, take the cash, and move on. Your title company can get you the information about out-of-town owners, and, again, it's free. Check Web sites or your own database source of real estate owners.

Changing Conditions

Life never stays in one place, but moves continuously through changing conditions. Property owners suffer setbacks, lose jobs, become ill, divorce, send kids to college, go broke. In other words, things occur that require them or their families to sell their property and get cash. Partnerships, like marriages, go sour, leaving the partners to cash out and sell properties under market. Part of any investor's success will depend on how attuned they are, how closely they pay attention to changes in conditions all around them.

HOW TO GET STARTED IN REAL ESTATE INVESTING

As you can see from this list of sources, you won't have any trouble finding plenty of leads. That's no problem. The problem is that there are a lot of folks just like you who are also chasing those same leads. So imagine this. You need to sell your property quickly, and six or seven real estate hounds call you about making an offer and getting you off the hook of your dilemma. That's the definition of a seller's market. Are you going to knock 25 percent off your asking price, the fair market value, when so many real estate investors are convening at your front door? No!

If done correctly, purchasing probate real estate can be much more profitable because you are the first and only one contacting the seller. Because there is no competition, you buy that property for 30 percent or more off fair market value—or you walk away! But more on that later.

Meanwhile, let's talk more about locating and purchasing investment real estate. It doesn't matter whether you're buying property conventionally or out of probate, the guidelines are the same. What kind of property would you look for, and where?

Get to Know Your Real Estate Market Thoroughly

Before you actually begin buying investment properties, you need to know intimately the market around you. I mean, you can't even buy a TV or a DVD intelligently until you know the price range, features, and advantages of comparable makes and models.

For most of the expertise you'll need to be a successful real estate investor, you can call on a knowledgeable, trustworthy expert—a real estate attorney, an accountant, even another investor—to advise and guide you. Knowing your market is your job, however. It's your homework, and no one can do it for you. You absolutely must become proficient in the art of evaluation.

I suggest that you become an expert in a small area. I worked just five miles from home for 30 years, and never ran out of good deals. Drive around your target area until you could do it blindfolded. You'll spot new yard signs and open house signs in a constantly changing neighborhood yardscape. Talk price with the owners and real estate agents. Stroll through those open houses and compare price and value. Within four to six weeks, you'll begin to get a feel for prices. Within three months, you'll be able to pinpoint a property's fair market value. Remember, there are database companies that sell property owner information. Get one. It's the same type of source that real estate brokers and title companies use. Also, as previously mentioned, Web sites provide the same information.

I once learned a hard and expensive lesson about staying in my market area. The fourth property I bought was out of my neighborhood, but after three successful investments, I was beginning to feel ten feet tall and bulletproof. I live on the West Coast where the volatility of home prices terrifies the boldest of buyers.

This was a little house in Beverly Hills that needed some fixing up. Okay, a lot of fixing up. It was a mess. I was well acquainted with a very experienced appraiser, a widely regarded expert in his field. We'll call him Bruce. Even though he wasn't that well acquainted with Beverly Hills, I asked Bruce to give me an appraisal of what the property's value would be after repairs. He assured me I could get $425,000 for it. After all, it *was* Beverly Hills.

Fantastic, I thought, and I bought that sucker for just $175,000. I put $100,000 of repairs and renovations into it, then listed it for $425,000. It didn't sell. It didn't sell for $395,000 or $349,000. In desperation, I called four local brokers and asked them to appraise the house. Two of them, experts in that neighborhood, agreed that the property was worth $270,000.

That's what I sold it for. You might imagine that was a cheap lesson. I invested $275,000 and sold it for $270,000. But I lost $18,000 in interest payments on the mortgage, another $15,000 interest costs on the signature loan I took out to pay for the fix-up costs, and $5,000 on the difference between my investment and the selling price. My closing costs were $8,200. My total loss was $46,200.

I made two fatal mistakes that I've never repeated. First, I trusted the opinion of someone else, an experienced and highly credentialed appraiser who wasn't qualified to give an appraisal in that area. Second, I bought outside my own market area. Had I first studied the market in that section of Beverly Hills, I would never have paid $175,000 for that house. All that glitters, even in Beverly Hills, is not gold!

Another way to become familiar with your market area is to study the MLS listings. Size up a home's location, size, and features with the asking price. Why is this house more than a comparable one on the next page? MLS listings aren't available to the general public, but if you've made a friend of a real estate agent, maybe you can get the information for honing your feel for price and value.

Your county recorder or county assessor's office will have the sale price information for new sales, but you'll have to go there to get it. Your title company can also get this information for you. Unfortunately, the database information is usually about 30 days late.

If the sale was through a real estate agent or broker, the Board of Realtors MLS is supposed to be notified within 24 hours. That means that any broker affiliated with that board will have access to that price and can share it with you.

Remember this about real estate. It's a small industry, so make friends and establish yourself as trustworthy, honest, and fair in your dealings. Goodwill is free, so pass around all you can. Chapter 3 goes into much greater detail about how and why to build yourself a team of real estate experts.

Establish Your Target Market for Best Results

In any business, the least amount of competition is at the very bottom or very top of the market, because most people stay in the middle trying to cut each other's throats. The middle of the market is the last to go up and the first to go down. Real estate is no exception.

At the upper end, it's much harder for most people to put together and/or find a good deal in a place like Beverly Hills than in a less affluent neighborhood. That's a good reason for beginners to start their real estate investing career at the "entry level" or starter market. That's where early success lies.

In addition, look for areas that are on the upswing in value from both a residential and commercial standpoint. Which way is growth headed in your town or city? Where is the proposed beltway going to be? Where will the big shopping center be built? Are there plans for a downtown restoration program that will provide tax incentives for new restaurants, shopping, and homes for upward mobile young urbanites? Look beyond the next couple of months and you'll get the vision of where your community is headed, and where you may want to have property when it gets there.

The best place to cut your investing teeth is with fixer-uppers. You can learn the real estate market from the ground up. By working with carpenters, plumbers, and painters—or cans of paint—you earn *sweat equity* that will pay off in valuable experience the rest of your career.

Buy Single-Family Homes, Condos, and up to Four-Unit Apartments

If you're a beginner, make it easy on yourself. Single-family homes and condominium units are nice and simple—easy to buy, easy to sell. Ten-unit apartments or commercial buildings, by contrast, require more sophisticated financing and are subject to more regulations and requirements. You may reach the point when you'll want to invest in something larger, but remember this: apartments larger than four units can require a resident manager and create more property management problems. Many investors believe that property management is the worst aspect of real estate investing. Besides, the income from a one- to four-unit complex is considered residential income. Five or more is considered commercial, and the lending criteria change.

On one- to four-units, you can get a simple home loan. You can get a 3 percent loan through FHA or, in the event of owner occupancy for one year, no-money down. Finally, one- to four-unit apartments are easier to sell than larger, multifamily properties, which are typically bought by corporate investors.

Buy Property No More Than Half an Hour from Your Home

Looking after a rental property that is an hour's drive across city traffic is just not worth it. Your time is too valuable to be driving all over your metropolitan area when there are plenty of available houses you can buy less than half an hour from your front door. It's far easier to know your market when it's all around you. There are so many probates, this will never be a problem.

THE NO-NOS OF BUYING INVESTMENT PROPERTIES

Investment property buying is not a one-day sale in Macy's basement. Examine the deal and inspect the property until you're satisfied neither will collapse and injure you. There will always be plenty of real estate deals, so proceed with prudence and caution.

Here are some no-nos of buying properties, particularly from owners who are still living.

- *Don't buy a fixer unless you have the money, the knowledge and time, or the skilled people to repair it.* I told you about my experience with linoleum. If you aren't a weekend carpenter/painter/plumber, you sure better know people who are. Once you buy a home that was a bargain because it was run-down, it's going to stay cheap until you get it fixed up to sell. I recommend you locate some independent, reliable, skilled craftsmen and, when the property is sold, offer them a small bonus over what they normally charge. That's terrific incentive for keeping your handy men handy! A very common mistake is to list your fixer property before all the fix-up projects are completely fixed up. It may be obvious to you what the property will look like when it's finished, but homebuyers and real estate agents only know what they see. Don't depend on their imagination to help sell your property.
- *Avoid a property in a bad location.* Avoid areas of declining value due to such factors as property decay and abandonment, high crime, gang activity, and drugs. Buying in a high crime area can be profitable, but when your toilets and sinks are being stolen at night, you waste a lot of time and

money replacing them. A "bad location" can also mean homes on busy streets, which are very hard to resell. Also be careful about properties with features that most buyers would avoid, such as a poor floor plan or dated architectural features, even a steep driveway or a lot that backs up to a busy avenue or freeway.

- *Be cautious about buying a property with negative cash flow.* A good rule-of-thumb is don't buy any property that has negative cash flow. That means if your monthly payments are $700 and you're only collecting $500 in rent every month, you have $200 in negative cash flow. But if you bought it for no money down, or bought it cheap and can handle the negative cash flow, and there's an upside potential to sell it for a profit—go for it. Some people buy properties that rent for a negative cash flow for the tax write-offs. If you're just getting started, go for the profit rather than the write-off. I go back to the necessity of buying at 30 percent off fair market value—to make the monthly payments low enough that the rent covers them if you end up renting it. Historically, if a property has a 25 percent equity position, it paid for itself, and that was when interest rates were 11 to 14 percent.

- *Don't get emotional over a transaction.* That's true of any business deal. Never let your intuition, impatience, that demon greed, or any other emotional factors influence your handling of a real estate transaction. Focus on the math. Decide based on your knowledge, experience, cold-eyed logic, and clear judgment.

- *Avoid properties with bad financing.* A lot of residential properties are saddled with high interest mortgages, liens, and loan terms and conditions you don't want to take over. If you want the property, restructure the financing to suit you, not the bank or the present owner.

- *Don't buy at less than 30 percent below market value unless you get some great terms.* I've already told you to aim for 30 percent under market value. If the interest rate is low, the owner is willing to sell under terms favorable to you, and the property can be rented for much more than the monthly payment—go for it.

- *Don't trust anyone else's numbers.* Use your calculator. The other party's figures may well be wrong or just misleading. "Figures don't lie, but liars figure." Knowing the numbers from your own calculations ensures that you don't lose control of the deal.
- *Don't give up. Stay persistent.* Yes, I know that this sounds like a cliché, but it works. A real estate purchase is like a lock into which you can stick any number of keys. The first few may not work, but ultimately one key will. Timing, for example, is important. The seller might be more willing to sell in three months or six months. Conditions change. Keep a file of deals you haven't yet made, and call back in a few months.

This chapter has covered the basics of buying real estate for investment, but I avoided discussing on a host of related topics: how to be a landlord, how to work with a bank, how to do tricky and creative financing to buy with nothing down, and how to help "motivated" sellers (i.e., owners in personal crisis) by buying their property.

Just ahead, you'll learn more about building that network of real estate experts, a team you'll need regardless of whether you buy probate real estate.

After we've covered the basics, we'll move to the techniques of buying probate real estate from people who, more often than not, are indifferent about the property you want to buy. And, because the owners are have already passed on, you can purchase at 30 percent, 40 percent, or more below fair market value—with a clear conscience!

3

GETTING STARTED
AS A PROBATE MINER

If you could buy a dollar for 60¢ or even 70¢, wouldn't you buy as many of those dollars as you could get your hands on? That's the way it is when you purchase probate real estate.

Why can you get more house for less money in probate real estate? The main reason is that most real estate investors cling to the techniques we discussed in the previous chapter. That means they all read the same classified, see the same signs, pursue the same foreclosures—and guess what a crowd like that does to the supply and demand ratio? It makes it a seller's market. If I'm a motivated seller and you offer me nothing more than 25 percent off my home's fair market value, and three other guys offer me only 20 percent below, who am I going to sell to? As far as 30 percent—forget it!

The point is that if you were relying on foreclosure notices, classified ads, and yard signs to find properties that you could buy for 70 percent of market value—or even 60 percent or less—you might starve to death. If the address of the property is in print, your chances of buying real estate 30 percent or more below fair market value are virtually nonexistent.

On the other hand, suppose you discovered two or three properties that were available for purchase, but that no one else knew about. You make a few discreet phone calls and the people at the other end are actually surprised that you called about buying their properties. "As a matter of fact," they say, "We just want to get rid of those properties. We didn't know what we were going to do."

"How much does the estate want for the properties?"

"Oh, my Dad put in new carpet just before he died. I'm not sure we want to . . . ."

"Oh, I can understand your hesitancy. How old was your father when he died?"

"He was 85."

"Well, I'm sure he lived a full life."

"Oh, how nice of you to say that. Well, we do want to get rid of the properties, and we have some bills to pay, and, of course, we don't want to continue paying his monthly mortgage payments . . . But it's still tied up in probate. We thought since Dad had a will that everything would be okay. But now it's costing us a fortune in attorney's fees, and it may take three years . . . "

"I understand. I'm sure Dad wouldn't want you to wait for three years to enjoy the benefits of the properties."

"That's what we thought. When can you come by?"

This is a hypothetical conversation, of course, and condenses several real-life visits with the heirs to Dad's house. But the question arises, even in this short exchange, "Why are they willing to sell that house they're inheriting for $70,000 below market value?"

Good question, and one of the answers is that poor, old Dad's beloved home, where he and his late wife, Doris, raised four children, means nothing to the four adults that the children became. Two live out of state, one lives at the other end of the county, and a fourth is a petrochemical consultant in Bahrain. Among them, they have nine grandchildren. None of them give two hoots about that house anymore. What they see when they look at it is a big pile of instant cash. They see some college tuition, a new Miata, braces for the kids, a Caribbean cruise—but certainly not that paint-flaked house.

They are not trying to save their home from the bank. They're not in love with the home. Their self-esteem is not tied up in keeping that home. Dad's kids have no emotional investment to pay off. They've got their own lives and families and mortgages. They sure don't want Dad's mortgage too! So their attitude is, "Let's get rid of that sucker and split the profit! And the sooner the better! But that blasted probate has everything tied up!" Then the phone rings, and it's *you.*

These are not investors. These are ordinary people just like you who are going about their own lives and now, through no fault of their own, they are inheriting something. They want their free cash! They are not as concerned about fair market value as they are about getting their unearned money, and as soon as possible—not three years from now.

The reality is that it doesn't make any difference what we pay them. They will probably squander it away. You might think I'm being a little rough on them, but years of observation prove that people have no respect for unearned money. Tom Brokow reported on *NBC Nightly News* in August 2003, that about 70 percent of those who win the lottery are broke within three years. Research by the Insurance Institute revealed that life insurance beneficiaries spend all their money, at varying degrees of foolishness, within three-and-a-half years.

Do you think most of these suddenly wealthy people are going to invest their windfall in annuities, real estate, or any other investing vehicle? No, because human nature whispers in their ear, "This is a bonus. You can spend the whole thing and it won't hurt you because you didn't expect it anyway. Eat, drink, and be merry!" So they stock up on Bud, buy a Harley-Davidson, get another doublewide, throw parties for their new friends, fight with their spouses about whose money it is anyway, and get a divorce.

The same attitude, no respect for unearned income or unearned benefits, is why government welfare programs hardly ever work. Recipients don't respect free government checks, or free government housing, or anything else free.

I've had thousands of people over the years tell me that would never happen to them. My response has always been, when you inherit a small fortune, call me three years afterward and tell me you still have it. To date, no one ever has.

YOUR FIRST SOURCE OF MINING NEWS IS JUST OUTSIDE YOUR FRONT DOOR!

Are you beginning to imagine glints of gold in this probate thing?

Then pick up your mining pick when you pick up tomorrow's newspaper. Over coffee, go straight to the classified section of your paper. Under Legal Notices, look for probate or death notices. Note: Do *not* look in the obituaries. You are not looking for legally required death notices. In most states, the notice is called *Notice to Creditors*.

Depending on your state, probate notices could also be called:

- Notice of Administration (Florida, Indiana)
- Notice to Debtors and Creditors (Georgia)
- Notice of Letters Testamentary Granted (Missouri)

- Notice to Interested Persons (Oregon)
- Notice to Administer Estate of _____ (California)

State statutory codes state that Notices to Creditors must be printed in a newspaper of general circulation in the county of residence of the deceased, usually three times in two weeks or ten working days. These notices appear in newspapers Monday through Friday. Attorneys and sometimes the Probate Court itself place them in the paper. In the interest of saving money, they will not place a Notice to Creditors in the big daily newspaper, but in a weekly business paper or other regularly appearing local periodicals of general circulation. No such notices appear in the *Los Angeles Times,* for example, or *The New York Times,* but they will show up in the *Orlando Sentinel* or the *Butte Gazette* (if there is one). If you have trouble finding them, simply call your local newspaper.

Notices to Creditors also appear in those legal journals that sell around the county courthouse. You can also subscribe to these journals. When I first started in Santa Monica, I subscribed to seven different newspapers.

What's in a Probate Notice?

The wording of a probate notice, or death notice, varies from state to state, but all of them provide you with:

- The name of the decedent (or deceased) and any "also known as" or "aka" names that he or she might have used in business, especially when buying real estate property
- The name and address of the court handling the probate case (see Appendix K)
- The case number or file number of the probate case. Every state has a different numbering system, but you can usually

locate that case number on the notice, because it is usually prominently displayed.

- The name of the attorney representing the decedent's personal representative, law firm, address, and phone number, and usually the name of the personal representative
- The statute of limitations (one of the two reasons for a probate judicial system) for making claims against the estate of the deceased

Notices to Creditors may also have additional information, such as the date, time, and place for a court hearing on the petition for probate, instructions on how to object to the granting of that petition, and permission to examine the file kept by the court, "if you are interested in the estate." (You certainly are interested—you want to buy Grandpa's property and sell it for a bundle!) In the event the deceased owned property in more than one state, attorneys from each state will also be listed.

THE PROBATE PROCESS BEGINS

Here's the legal process for turning one's late, lamented loved one into a number at the courthouse. Within ten days of a death, the funeral home will receive an official Death Certificate from the coroner's office, county registrar, or Clerk of the Courts. The petition or application that is sent to the Probate Department at the courthouse by the law office of the probate attorney will start the process. The probate file will be established by the Probate Department.

There is absolutely no time requirement for this file to be established after death, so it can be years later, and sometimes it is. If there is nothing to probate, no file is established.

Why could there be nothing to probate if there's a will? There are several reasons. The deceased could have been smart enough to establish a living trust, whereby all properties including real estate could be passed directly and privately to heirs without having the enormous expense of a probate attorney and executor, as is discussed in Chapter 1.

Another reason there's nothing to probate is that everything of any value, including the deed to the ranch, all checking and savings accounts, automobiles, boats, and stocks and bonds, were held in joint title, in most cases by the husband and wife, in joint tenancy. That means, much like insurance, those items of property pass directly to the surviving spouse.

GET YOURSELF ORGANIZED FOR PROSPECTING

Organization is everything when you're pursuing a list of probate cases, each with its own names, dates, and case number. In the interest of keeping things simple, I long ago devised what I call a Working Case Sheet. You can create your own, or you can make copies of the one in Appendix F if you like, in the interest of not reinventing the wheel. Note that I leave space for the actual Notice to Creditors from the newspaper to be attached. The Working Case Sheet has space provided for every pertinent detail about the heirs, the probate attorney, the personal representative, the real estate property, and even the sales prices of comparable properties, so that you can keep track of market values from which to knock off 30 percent or more in your purchase negotiations.

Another source of information about probate cases is the Probate Department at your local courthouse. They maintain a file of probate cases, but it is only by name, not number. That's the reason you write down the case number on your Working Case Sheet and keep it handy.

You also record the case number—but not the name—on what I call a Master Numerical List (see Appendix G). This is a quick reference sheet that enables you to keep track of cases that have or do not have real estate. We're not talking rocket science here:

BATCH RUN DATES				
FM: 7-31-04 TO: 8-31-04	**R.E.?**		**STATUS**	
48-2004-CP-001476-0	**Y**		**W**	
48-2004-CP-001501-0		**N**		**O**
48-2004-CP-001504-0	**Y**		**W**	
48-2004-CP-001515-0		**?**	**W**	
48-2004-CP-001125-0		**N**		**O**

Y = Real estate is in the estate
N = No real estate in the estate
? = Uncertain about real estate in the estate
W = Working File
O = File Out

This system is a good, simple way of tracking case files. As you come across a probate notice in the newspaper, check the case number against your Master Numerical List. If you've got a *Y, N,* or *?* beside it, you're already covered. If not, cut the notice out and attach it to a new Working Case Sheet.

What happens if you get a lead on a probate case rattling around the courts, but you have no documentation? You don't know the deceased owner's name, and you have no case number. In fact, all you do have is the address of the property. Visit the county assessor's office or the county recorder, or whatever your state calls it. They have on computer the name of every property owner of every address in the county. Faster than you can double click, the name you want is on the screen—but not the probate case number.

Jot down the name of the deceased. Then go over to the Probate Department where, if you have the name, you can get the case number. I suggest that you go in person the first time to get a feel for where everything is located. From then on, depending on what state you're in, you may be able to get information through the Internet.

Still another source of probate information is a monthly alphabetical list of cases heard by any of the probate courts. It sounds like tedious work, but in smaller counties or small jurisdictions within counties, the alphabetical list is a better source than newspaper notices.

So now that you've got the name of the deceased and the probate case number, proceed to the file room. These files are public record, so don't be shy. Pick up a standard request form at the desk and give it to the desk attendant, who will pull the file for you.

During your research at the courthouse, look around you. You're likely to be alone, because 99 percent of the other real estate investors in your community are out chasing down For Sale signs, foreclosures, tax sales, REOs, resales via broker, and the real estate classifieds, where every property's address is printed out and/or listed. Everybody who can read and wants to make money in real estate knows about them—and are your competitors! Lesson?

Yes, it's lonely there in some dusty backroom of the courthouse. Like any other gold mine, though, it's not the number of prospectors that make a strike rewarding, but the amount of gold you take home!

TYPES OF REAL ESTATE PROPERTIES IN PROBATE

Your courthouse maintains an individual file for every probate case. As I pointed out, these are all public record, and since you're a member of the public, you can start digging to your heart's content.

The real estate you find in the probate files will consist mostly of single-family residences. However, there is every type of real estate in probates—multifamily units, commercial and industrial property, raw land, and farm land. The vast majority of those passing away lived their lives in freestanding homes—just the kind of properties you want to add to your investment portfolio.

By the way, there's a persistent myth that most probate properties, especially homes, are fixer-uppers. In my 30-something years in probate real estate investing, my experience is that fixer-uppers only account for about 12 to 15 percent of the cases. Because most people pass away in their later years, they cannot maintain the properties exactly the way they once did. A lot of homes, may need paint and carpet replaced or the drapes thrown out, but those improvements are all cosmetic, not in the same category as a fixer-upper.

Also, keep your eyes open for commercial, industrial, and multifamily income property, and even vacant lots. One of my greatest finds was a rundown bowling alley that I renovated and reconfigured into warehouse space. The purchase price was $700,000. The cost of repairs and renovation was $75,000. The property later sold for $1,200,000. Gold is where you find it.

HOW TO READ A PROBATE FILE

Here's a partial list of the forms you'll find when you open a probate file.

- Petition or Application for Probate
- Proof of Publication
- Inventory and Appraisement
- The will of the deceased
- Notice to Creditors (or its equivalent)
- Order (Decree or Statement) for Probate

See Appendix A for a sample of the forms to be found in the probate file.

Petition for Probate or Application for Probate

As you peruse the files of a probate case, look for the *Petition* or *Application for Probate*. This form, if properly filled out, gives a great deal of information about the decedent and the assets he or she left. In our sample form in Appendix A, Line 3c lists the value of real estate and personal property that has been established, usually by the executor and/or the probate attorney.

There are two primary sources of appraisal. Typically, either a professional appraiser drives by the house, takes a look, and pulls a dollar figure out of his ashtray, or the executor has attached what he or she believes to be a fair market value, usually either a "guesstimate" based on sales prices of other homes in the neighborhood, or from a crystal ball. Rather than reflecting any fair market value, that figure is more indicative of what the estate expects in the way of a price, and gives you a ballpark figure for you to begin working on your own purchase offer.

An appraisal is good for one year, after which the property must be reappraised. If the property has not been appraised for inheritance tax purposes, or if the court believes the previous appraisal is too high or too low, it can order a new appraisal.

Peruse the probate files with an open mind. Look for little clues, little slivers of gold that suggest bigger things behind the mine wall. You just never know what you're going to see. Look on this form, for example, for the names of all the heirs. One good lead can be found on Line 3b of the Petition for Probate form. This line tells you the location of the decedent's residence at the time of death—and an address for you to research.

Now think about this. You can be reasonably sure that a probated residence is free and clear of debt. Why? Because the original lender, usually a bank, probably had a life insurance policy—mortgage insurance—tacked on to the monthly payment, with the lender named as the beneficiary. Much of the time, it just shows up as a quiet little line item on the purchase contract, and the purchaser never really understands what it is or that it's not required by law. This is a fairly common practice, enabling lenders to rest easy that they'll get their money back if the owner passes on to a place without check mailing service. (It's always laughable how banks justify mortgage insurance. They sell it as protecting the owner's family in case of the owner's death. "You'll have the peace of mind in knowing that your family can continue to live where so much love has grown up." Gag.) Remember, the deceased is usually in his or her later years and the residence is very often paid off.

Proof of Publication or Affidavit of Publication

If you still haven't found an address for the probated real estate, look for the *Proof of Publication* form. This is a statement by a representative of a local newspaper that attests to the fact that the Notice to Creditors or other probate notice has indeed been published according to law. This form sometimes includes the address of the deceased homeowner.

Most real estate in probate has served as the decedent's own domicile. That domicile is determined by confirming the place from which the decedent filed his or her last income tax return, or the place where he or she voted in the most recent national election.

Remember the story of Howard Hughes in Chapter 1? When he died, his estate was in excess of two billion dollars. In addition to the U.S. government seeking $821 million in inheritance taxes, three states that wanted other millions in inheritance tax—Texas, Nevada, and California—eventually fought over the issue of Hughes's domicile (i.e., where he called home). The fact that he expired in a private jet plane "somewhere in the international sky" only complicated matters.

Inventory and Appraisement

A surprising number of Americans die owning more, often much more, real estate than just the roof over their heads. This real estate may include a second home some distance away, an obscure vacation cottage where the kids had to endure mosquitoes every year for a week, or various investment properties that mean nothing to any of the owner's survivors. The heirs have absolutely no emotional attachment to any of these places. As a result, you may pick up one or more of these properties for 30 percent or more below fair market value.

But you need to know where and how many there are. That's when you go digging through the probate file for the Inventory and Appraisement Form. It usually lists the exact address of all real estate properties and their appraised valuation. (By the way, I have purposely used vague words when discussing these forms: *usually, sometimes, often.* That's because law offices are often pretty lax about filling out every line of a form. The line they leave blank is *usually* the one that would have contained just the info you need.)

Remember to record on your Working Case Sheet all the real property owned by the deceased as listed on the Inventory and Appraisement form. Also, from the top of any form, copy the probate attorney's name, law firm, address, phone, and e-mail address if possible. Just below that area is where you can find the name of the petitioner or the estate representative.

At the bottom of the Working Case Sheet, I have reserved a space for "Comparable Sales," so you can record the selling prices of other properties in the same area. Where do you get that information? Remember we discussed making friends with a title company? They'll be delighted to give you all the comparative sales information you want, because you've begun to use their services. (As a suggestion, use one of their representatives for all your title business. Cultivate a one-to-one relationship that will enable you to ask for freebies when you need them.) Also, your database information will do the same thing.

You also have room for other information from other sources, so list such pertinent items as parcel number; date purchased; zoning; square footage; number of rooms, bedrooms and baths; and other data. All of this information is on file in the county recorder's office or county assessor's office.

The Will

In our search for bargain basement gold in probate real estate and personal property, the most important source can be the will, the *Last Will and Testament* of the departed. You can *always* find that will in the courthouse probate file.

There are three different kinds of wills. By far the most common is the *witnessed* will, a typewritten, legal declaration of a person expressing his or her desires for the disposition of that person's property after his or her death. It is signed by the maker and declared to be the maker's will in the presence of at least two witnesses. At the maker's request, and in the maker's presence, they sign the document as witnesses.

The *holographic* will is entirely handwritten, dated, and signed in the testator's own handwriting. No other formalities are required. Not all states accept such a will as valid.

The *nuncupative* will is an oral, not written, will. It requires neither writing nor formalities, but can be made only in contemplation of death under special circumstances. This will is rarely used. It may dispose of personal property only, and is limited to $1,000. Again, not all states accept such a will.

Let's return to the witnessed will you'll find in the probate file. Sometimes real and personal property are not mentioned in this document. Sometimes it's impossible to find the exact address in the will because the property happens to be recorded in the name of a corporation, trust, or limited liability company instead of an individual.

Read this document carefully. Because your time perusing the probate file is limited, it will benefit you to learn to read the will as quickly and as carefully as possible.

One of the most important elements in interpreting a will is in the Testamentary Power of Sale statement, which reads, "with or without notice." This phrase doesn't appear in all wills, but when it does, it suggests a superb opportunity. The phrase means that no address of any real estate will be put in print if the wishes of the deceased are honored. Other than the Notice to Creditors, no publication of any kind will be printed, and no item being sold will be exposed to the public. Because the assets will not be exposed to any competitors you might otherwise have, you will be far more likely to get a significantly below-market price.

In looking through the will, you will find a list of all the heirs and their addresses. You may discover who will be inheriting what percentage of what asset. Once again—and I can't emphasize this enough—get all the information you can about the heirs and the estate representative: names, street addresses, city, state, zip, telephone number(s), and e-mail addresses if they're listed. You may be talking to them, and you want all this data in one location and at your fingertips—on your Working Case Sheet.

Notice to Creditors

Sometimes also known as the Notice of Petition to Administer the Estate of . . . , this notice is sent to the decedent's survivors, known creditors, and others who might be interested or have a stake in the disposition of the estate. Known by different names in different states, these probate notices are required to be run in local newspapers. (See Appendix E.)

If there is no mention of a personal representative in the will, or if the appointed personal representative has declined to serve, look for the Notice of Petition to Administer Estate in the probate file.

Now that you've gathered all the information you can about the probate cases listed on your Numerical List, it's time to use that wealth of data to become a skilled and knowledgeable purchaser of probate real estate and personal property.

You've found some gold deposits. All you have to do is stake your claim and take possession!

4

ASSEMBLING YOUR
REAL ESTATE EXPERTS

No one succeeds alone. Especially in the field of real estate investing, nobody ever made the big bucks without a team of experts, people in other disciplines to help make the money and who also benefited from the process.

Let's discuss them all, and then focus especially on the team member that has the power to make or break you as a real estate investor—the lender.

THE REAL ESTATE BROKER OR AGENT

A real estate professional has the ability to help your investing career get off the ground—or crash on takeoff! He or she should know the market and property values, be able find you likely properties, and give you quick "eyeball" appraisals based on their experience. If they'll do all that and help you fill out a purchase offer form, you've got a good agent that'll cut your work in half.

But you need to check around. Call a few agents in your area and make an appointment to visit their offices. Find out whether they are full-time agents or weekend wonders, and whether they themselves invest in real estate. An agent that looks at property the same way you do, through investors' eyes, will be more likely to throw a property you way if it fits your investing profile. At the same time, the implied obligation is that you throw business his or her way as appropriate.

But heed this caveat. Never allow yourself to be vulnerable to someone else's opinion. When I first started, I wanted to sell a triplex. I called four agents to give me a quick appraisal, including their estimate of monthly rental income and property price. The first agent worked for a large corporation from which you can also buy appliances. The second worked for a national company from which you can buy stocks and bonds. The third and fourth agents worked for the two largest real estate brokers in the area. Each agent was to give me an opinion, and each knew that he or she might get the listing.

The first agent showed up 15 minutes late, glanced at the property, and decided that the rents should be $1,900 a month. The second agent also arrived 15 minutes late, and said that the rents should be $2,100 a month. The third never showed at all. The fourth sent an underling, who told me the rents should be $2,600 a month.

I agreed with the fourth agent. In fact, that's what I subsequently charged my tenants. But he appraised the property at $40,000 less than the appraisal of the second broker. Obviously, if I had put my faith in any one of these agents, I would have done so at my peril. By all means, call in a professional in the industry to give you an educated guess, but recognize it for what it is: a personal opinion. After all, these are real dollars you're playing with, not Monopoly money.

A TITLE COMPANY

If you've ever bought real estate, you've dealt with an officer at a title company. When you bought your title insurance, you became a permanent listing in his or her databank. Now's the time to give that title officer a call and renew your acquaintance, because you're going to be tossing some business his or her way in the near future.

Title insurance is very important because no one is going to buy a property from you if you cannot arrange title insurance.

Every title insurance company on earth has been burned on having to pay out on a claim on a probate deal. The reason was fraud! So title insurance companies are very careful when issuing title insurance on probate.

Interview at least three title companies as if you were hiring them—which in a sense you are—and choose the one with whom you can best work. Let each one know you will be investing in a lot of properties and that you are looking for a long-term and mutually profitable relationship with one title insurance agent. They have access to some property profile information you can't get from the county assessor or your own database of information.

OTHER REAL ESTATE INVESTORS

Strange as it may seem, other serious real estate investors can become invaluable sources of information. There are an infinite number of houses for sale, so you won't threaten an established, successful investor. That's even more so in probate real estate investing.

Investors call me all the time, sometimes to borrow money to finance deals, sometimes just shopping for deals. When I'm teaching a probate real estate workshop, I sometimes tell the audience, "Hey, you want to network? Look around. Get acquainted.

You're surrounded by dozens of new investors who'll be able to help you one day soon, and who you can help in return.

Here's another tip about investors. They're a talky, gregarious bunch. They love to tell stories of how they did this or that deal. Most of them enjoy passing along tidbits they've learned over the years to new investors. I'd suggest you find the names of active investors wherever you live.

One way to find such investors is to call your contact at the title company. Ask for a cross-listing from the title company's database that will reveal the name of an individual who owns several properties. Your contact hits a few keystrokes—click, click, click—and says, "Here's one. It's owned by a gentlemen named Max Gross."

"Oh, how many other properties does he own?"

Click-click-click. "According to our records, he owns 14 properties."

"Great. What's his phone number?"

Call up Max and introduce yourself. "I'm a new investor just getting started and your name has come up as being very successful in this field. Whenever it's convenient, I'd like to buy you lunch and ask you a few questions."

When you sit down with an experienced real estate investor, ask him or her, "What are a couple of recent deals that stand out in your mind? What interested you about this deal? What did you learn from it?" Then sit back and listen. What you hear will far exceed in value the price of lunch.

A MORTGAGE BROKER

People in the mortgage business have their finger directly on the pulse of what's happening in the local real estate market. The trick is to find one with the knowledge, credentials, personality, and general professional profile with which you're comfortable.

Just like in any other industry, there are terrific mortgage brokers and mediocre mortgage brokers. How do you tell the difference? You interview several potential mortgage bankers as if you were looking for a partner for your enterprise. Ask about their services. For example:

- *Do you offer creative financing?* Can they get you a no-money-down mortgage, and can they structure and customize mortgage terms to handle your needs? A mortgage broker is paid for being innovative. Otherwise, homebuyers might as well buy an off-the-shelf mortgage product from the bank.
- *Do you handle government programs?* FHA is a prime example. If a mortgage broker doesn't deal with FHA, he or she is ignoring an enormous source of mortgage possibilities. This is also a sign he or she lacks the capacity for imaginative thinking. Move on. You might make an exception for areas where the prices are so high that FHA limits make FHA loans nonapplicable.
- *Can you do subprime lending?* A homebuyer with bad credit or a history of late payments is not a prime customer, but mortgage programs exist for that segment of the buying public. You need a mortgage broker who can handle such subprime lending for a potential buyer you may be working with, as well as for yourself, if applicable.
- *Can you do hard money?* A good, well-rounded mortgage broker can do all the no-money-down programs, including those offered by the government, such as FHA and VA loans.

The point is, go to a mortgage broker who does everything, not just conventional loans. Go to a creative broker, one who thinks outside the box, and who has all the funding connections and resources necessary to customize a loan that banks can't or won't handle.

APPRAISERS AND OTHERS ON YOUR REAL ESTATE INVESTING TEAM

Establish a relationship with a good, reliable appraiser. These specialists see a lot of properties. They've learned to make solid appraisals, often based on a single walk-around. (An appraiser who assures you that he or she can do a drive-by appraisal is just lazy. Who knows what deterioration or decay lies in the backyard or the back bedroom?) However, never allow yourself to be dependent on the evaluation of an appraiser, or anyone else. Do your own checking and verifying.

Just as important as their expertise at assigning value, appraisers have a wealth of contacts in other professions. They can recommend a good real estate lawyer, or a reliable home repair contractor who won't charge you an arm and a leg. They know others like Max Gross who are involved in investing as well, people you can talk to about the market without threatening their livelihood.

A talkative appraiser might even recommend a lender.

SELECTING A LENDER—AND SURVIVING THE PROCESS

Let's spend some time talking about lending institutions and the people who work for them. If I can help you eliminate some of the mystique bankers have programmed into your mind, and put *you* in charge of your lending relationship, that feat alone is worth the price of this book.

If the idea of walking into a banker's office strikes mortal fear in you, let's put this in perspective right now and move on. A recently published news article titled "What Kills Us" listed the statistics for the most frequent causes of death in America. Heart disease is the number one killer, followed by cancer, then stroke and lung disease. But not one death in the U.S. has ever been attributed to rejection by a banker, or indeed the rejection of any lending deal. Asking for a loan is not terminal, so get over it!

The techniques of dealing successfully with bankers remain a mystery even to some seasoned real estate investors. Why do you want the money? Well, unless you're independently wealthy, have incredible credit, and don't need the banker's money, the bank will not lend you mortgage money on the strength of your smile, especially if you're trying to buy several properties.

Oh, sure, you can get a signature loan. In fact, I suggest that you start now—today—and take out a small signature loan based on whatever credit you have, say $1,000. Hold the money for a month, then pay it back. Your banker may actually smile for you, but more important, you've established yourself as an individual who pays back loans. (While you're at it, open a few credit cards and charge a few items. Pay off those charges, then put that stack of credit cards in the back of your sock drawer. Forever. They've done their job, establishing that you're a good credit risk.)

Bankers and other lenders are wonderful people. All they want is a little interest, some points, a small fee—and no profit at the back end. A partner lends you money, on the other hand, will want all of the above and a percentage of your profit.

A loan officer at a bank or a mortgage broker is an element of your success. You'll find that your relationship is with the person—not the institution that person works for. Lending is a people-to-people business. So when a loan officer moves to another company, go with him or her if you can. You don't want to start all over building a new relationship every time you desire a loan.

ADDITIONAL MEMBERS OF YOUR INVESTMENT TEAM

Another member of your investment team is the hazard insurance agent. If you are flipping properties, the commission the hazard insurance agent receives is charged back—if the policy is not held for at least one year. So, as a thank you to the agent, he or she handles all my personal insurance needs, and I always recommend that agent to others every chance I get.

Another key player on your team is the individual who does your closing, or the escrow agent on your real estate transaction. In the Southeast, attorneys handle most closings. In other states, title companies do the closings, usually a different person than the one who issued the title insurance.

In Southern California, where I live, escrow companies handle closings as an independent, bonded third party. As highly professional specialists, they handle everything and send you a check. You don't even have to be in the state! There is no better way to conduct a closing. In Northern California, which is virtually another state and another state of mind, both escrow companies and title companies handle closings.

Though real estate brokers can do closings, I do not recommended it. They do not have the depth of experience, nor do they have the financial resources or "deep pockets" to sustain the impact of a lawsuit should a critical mistake be made in the closing documents.

LOCATING YOUR "FINANCIAL PARTNER"

No matter where you live, you have a choice of financial institutions to consider when you begin thinking about financing your real estate deals: banks, savings and loans, mortgage companies, finance companies, and other sources.

Wherever you are, look in the phone book. Read the business section of your newspaper. A lot of major metropolitan newspapers publish quarterly a list of banks looking for borrowers. Call the business desk of your newspaper and secure a copy of the most recent edition of that report.

Using all the resources available, make a list of banks that begins with "First Megabig Bank," headquartered in the most arrogant skyscraper in the state, and ends with "Community Corner Bank," down at the strip mall by the gas station. Then find out who the managers are of your most likely prospects, and who the lending officers are. Go down the list, call each bank and ask. The names of these bank officers are not a state secret. Stop by and ask the receptionist or even the security guard.

What financial institutions are most likely to lend you the money you need? At the very top of the list is any newly opened branch office. New banks have no customers. They are stacked to the ceiling with money they need to shovel out the door in order to begin generating income, and they're run by a shiny new manager who has a desperate need to prove himself or herself by generating loans. Consider this actual promotion recently written for a new bank in Florida:

> Midstate Bank of Florida is now open at the corner of Rolinson Street and Magnolia Avenue to handle all your personal and business banking. At MBF, our style of community banking is based on building personal relationships with our customers. We get to know the needs of your business, so we can provide the best mix of financial services, adapting them to meet your specific business requirements. When you need a loan or a line of credit, relationship banking means that approvals come quickly from local management people who already know you.

This bank is saying, "Please give us the chance to lend you money." In the world of finance, we call this bank a *laydown*. The bank should have its grand opening in the vault. If I were shopping for mortgage capital in Florida, I'd be all over this bank like fleas on a hound!

I recently read where two women banking executives had joined together to open their own bank. If I were a woman trying to secure funding for my dream, I'd be on the phone to them in a heartbeat. That's not a sexist observation—who can deny that, all other factors being equal, a strong chemistry pre-exists between the founders of this bank and any female entrepreneur?

For lending purposes, there are basically two types of banks: centralized loan institutions and branch bank institutions. The centralized bank pools its loan requests from several branches, and this bundle of requests is forwarded up to people who've never heard of you. Your deal will be weighed objectively in competition with all the other requests, and regardless of its merits as a splendid opportunity, it's likely to get lost among more promising deals, backed with stronger collateral and other advantages.

Instead, you want to approach a branch bank institution with local lending approval power. Like Midstate Bank above, this is likely to be a "community" bank or a "hometown" bank, run by "your neighbors in the banking business." The loan committee is comprised of your individual banker, who becomes your advocate, and three or four other bank officials or directors, community businesspeople to whom bankers look for guidance. Also, these hometown good ole boys usually have another agenda. They want to build up business quickly and portray an aura of success, so that in three or four years they can sell out to United MegaBank and make a small fortune for every good ole director on their good ole board.

Suppose you've picked five banks as possible lenders. Which one do you try first? The one that's least likely to provide you financing. That's because you need to practice your presentation skills, both on the phone and in your face-to-face meetings. Make all your mistakes, expend all your butterflies before you get to the serious prospects.

What's your first point of contact? I recommend that you have your accountant or attorney make the first call on your behalf.

Either one of these individuals is likely to have more clout with the banker than you do. In fact, the banker will take the call of an attorney or accountant long before taking or returning your call. And an intercessory call made on your behalf suggests you are a significant or at least knowledgeable player in the local business community. ("The perception of reality is greater than reality itself.")

Your accountant, hopefully a prominent CPA associated with a respected firm, calls the banker and says, "As [YOUR NAME HERE]'s accounting firm, we've recommended that he consider your bank to establish a business relationship. He's a real estate investor. Do you foresee any conflicts?" Of course not. "Good, I'll have him call you and set up a meeting."

What if you have to make that first call yourself? No problem. You start with the manager. You may be passed to the vice president responsible for lending. Most likely, however, you will find that Mister Big Banker is "not available," and some assistant will take your number. Do not sit by the phone and wait for a return your call. Most bankers are very busy individuals, being phoned constantly by people he or she already knows who are more important than you, a total stranger. Call back. Call again. If he or she has a voice mail, saturate the system with your patient, professional messages. (If I find out a banker has no time-called indicator, I'll call 13 times in ten minutes!) Finally, it will become clear that you are persistent—you may even screw up the banker's voice mail if you don't get a call back. So the banker will call.

Introduce yourself, graciously thank him or her for returning your call, and begin with, "I'm a real estate investor, and I'm looking to establish a financial relationship for my business. I'm in the process of interviewing several banks that have been recommended. Rather than go into details over the phone, I'd like to set up an appointment to meet you and talk personally. When would be the best time for you?"

Notice you didn't say, "I need to borrow some money, and I need it by next Thursday." Bankers, you see, are very much into relationship banking. They want to know who you are, see your face, understand what the hell you do, and begin forming a judgment as to whether you can pay back any capital lent to you. Personal chemistry—not the numbers—is absolutely key, for both of you.

By the way, it's an important part of your strategy to mention that you're "interviewing" banks. This puts the banker on notice that, as far as you are concerned, you're the one doing the selecting, that you're in control of hiring a bank, maybe this bank, to handle your affairs. It also tells the banker you're talking to the competition, and if you are a significant account for this banker, he or she will have to earn it. Doesn't that approach beat how you always thought it would be—crawling in on your knees to grovel for a loan?

So, in order to begin developing your mutually beneficial relationship, you might suggest lunch. Bankers always pick up the tab. It's part of their training. I've been dealing with bankers for years, and I don't recall ever buying a banker lunch. It's even better if you can arrange for one banker to see you having lunch with another banker.

The purpose of your first meeting is to get acquainted, for each of you to see what the other looks like and sounds like, so the bonding process between you can, you hope, begin. Your initial discussion of your business should be general, because you also have two other things to do during this meeting: listen and ask questions.

As you discuss your ideas, give the banker a chance to react to what you're presenting. He or she can probably offer some suggestions and ideas you can incorporate into your thinking, help you sharpen your focus, and give an even better presentation to the next banker you talk to. The banker's advice is free, and it's based on experience. So listen.

Most wannabe borrowers sit in front of a banker with no idea of what to ask beyond "Can you help me?" They don't understand that they should be in interview mode, asking questions to clarify just what this bank is all about—and if it's the best bank to fund their project. Let's talk about some of the questions you need to ask each banker with whom you meet, and why each question is important.

- *What is your personal lending limit, both secured and unsecured?* Every bank manager and loan officer has a credit limit that he or she can approve without having to check with a superior. Ask. In fact, ask this question on the phone before your first meeting. You may be talking to the wrong person. Don't let them hedge around with relationship doubletalk. It's a specific number. If they tell you $50,000, you're going to probably need about $48,000. If it's $100,000, your requirement will coincidently be asking for about $95,000. If you determine that this person does not have the authority to approve as much as you may need, move on to the next candidate immediately.
- *Who do I have to go to for an approval on the next level of financing?* When your new banking friend tells you who the official is at the next approval level, that's the person you want to meet. Don't waste your time making presentations to the wrong people. While you're asking about lending limits, inquire about the credit limits of the bank itself. When you ask a banker about his or her employer's unsecured credit limit (usually 1 percent of assets), the banker begins to think of you in terms of maximums.
- *Are you a centralized loan institution that pools loan requests, or a branch-based lender?* We've already said why you're looking for a branch-based lender.
- *Is your bank presently in a lending mode, or in a downsizing mode?* This is code for, "Have you made some bad loans in

the recent past, to the extent the government is watching your lending practices very closely?" It's not classified information, and your banker will respect you for knowing to ask the question. If the answer is something like, "Well, we're in a holding process right now," that's a coded response for, "We're in a death spiral right now. Do you have any openings for a former banker?" Before you escape, you may want to buy his or her lunch.

- *On what type of real estate ventures do you like to make loans?* Some institutions focus on commercial development, others on residential development or even real estate investment. If you're thinking of buying two or three mid-priced properties, you want a bank that's comfortable lending on such properties.

- *Can your institution take me to the next level of my growth?* What if you want to move into major commercial property investment? Once again, as a rule of thumb, banks can lend 1 percent of total assets unsecured, and 2 to 3 percent of total assets on a secured loan.

- *What is your bank's policy on asset lending versus cash flow lending?* By now your banker buddy is regarding you with a degree of awe. You're already sounding more sophisticated than 90 percent of the morons he or she talks to about loans. You know that in asset lending, the loan limit is determined by the loan-to-value ratio of an asset. Take 50 percent as an example. If you've got approximately $100,000 in tangible assets, the bank will lend you $50,000. Many banks these days steer away from asset lending, because in the past, loan defaults have forced them to become reluctant property owners. You should look for an asset-based collateralized loan, since most banks will bend over backwards to work with you in a pinch rather than take possession of your chain of dry cleaners or pet stores. Cash flow lending, on the other hand, bases lending parameters on a percentage of existing cash flow revenues, less operational expenses, cash costs, and taxes, typically between 50 percent and 65 percent of cash flow (without "smoke and mirrors"). If you're already producing income, many banks prefer this basis because they can get their hands on income without the hassle of property ownership. If you're just starting, show them how much income your investments will generate, so that they might consider giving you the loan based on future cash flow.

- *Are you an interstate bank, or do you operate just within this state?* I'm talking U.S. banks, of course. You'll already know the answer to this one by the time you and the banker sit down. You will prefer an intrastate bank, since it's simpler to deal with an institution that operates in only one state. Besides, interstate banks are subject to more federal red tape and regulations. The fact of the matter is that these days, as bank consolidation continues, there are fewer local banks and more megabanks than ever. But again, you'll bank with whomever has the funds and wants to give you mortgage money!

Suppose you establish a working chemistry with an individual banker. You meet for lunch periodically. You play golf. You nurture the relationship for months or years, and then he or she takes a position with another bank. Do you stay with the bank? No! Remember that the spirit and substance of that relationship is with the individual. The bank is nothing more than a mechanism for getting the capital your banker is willing to arrange for you. Unless there are unanswered questions about the move, always go with the banker instead of the bank. Otherwise, you're back to square one at your present bank.

One last thought about choosing a bank: Don't overlook the option of spreading your capital requirement out over two or even three banks.

HOW TO DEAL WITH FINANCIAL INSTITUTIONS

Most business people make two false assumptions about lending capital: first, that there is a finite amount of money available for an infinite list of potential lenders; and second, that bankers are their adversaries, using their office to keep them from borrowing money. If you forget everything else about dealing with bankers, remember these two statements:

1. There is more money out there crying to be borrowed than there are people trying to borrow it.
2. Bankers want to lend you money, because that's how they put food on their own tables.

Their money does not produce revenue sitting in the bank. That means if they're even halfway convinced of the viability of your plans, they'll give you the benefit of the doubt. No wonder most banks, regardless of what they'd have you believe, are laydowns, especially with the right romancing.

The fine points of how to deal with your financial institution begin to surface during the selection phase we've just discussed. The operating premise is that you want to develop rapport, understanding, and chemistry with a banker from the first words you speak, and from the first time he or she lays eyes on you. That's why you practice what you're going to say before you blurt it out to the banker. That's why you dress like the sort of business executive that a banker feels comfortable talking to and being seen with in the restaurant where you lunch. Bankers, like the rest of us, have comfort zones, and you want to put yourself smack in the middle of it!

Let's talk about what you say first. Words have meanings. Remember the term *interview* and what it signals to the banker? If you haven't guessed it by now, bankers like to hear words like *relationship*, *partnership*, *long-term*, and *mutually beneficial*. When you're communicating to a banker you don't ever *need money*. To a refined and sensitive banker, that's pretty coarse. Instead, you have *capital requirements*. You don't call your accountant a *CPA*. Everyone assumes you have a CPA, but if you use that term, it sounds like you're impressed you have one. Use *accountant*. These are details no one ever told you in a real estate workshop.

You live in laid back Southern California, or casual, steamy Florida, or in the rural farmland of north Texas, and you need financing to buy some modest residences. What do you wear to go see your banker?

A conservative business suit. Period. I don't care if you're about to buy condemned drug houses in South Chicago, you show up for your banker meeting in a black, dark gray, or dark blue suit with a white shirt, patterned power tie, dark socks, lace-up shoes, and no-nonsense haircut. Leave your gold chains and faux Rolex at home.

If you're a woman, of course, you know which business suit in your wardrobe corresponds to the male attire I've just described. You already know why, but I need to remind you that a banker is most comfortable talking to and being seen with a person who looks like him or her and his or her associates. You'd be surprised how many otherwise bright business owners stroll in for a major lending presentation in golf shirts and Dockers.

WHAT YOUR BANKER WANTS TO HEAR— MOST OF ALL, LOUD AND CLEAR

All this preliminary stuff—lunch, meetings, conversations—is foreplay, so that the banker becomes comfortable with one fact: *You fully intend to pay back the money he or she is going to approve.* No matter what! The amount and payback schedule of interest is negotiable, but it's absolutely indispensable to the approval process and the banker's personal comfort zone that he or she knows the bank is going to get the principal back. The banker *wants* to believe. The banker *wants* to sell you some money.

Your banker also wants to know that you plan to bring as much business as you possibly can. Give your banker all the reasons you can think of to go to the loan committee, more than once if necessary, to pitch your deal.

WHAT YOU NEVER TELL YOUR BANKER

If you're unsure about some element in your plan, if you have a seed of doubt that it won't work, never mention those doubts to your banker. Never share a doubt. While you're keeping things to yourself, never say something like, "The last time I tried something like this I lost my butt." Keep the conversation focused on the positive—on future success, not past failures.

You have a couple or three meetings with a promising bank, and the requirements become more and more specific. The bank may want to look at your recent financial statements. That's fine, because your accountant has prepared audited financials on his or her firm's embossed letterhead. It's an impressive document before the banker even picks it up. It spells out your cash flow, existing capital, long-term debt, and short-term debt. It is an accurate snapshot of your business.

Your accountant can provide several levels of documentation. The most basic is a compilation and review without opinion, which essentially reports the figures you provide on prestigious CPA letterhead. You might get an assurance letter that deals with an isolated specific, such as receivables. The most expensive and comprehensive documentation is a full-blown audit, with an attached opinion, which tells the banker that your accountant has personally audited and checked your figures, and they are true and correct to his or her best knowledge. Pay the fee and take audited financials to any banker who requests financial statements. Banks will always lend more on audit numbers.

As the time approaches for the bankers you've been courting to make a decision, they'll have for their consideration any or all of the following elements:

- Your articulated enthusiasm for your real estate investment and its overwhelming chance for success
- Your audited financials, prepared by your prestigious accounting firm
- The answers to as many questions as they can think of

What about a question you haven't anticipated? The rule of thumb is that if you don't have an answer, never try to wing it. Chances are that the banker is asking some questions he or she already knows the answers to, just to check your level of forthrightness. Simply say, "That's a good question, and, frankly, right now, I don't have an answer. But I can certainly get you one." Then you dutifully make a mental note, as well as one on your notepad.

What happens if you get turned down? What do you do? The reason you've been turned down may well be that somewhere along the way, one of your selling points fell through the cracks. A no really means, "You haven't given us sufficient data to approve your concept. You haven't covered every base and done your job adequately."

Your response should be, "What element do you feel you're missing from the proposal equation? Where do you have a problem?" Ask! There's a legitimate reason you've been turned down, and you're not out of line to ask what that reason is. It could well be something you can fix.

Bankers are not gods, regardless of what some of them would have you believe. They're people with human needs, representing an institution with corporate policies and guidelines that have a great deal of resiliency. Make your banker your partner, your co-conspirator in helping you realize your dream. If you're prepared, if you're knowledgeable and professional, and court your banker step by step into what promises to become a long-term, mutually profitable relationship, it will suddenly seem that your banker is working for you instead of his or her employer.

5

SHOPPING AND CLOSING PROBATE DEALS

Successful real estate investors, regardless of where they get leads, carry a theatrical trunk around in their cars just as sure as they carry a spare tire. By that I mean they carry a number of masks—tragic, comedic, sympathetic, enthusiastic—whatever mask best reflects the mood of the potential seller.

They also carry an encyclopedic knowledge of real estate financing, which means how to structure the deal to make it absolutely irresistible. At the same time, the astute real estate investor is constantly calculating how to buy the property in question for the lowest possible price, with as little down payment as possible, and to keep the monthly mortgage payments as low as possible.

The classic real estate investor, as you may recall, is the white knight riding to the rescue of motivated sellers, creating a win-win situation by which the sellers can sell their treasured homestead for 10 to 15 percent under market value, for the cash to pay for mother's operation or that pilgrimage to the Holy Land—or to stop a foreclosure.

As I've stated, I've long since left that "motivated" seller scenario to others. The main reason is that the addresses are all listed in print, and I've never met a real estate investor who couldn't read! Besides, the most recent owners of the homes I purchase have no motivation whatsoever. They're dead. They're history. While some sensitivity is certainly required to negotiate a price for one's late father's home, usually there are no illusions about why I'm buying it—to resell it and make money while getting it out of the hair of the heir. But I've also bought probate properties and made them my home.

With that in mind, let's go shopping.

Sales of estate assets occur frequently in probate practice, and are common to estates of all sizes, types, and conditions. They require a detailed knowledge of both relevant statutory law and of local practice.

The power to sell assets is derived either from a state's Probate Code or from a provision in the decedent's will. The will frequently requests a general power to sell estate assets. This is called *testamentary power,* because it comes from the Last Will and Testament. The decedent may have directed the sale of a particular asset, or possibly all the estate assets, thus imposing an obligation as well as the power to sell.

In the absence of such a testamentary provision, the estate cannot sell real or personal property unless it can point to a state statute under which it is acting. There are two significant differences between the statutory and testamentary power of sale.

First, usually, notice of the sale must be given when following the statutory procedure, so that every potential purchaser has the opportunity to put in an offer. Notice need not be given, however, when there is a testamentary power of sale. Second, if the representative proceeds under a statutory power, he or she must be able to show a statutory reason for the sale. The testamentary power of sale doesn't require justification under the law. At the same time, it does not relieve the estate of the necessity of reporting the sale to the court for confirmation.

A general discretionary power of "management and distribution" of the decedent's property granted to the estate under the terms of the will does not necessarily include a power of sale. A testamentary power to carry on the decedent's business carries with it the power to sell property in the ordinary course of the business without reporting these sales to the court for confirmation, but this power is limited exclusively to sales relating to operating that business.

When the estate is directed by the will to sell estate property to a specified person, this should be done and reported to the court. A general power of sale given to the representative by the will does not impose a duty to sell estate property, but if the will directs a sale, for any reason, the estate is required to carry out the direction. The duty of the estate to sell property is enforceable by the court upon the petition of any person interested in the estate after the summons to appear by the estate.

Under a testamentary power of direction to sell, the representative may publish notice of the sale, but is not required to do so. If the representative does publish a notice, he or she is bound to comply with the notification requirements and to sell under the terms of the notice.

Local rules for probate sales vary from court to court across the country. However, they share the basic requirements and guidelines. The published notice of sale of real property constitutes a solicitation for offers. There cannot be a variance between the terms of the notice and those of the sale. Subsequently, if a technical defect appears in the terms after the sale, the court can nullify the sale.

The estate may sell real property through a private sale, a public auction, a private auction, or listed with a real estate broker. A good number of estate sales are completed as private sales, so let's discuss this method first.

BUYING PROBATE REAL ESTATE AT A PRIVATE SALE

A private real estate sale is one in which bids are solicited independently of each other. A private sale is usually handled by the attorney because the estate allows the attorney for the estate to control the entire probate process.

The attorney will invite all bidders or their representatives to come to his or her office at a given time with sealed envelopes. The highest bid is the one that is accepted.

A determined buyer knows, like Yogi Berra, that, "It ain't over 'til it's over!" The buyer will not stop there, and since you've read this far, I can assume that you intend to be a determined buyer! So you learn that your offer was not the highest. Don't roll over and play dead. Go back to the attorney with a better offer. The attorney will probably tell you that he or she cannot accept the new offer. Then you explain that if your offer is not accepted, it will be filed in the Probate Court in the county where the proceedings are pending.

There's no need to say much more. The attorney would look foolish in front of the judge if he or she did not accept your new offer. So to avoid embarrassment, the attorney will usually accept your offer. Notice I said *usually,* since occasionally you run into a lawyer who will not be bluffed.

If the probated property is going to be listed in the real estate board's multiple listing service (MLS), it's critical that you buy as quickly as possible after it is listed in order to limit its exposure to competition. *Exposure is the enemy of the investor.* The more the exposure, the higher the price you're going to pay. As you recall, the whole reason for pursuing probate real estate is that there's no competition. On an empty playing field, you're always the winner!

Avoiding MLS exposure is not so important in large metropolitan areas as it is in smaller communities. In larger cities there are so many properties listed in the MLS that a lot of them go unnoticed, especially new listings, and especially if they include the usual 5 percent probate commission, as opposed to the customary 6 or 7 percent real estate commissions. Regardless of the market, the best way to avoid exposure is to hurry and get your offer accepted quickly.

One observation about the use of MLS to sell probate properties. Attorneys and personal representatives go through the MLS to cover themselves and to make the sale easy on themselves. They can point out in court that the property has been given the greatest exposure by having it listed in the MLS, putting it in the hands of a professional real estate broker, and so on. Going the MLS route also eliminates the work they would have to do if they sold by private sale or public auction.

From the estate's point of view, the private sale is the best method of selling real property. In my personal opinion after doing this for almost 34 years, the private sale gets the best results for the seller, largely because a good and competent broker will really work hard under those circumstances. Hungry, committed real estate brokers will comb the newspaper listings for private offerings. Even though they get only a 5 percent commission, there is usually no listing broker with whom the commission has to be split. Sometimes the selling broker will actually make two-thirds more in commission for the same job—even as much as 100 percent! Otherwise, few brokers accustomed to getting 6 or 7 percent are going to shortchange themselves by even 1 percent. I certainly wouldn't.

So remember, if you're going through the court process, it's important that you be right there when the bid is going to court—*before* it gets to court. Timing is critical! That way you can control the amount of the first overbid and set the terms of sale.

Personally, when I find a property listed that already has a court confirmation date, I walk away from it. I know that it will have had too much exposure. I may miss a good deal once in a while, but usually I save myself time and effort.

BUYING PROBATE REAL ESTATE AT PUBLIC AUCTION

A public auction sale is similar to the private sale in that it is usually controlled by the attorney, in his or her office at a specified time. The difference is that there are no bids. The customary auction format is followed, with open oral bidding. The highest bid is then petitioned for court confirmation.

As with private sale proceedings, as we talked about, it is still possible to circumvent this decision by filing a counteroffer in the Probate Court.

BUYING PROBATE REAL ESTATE AT PRIVATE AUCTION

In this type of real property sale, a professional auctioneer is contracted by the estate representative or attorney to conduct the auction. This is particularly true in large cities, while in smaller communities the attorney might supervise the auction. The contract with the auctioneer must permit the estate to reserve the right to withdraw the property from sale. Probate property may be sold as a whole or in lots or selling units.

Sometimes, especially in a slow market, a property held for public auction will be listed by a broker. Once again, this is to cover the attorney and estate representative with the court, and take the hassle of selling the property off of these two people.

In a private auction, the outcome is the same as in a public auction or a private sale. The highest offer will be accepted.

BUYING PROBATE REAL ESTATE "WITHOUT NOTICE"

Buying real property being offered without notice requires a great deal of hard work. However, the great advantage is that it virtually guarantees that you will get that property well under market value.

In order to be successful at buying probate real estate, the first rule is: *The early bird gets the worm!* Be the first one to help the estate. You'll be surprised to discover how many times they'll look to you for advice. By being in there from the beginning, you can ascertain what's on their minds, what they plan to do with the property, what the price and terms are likely to be, and, most important, who will make the final decision.

Be knowledgeable, polite, and businesslike, and exude the quiet confidence of a professional. You're there to help them settle the estate.

BUYING PROBATE REAL ESTATE DIRECTLY FROM THE HEIRS

Another opportunity to buy probate real estate and personal property comes after it is no longer in probate. Once you have agreed on the price and terms, you then immediately get the agreement in writing, witnessed by two people or notarized. Then initiate the closing. Now you have a deal! By doing this, you've bought a property the address of which was never in print!

Buying this way directly from heirs ensures that the property will receive little or no exposure, and therefore be subject to no competition. This is absolutely a great way to purchase probate real estate.

Community property and joint tenancy property can be sold without going through any probate at all.

PERSONAL PROPERTY—A TREASURE OF EARTHLY DELIGHTS

We've spent a lot of time talking about purchasing real property out of probate, but never forget that when you buy, say, the home of the late resident, you buy it *as is.* Of course the heirs and family friends are going to enjoy first cull of various personal items, ("I'd love to have that broach Aunt Sally wore all the time, to remind me of her." "I could use some of those tools in the garage.") but in most cases, the family says, in effect, take all that stuff and get rid of it. In the event there are no family members, you get everything in the house when you take possession.

Chapter 7 is a series of vignettes, good and bad, that includes some stories of hidden treasure that become legends. Right here, let me tell you about the late John Harley, a bachelor and the town barber in Medford, Wisconsin. He died at age 78, and a young couple bought his house and all its furnishings out of probate. Included was John's old piano, a broken down, out-of-tune relic that may have been his mother's. Who knows?

The couple decided to keep this antique piano, but realized that it needed serious restoring—stabilizing the frame, refinishing the woodwork, replacing broken ivories and strings, and of course a good tuning. They had the time and handy skills to do most of that themselves, but when they dismantled the piano, they discovered that, in the 60 years John had owned the piano, he had stuffed it with some $140,000 in cash.

It wasn't a piano—it was John's piggy bank! That was $140,000 counted at face value. Some of those bills were old silver certificates and other currency that had long been out of circulation, which they sold to collectors for far more than face value.

The point is, you never know what a house, especially an old house, is going to hold. When you walk into an antique shop, where do you think all those antiques and "collectibles" come from? Estate sales! They've been bought by the cardboard box at pennies to sell for dollars.

When you buy your first real property filled with a lifetime of personal property, you need to understand the *mathematics* of personal property. You should never pay more than 25 cents on the fair market dollar for any personal stuff—furniture, jewelry, artwork, china, crystal, and silver included. Here's why. You want to make the standard keystone markup of 100 percent when you sell all that stuff to an antique dealer. That antique dealer, selling retail, wants to make his or her keystone markup of 100 percent as well.

For example, Grandma Jones' nice cut-glass lamp would probably sell for $100 at Joe's Antiques. You pay the estate $25 to take it off their hands. You sell it to Sam's Antique Shop for $50. There's your 100 percent. Sam puts a $120 price tag on it, giving him room to let a likely buyer haggle him down to $100. Sam gets his 100 percent and everybody's happy.

Now that you've shopped and closed on your probate deal, it's time to fix that baby up and sell it for a tidy profit.

6

FIXING UP YOUR FIXER

Volumes have been written on what to do with your recently purchased investment property that is slightly or even critically in need of fixing up. After all, that's why we call them fixers or *fixer-uppers*.

Properties acquired out of probate are always purchased *as is*, and are likely to be at least moderate fixer-uppers. The majority of these properties had served as the decedent's most recently owned residence. In instances where former residents were elderly, particularly, household repairs they would have had made immediately in previous years have slipped by undone or even unnoticed. One contributing factor is that they often were living on a fixed income, and necessities took precedence over a new exterior paint job, fresh carpeting, or a new roof.

Don't be afraid of fixers. Don't be intimidated because a potential investment is a little run down. Just make up your mind to appraise the costs, make your decision, and get it fixed. The key is to squelch the question, "Can I do it?" and ask yourself "How can I do it?" and "How soon can I start?"

INSPECTIONS—INVESTIGATING BEFORE YOU INVEST

Some conditions are not readily evident, and are potential deal breakers. Termites, for instance. Get permission from the estate to have a termite inspection done at your own expense. Also with permission, get a professional structural inspector to go through the property from roof to basement. Accompany this inspector so you can learn the details about any structural problems he or she encounters.

Sometimes before you can sell, you have to upgrade such items as the electrical system (from 110v to 200v), and plumbing from lead pipe to copper or PCV, all of which often gets costly.

Another inspection you may want—at your expense—is for toxic mold. This is new, and if it is not a big deal in your area now, it will be. I've talked to a man who is familiar with toxic mold lawsuits all over the country. He claims it's a nonissue. He said, "I'll buy all the houses in America that have toxic mold." So regardless of how fictitious the problem may be, the lawyers have made it an income source for themselves. It exists as a perceived problem, so you may want to check for it.

PUTTING YOUR CREATIVITY TO WORK

As you walk around a potential investment property looking at small tears in the screens or peeling paint or a lawn gone to weeds, look beyond what it is to what it could be—and what you could get for it as a resale. Take along a copy of the Property Expense Repair Survey in Appendix H, and figure up just what it will cost you to get that house back to its old eye-appealing self.

In fact, I always look on a fixer as an opportunity to exercise what creativity I have. That may include bathroom or kitchen curtains in cheerful patterns and colors, a nice bed of multicolored flowers near the front door, even a few household tools hanging in the garage that you just "throw in" as part of the deal. You can never tell what little extra will make the sale.

A friend of mine once owned a condominium in Florida, in one of those condo communities in which all units are essentially the same. They all included a so-called backyard, a fenced-in square of ground off the kitchen that could accommodate at most a cookout grill and a playpen. When he decided to sell, he surveyed the community and discovered that four other identical units were for sale at virtually the same price. He visited each one, and observed that the yard in every case had deteriorated into a weed patch, much like the one behind his own unit.

He went back to his unit and cut down the weeds, then he went down to the K-Mart Garden Center and bought 25 small annuals—red and white impatiens, orange marigolds, perky petunias—for 85 cents apiece, and plunked them in the dirt around the wood fence.

An hour later, a young couple arrived to look at his unit. They strolled around gazing passively at the fourth or fifth such condo they'd seen in an hour. Then they opened the back door and stepped into yard area.

"Oh, honey, I like this yard. It's so pretty, and it's like . . . bigger than the others," cooed the young wife.

"Yeah, it may be," fudged my friend. "I just love it out here," he added, as if it were Cypress Gardens. More important, he mentally added a grand to his asking price and sold it to them on the strength of $23.58 worth of tiny flowers and half an hour's gardening.

DECIDING WHAT TO DO AND WHO TO DO IT

Once you've run the figures and are certain you can cover the repair costs and still make a profit, you have two choices with regard to repairs and improvements. You can do it yourself for several reasons. You are, for example, quite handy with every home improvement tool. You also have a high pain threshold that does not acknowledge cuts and bruises caused by stupid equipment.

You have a great deal of time on your hands. You've watched a professional home repair team work and said to yourself, "I can do that." Finally, you love to work for countless hours on a house to realize a sense of personal achievement.

You could also do what I do and contact professional repair people. How do you know who's reliable and honest? Get recommendations. Ask other real estate investors. Ask that real estate agent you've been nurturing. The discovery of a skilled, dependable, and affordable repair and fix-up source is like hitting a side vein in your gold mine.

Have three repair contractors come out and give you estimates. Before they come, type out a list of what you want done and make three copies. Put your name and phone number on it and give one copy to each contractor. If one of them has other suggestions for you to consider—and to charge you more—add them to the list you're giving to the other two. Remember, apples to apples. Otherwise you're likely to slide into "repair dementia," a degenerative condition in which a homeowner no longer remembers what he or she wants done.

Actually, you have two options, depending on who's available and reliable in your area. You can hire a recommended contractor who has friends and no doubt relatives who do the actual labor, such as paint, repair, and resurface. The contractor supervises a crew, handles all the details, and is answerable to you. Instead, you can call a recommended painter, a recommended carpenter, a recommended electrician, and so on, and be your own contractor.

The following is a list of fix-up recommendations that I have found useful in the lower end or starter market, and that may add to your own success:

- Texture all interior walls. A textured paint covers cracks caused by ground settling and makes the house look ten years younger. Apply a popcorn finish to all ceilings, again to cover water spots, cracks, and other imperfections.

- Paint all walls an off-white—eggshell, oyster, whatever. Darker colors make rooms appear smaller. Do not get creative with interior wall colors. You might think that Misty Coral or Jungle Jade is just darling for the den, but restrain yourself. Others might disagree.
- Install beige carpets. Few homebuyers overtly dislike wall-to-wall carpeting, and it makes the room look larger. The same advice about wall colors applies to carpeting. Carpet that calls attention to itself is inevitably detrimental to a house sale. That means nobody likes it. If the floors are an attractive wood, especially parquet, refinish them and leave them uncarpeted. Really nice wood flooring is more prized than carpeting.
- If you need to restucco the exterior, use colorcoat and texture it, for the same reasons you would texture the interior. You can cover those cracks well—unless the house sits astride a recent fault line.
- Paint the exterior with anything but a dark color. Some wisdom says that if you want to sell a house fast—especially a small house—paint it yellow. Don't ask me why. Again, basic off-white is good.
- Clean up the yard. Put in a few flowering bushes. Remove the debris that a vacant house collects. Get a new welcome mat for the front door. Straighten the mailbox. You want this house to look lived in—not died in! Give the property "curb appeal," so that it conveys a positive first impression the moment prospects step out of their car.

It's a good idea to match décor trends at the level of the neighborhood surrounding your property. For small or starter homes, this means mica counter tops, medium-grade carpeting, and shower curtains.

Medium-priced homes require tile countertops, wood flooring, and plastic or glass shower doors.

High-end homebuyers expect granite countertops, stone floors, tiled Roman bathtub and shower with adjacent Jacuzzi, walk-in closets, four- or five-car garage, subzero refrigerator, Viking stove and oven—maybe two—plus Anderson or Pella windows.

Doing much more than is standard is wasting your fixer-upper money, but make sure your property offers the same amenities that everyone expects for the price range—and do it better.

In addition to these areas of fix-up, you'll have other decisions to make about the finishing touches—kitchen and bath fixtures, crafted wood cabinets versus prefab, decorative glass and stone surfaces. One measure of your success in making your fixer stand out in buyers' minds comes when you follow them around the house. Count the number of "Look Dears." "Look, dear, that's real parquet in the living room." "Look, dear, aren't those nice bath curtains." "Look, dear, how well they've kept this house."

One homeseller I know puts a small table in the dining room of an empty house. Then, before a showing, he puts a vase on it with fresh-cut flowers, and another one on a kitchen counter. I just can't overemphasize the persuasive power of the small touches— thoughtful, inexpensive little things that ring a bell with a buyer's emotions. I have heated vanilla extract in an aluminum pan in the oven before a prospect arrives for a house showing, just to add a pleasing "home-baked" aroma to the property.

When you go beyond just fixing a fixer, and add touches of personality and warmth, eye appeal and heart appeal—call it livability—you'll get top dollar return and get it faster.

That's what investing is all about.

7

TRUE TALES FROM THE WORLD OF PROBATE

I almost called this chapter "Horror Stories from the World of Probate," except that some of them are more hilarious than they are horrific. Almost all of them play out just beneath the horizon of the daily news, so that, like the gold mine of probate itself, most folks never hear about them.

THE LUXURY-LOVING LOOTER OF TEXAS ESTATES

A former probate specialist in the Bexar county clerk's office hit on a great idea for financing his fantasy life as a gentleman auto racer. Using 20 years of experience in probate, Mel Spillman took fraudulent control of at least 120 estates in the San Antonio area, selling the assets of the recently deceased, which included houses, cars, antiques, jewelry, and furnishings. Over some 15 years, the soft-spoken, friendly clerk, whose annual salary was $33,000, quietly pocketed $4.9 million in cash. He took other proceeds to purchase a $450,000 mansion, and six Ferraris and other exotic racecars to compete on the high-rolling Formula One racing circuit.

Because the area of probate is so complex, few people, including county government bureaucrats, understand it, and many attorneys avoid it. Spillman's years of dealing with probate cases enabled him to use the system to take control of estates, sell their real estate and personal property, and set up several bank accounts in which to funnel the money—and remain undetected.

He was finally caught when some of his false documents caught the eye of investigators, who then videotaped him using those documents to take control of yet another estate. In June 2002, he was sentenced to ten years in prison.

THE GUN COLLECTOR'S TREASURE

A former student of mine did a follow-up on a probate case. The widow of the deceased didn't sell the house, but she did want to unload some personal items, starting with her late husband's gun collection. She hated guns so much that when he died, she had put all those guns out in the garage.

My student went over to purchase some of those personal items—you never know what you'll find—and the widow told him about the guns stored in the garage. He went out and found 18 guns packed away. It turned out to be quite a collection, and included antique firearms that went back to the Civil War. He returned to the house and asked the widow how much she wanted for them. She said, "$150."

"Each?" he said.

"No, for all of them," replied the widow, no doubt delighted at the chance to unload all those menacing weapons. So my dismayed student purchased the entire collection, helping the lady get them out of her life forever. The least of them was worth $150.

THE MOBILE HOME CASH COW

Another student, Joe, (not his real name) came across a probate case that included three mobile home parks. He purchased them for substantially less than fair market value. In each park he found a resident who was glad to act as manager and collect rent from the neighbors for a reasonable commission.

The first time Joe went to collect the rent receipts from his managers, he was astounded. They were almost all in cash! As he explained to me later, most of the tenants didn't have checking accounts.

Before long, he also discovered that mobile home residents who fall behind in their rent often just pick up and disappear, leaving their mobile home behind. Joe found he could clean up these abandoned homes and sell them almost immediately to new families. He would ask for a substantial down payment, and if the new tenants didn't keep up the monthly payments, he could always repossess the homes and resell them to new owners, again for pure profit, and do it again and again.

Joe told me one time that "the hardest money to make is tax-free. Cash is that kind of money." Now you know why "Joe" is not his real name.

PROBATE DOESN'T GO BETTER WITH COKE

When her husband died, Elizabeth was living in their 13-acre New England estate. Her late husband had appointed his son, "Harold," as executor of the estate, in charge of rounding up assets, paying debts, and distributing the balance according to the will. Trouble was, Harold was a cokehead, and the estate began to disappear up his nostrils.

He sold the estate and put Elizabeth in a $400,000 condo. Then he mortgaged the condo and spent those proceeds on his drug habit as well. When the bank foreclosed, Elizabeth was forced to move in with relatives. Elizabeth, ever the lady, never challenged her stepson's action because she didn't want to cause an ugly family scandal.

So instead, she's penniless.

TURNING RAW LAND INTO A RAW DEAL

Even when a beneficiary sues an executor, justice can be elusive. Susan's mother left a $13 million estate, naming Susan's brother as executor. Some $10 million of that estate was 383 acres of raw Texas land, valuable real estate positioned in the middle of an oil field. The brother neglected to sell the land at the height of an oil boom, passing up an enormous profit. Susan sued her brother. In 1996, a jury found that the loving brother had overpaid himself $2.4 million and deprived the beneficiaries of $169 million by not selling the land parcel to oil companies.

The judge was unmoved by the jury's decision. He ruled that the brother should return the $2.4 million, remain the executor, and use estate funds to pay his lawyers $1.5 million.

As usual, the lawyers won again.

MAKING A FORTUNE IN DEAD ERNEST

More than 20 years ago, a woman bought a probate house in the mid-Wilshire district of Los Angeles. While exploring her purchase, she ended up poking around in the crawl space above the ceiling, and came upon a small chest. Upon opening it, she found the chest filled with bundles of old letters. A quick read or two revealed that they were obviously love letters.

This was long before the days of eBay, so she took a sample of the letters to the renowned auction house, Butterfield and Butterfield, on Sunset Boulevard, to see how much she could get for them. She got an average of $5,000 per letter. Today, those letters would sell easily for about $20,000 each. Why? It seems that the letter writer had had a long affair with the previous owner of the house. The writer signed his love letters "Ernest," for Ernest Hemingway.

THE HOLE-IN-THE WALL HOAX

Back in 1978, a good friend of mine, Bob, bought a probate house in Venice, California. It was a fixer-upper, and while he was looking it over, a neighbor dropped by. She confided to Bob that the man who had owned the house prior to his death was a little eccentric, and there was a persistent rumor that he was supposed to have hidden $50,000 in cash inside one of the walls.

Bob got all excited. He grabbed some tools and proceeded to punch holes in every wall in the house, looking for that $50,000 in hidden loot. He probably found mice and mold, but never found the money—it was just an old wives' tale—and it cost him $11,000 to repair the walls!

THE SECRET OF THE CAST IRON STOVE

It was Bob's bad luck he didn't buy the home of Mary McGinnis. Mary, of Philadelphia, lived alone for years, wore cheap clothes, and lived in a rundown house with no heat, TV, or even a radio. Even at age 87, she rode the bus every day to get free meals at a local senior center. At her death she left $1.4 million to her parish church for a scholarship fund. Then her pastor, visiting her home, happened into the kitchen and discovered $500,000 in bonds and cash stuffed in a tin box inside her old-fashioned cast-iron stove.

A FORTUNE IN CORN FLAKES

Rumors of secret wealth are fueled by such stories as that of Edith Agnes Plumb. For 58 years, she lived in a modest North Hollywood home. She had inherited some Kellogg Cereals stock, and over the years it kept splitting. By the time she died at age 88 in 1995, she had accumulated 1.3 million shares worth about $98 million. Plumb was so casual about her stock holdings she never bothered to stash her stock certificates in a safe deposit box. After her death, her attorney found the latest 2-for-1 split, worth $48 million, stuck in a little black book beside the telephone.

THE HIDDEN ICE BOX

A lady from Albuquerque—we'll call her Lilly—attended one of my seminars for the sole purpose of buying a larger house for her family at a healthy discount through probate. She did just that, but the house needed painting throughout. Lilly and her husband decided to do the painting themselves.

Around the fireplace there were two built-in brick-and-glass breakfronts. As they were detailing the cabinets, they noticed a loose brick. Lilly removed the brick and found herself peering into a black hole. Being a prudent woman, Lilly asked her husband to stick his hand into the hole. He did, and pulled out a small white cardboard box.

Inside the box were 71 diamonds! They were in all the finest diamond colors—white, blue, even precious yellow diamonds of various sizes. She sold them to a gemologist for a tidy profit. Who says there ain't gold in them probate hills!

THE FAIR MARKET VALUE SWITCHEROO

The gemologist in the above story is a friend of ours and a former student we'll call Ralph. He specialized in gems that turned up as part of the personal property in probate, and had made up to that time about $175,000 on probate gems. He and his wife decided to try the real estate side of probate deals, and found a house painted a color we in Texas call "burnt orange," or maybe "sunset sienna." Anyway, it was a pretty distinctive color.

Buford, the estate representative for this case, was not exactly the sharpest knife in the drawer, and when Ralph came into the house, he spotted the tax bill for the property that Buford had left lying on the table. As any homeowner knows, the assessed value of any property for county tax purposes is far less than the fair market value.

Ralph quickly said to Buford, "You know, the government is going to try to get every penny it can out of this property—the 'pound of flesh' so to speak? So you know this tax bill appraisal is the property's fair market value."

Buford agreed, and that's how Ralph bought the property at 34 percent below fair market value.

THE LONELY LADY OF BALBOA ISLAND

An eccentric elderly woman had a small home in a beautiful community on Newport Beach Bay called Balboa Island. She lived alone and was kind of a local character, walking around the neighborhood making friends with everyone, and liked by all. No one had ever been inside her home, and her life was obviously a lonely one.

Then one day, someone found her sitting up and long dead. They also found that she had collected so many jars, cans, old newspapers, and other trash that there were only narrow paths through her house. One led to a small cubbyhole where she had slept sitting up for lack of room, and where she had died alone.

The house was only 700 square feet, but five tons of trash had to be removed. The individual who bought it out of probate had the house bulldozed, put up a two-story home on what was a very desirable lot—and made a net profit of $285,000.

REWARDING NOTES FROM AN OLD PIANO

Out on Long Island, Alan Sherman and Jay Nicolai bought a 1930s-era Baldwin Arcosonic piano from an estate in Farmingville. Nicolai, a piano tuner and repairman, opened up the old piano to discover a manila envelope filled with 62 U.S. Savings Bonds to the tune of about $30,000. Being the nice guys they were, Sherman and Nicolai searched Long Island for any descendents of the couple who had owned the piano. Finally, they found a daughter and presented her with the bonds. The money will go to help finance her three kids in college, she said, and also a reward to Sherman and Nicolai along with her gratitude.

THE DISGUSTING CAT HOUSE

Several years ago, Ben, a buddy of mine, bought a house out of probate. The late owner had lived alone there—with 39 cats. The house was a catastrophe. It was as if the cats played in the backyard but came inside to relieve themselves. Every drape in the house was stained with cat urine up to three feet from the floor. The floors were covered with layers of defecation piled as much as six inches high and covered with old newspapers.

Ben got a high-pressure hose and blasted unmeasured pounds of manure out of the house, down the driveway and into the sewers. The EPA would have put him away for doing that today. It took seven months and gallons of ammonia and polyurethane, and a lot of elbow grease, to rid the house of stains and odors, even to the point of replacing some of the flooring. Then he restored and redecorated it and, finally, the house was livable once more. Ben made a net profit of $157,000 when he sold it.

But there was another reward. While he was in the process of selling what was now a very lovely house, the grown daughter of the former owner dropped by. She walked slowly around, spending time in each room. Then, with tears in her eyes, she said to Ben, "This is the way I remember it, growing up." She thanked him for what he had done for her childhood home.

PLAYING THE PIANO BLUES

All probate piano tales don't end on a bright note. Years ago I partnered with a couple I'll call "John" and "Mary" to buy a probate house. I had no interest in the personal property, but John and his wife did. In fact, they bought everything but an elegant grand piano, because they didn't know where they could store it until they sold it. The estate's asking price for the piano was just $1,000. Still, they declined.

The estate representative lived out-of-state, but was nice enough to let John and Mary hold the estate property sale on everything they'd bought there in the house, everything from the estate except the piano.

Meanwhile, the estate representative called a local company that bought and sold used pianos to see if they would buy it and get it out of the house. The piano company said they would, made the estate an incredible offer of $5,000 and said they would pick it up later. The estate rep notified John and Mary of the deal, in case the piano movers showed up. He also told them how much the estate was being paid.

Back at the house, as the estate sale progressed, John and prospective buyers found themselves walking around the piano to get to other items in the house. "What was the problem in finding a place to store this thing," he asked Mary. Then they both realized that they could have bought the piano from the estate for $1,000, kept it right where it was, and with just a small walk through the Yellow Pages found the company that was paying five grand for it—and cleared a $4,000 profit!

Sometimes you just can't see the forest for the trees.

Chapter

8

PROBATE IS DIFFERENT
IN CALIFORNIA

Calilornia, long noted—or branded—for marching to the beat of a different drummer, holds a unique distinction among the country's the probate systems as well. It is the only state that maintains state-appointed board of more than 160 Inheritance Tax Referees, also called "probate referees," whose part-time job it is to evaluate estates for California probate courts.

Here's how the system really works. After a state-appointed probate referee, an officer of the court, appraised a property, the ultimate sale price of that property had to be within 9 percent of the appraisal. Then, after a sales contract was in writing, it would be submitted to the probate court. Next, in open court, anybody could come along and overbid the original sales contract by the following formula: the first overbid would be a minimum of 5 percent over the original purchase price, plus $500. Then all additional increments of the bid were at the discrimination of the judge. The last person standing would be declared the buyer.

In 1993, when now ex-Governor Gray Davis was still serving as state controller, the *Los Angeles Times* did a series of articles focusing on the fact that Davis, and controllers before him, had used the probate referee system to reward political contributors, personal friends, and Democratic associates. The article's headline said it all: "Gray Davis' Political Pals Get Lucrative Posts." It reported that Gray had appointed to referee posts the son of Democratic California Assembly Speaker Willie Brown, a daughter of a Davis campaign contributor, and various wives of labor leaders in unions supporting Davis' campaigns. In many cases, referees were appointed even though they failed to pass a qualifying test. Working part-time and on an as-needed basis, some of these appointees were making up to $100,000 a year, yet able to continue any full-time employment they already had.

Reform-minded politicians questioned how individuals with no background in either appraisal work or real estate could evaluate homes of every type and value, as well as personal property. How could a political appointment, for example, place a value on a rare painting or a piece of antique furniture without a background in appraising art or antiques? Or rare coin or stamp collections, or even cars, boats, or private planes, for that matter? Critics cried that the nonpolitical positions had simply been politicized to foster an outdated spoils system. They also questioned that if the system is so effective, why hadn't any other state in the Union, including other Democratic-controlled states, adopted the Inheritance Tax Referee system?

CALIFORNIA PROBATE REFEREES—IN MARYLAND AND CHINA!

The qualifications of the referees was held suspect not only because of the referees' lack of appraisal knowledge, but also because of their lack of availability. One particular situation the *Times* newspaper indicated was that two of the current referees were not even in California. One of them, Michael Steed, was a former director of the Democratic National Committee, maintained a Washington business office, and was registered to vote in Maryland. His wife told reporters that her husband spent about half his time in California.

The other referee, accountant Lawrence Lipsher, was trying to start a pharmaceutical business in southwest China and was spending half his time in China or working in an office in Hong Kong. Lipsher countered the charge by saying, "I do not live in China. I travel back and forth." Nevertheless, he listed the Hong Kong office as his address with the State Board of Accountancy. Lipsher had been a referee since 1975.

Another criticism of the referees was that, too often, they never saw the properties they were supposed to be evaluating. Instead, they had staffers, called "shadow referees" by critics, actually perform the evaluation for a percentage of the commission. One referee said all he had to do was sign the evaluation document, and he could do that by fax from any place in the world. Presumably including China.

GRAY DAVIS DEFENDS AND CONTINUES THE TAINTED REFEREE SYSTEM

After the October 1993 expose by the *Times*, controller Davis initially defended the referee system, pointing out that "not a single penny of taxpayer money" was used to compensate referees. Instead, referees earned their income by receiving one-tenth of one percent of each evaluation they performed.

Despite Davis' defense of the system, what it was doing, in effect, was creating an enormous Democratic slush fund. Every real estate property and every item of personal property in California's probate system contributed to a fund approaching five billion dollars. Adding to the take was yet another rule: If an individual sold a second property, even if he or she were a Californian, 3.3 percent of the sales price would be held until the tax return from that year was refunded, between 9 and 15 months later! The *Times* calculated that this would create an $87 billion private slush fund that would never be depleted.

Feeling the pressure from both the public and California Republicans, he then vowed to reform the referee system. Yet over the next year or so, in his final year as controller before becoming lieutenant governor, Davis appointed a number of politically well-connected individuals to referee posts, including David Elder, a Democrat who had raised campaign funds for his own campaign, in violation of a law prohibiting fund-raising by acting referees. Others had donated to the candidacies of Democrats Barbara Boxer and Dianne Feinstein.

KATHLEEN CONNELL—A DEMOCRATIC REFORMER WHO RILES DEMOCRATS

Two years later, in the summer of 1995, a new state controller, Kathleen Connell, also a Democrat, vowed to further reform the probate referee system. For the first time, referees up for reappointment were required to take a tough new qualifying test. Under Gray Davis, grades as low as 45.5 percent were considered passing; Connell now required a far more stringent 75 percent. As a result, 44 percent of the existing referees failed to pass. In addition, she began a program of interviews by an independent panel to further determine the qualifications of existing referees. As a result, only 16 of 35 referees up for reappointment in 1995 were reappointed. (Sliding over the issue of job qualification wasn't new in California. The following year, 1996, the State Bar Association voted 20 to 3 that newly appointed state Supreme Court Justice Janice Rogers Brown, a Democrat, was unqualified for the high court, but thanks to a Democratic-controlled state legislature, she kept her job.)

At the same time Connell was tightening up referee qualifications, she began to question aloud whether there was even a need for probate referees, especially since California was the only state to use them. Her campaign to reform or even eliminate referees was seen as a direct slap to Lieutenant Governor Davis, who was now being considered as a candidate for governor in 1998.

Connell had ambitions of her own, and began to gather support to run for governor herself. She was bright, energetic, photogenic, and gave a fresh voice to calls for reform in state government. She was also working closely with Pete Wilson, the Republican governor.

Connell's determination to reform the probate system, her veiled criticism of fellow Democrat Gray Davis, her obvious ambition to climb the political ladder, and her threat to end a spoils system through which Democratic supporters were being rewarded—these four factors turned powerful factions of her own party against her.

It was about that time that the Democratic-led state budget committee got bogged down in preparation of its 1998 budget. In what was a final straw, Connell distributed to reporters a summary of legislators' salaries and expense payments during the summer budget impasse, saying, "$1,365,240 per month for what?"

KATHLEEN CONNELL FADES FROM MEMORY; REFEREE SYSTEM SURVIVES

Although they denied it was an act of retribution, the budget committee voted to strip Connell's authority to appoint probate referees. As support within her own party dissipated, Connell's chances of nomination for governor against fellow Democrat Davis, and ultimately her political career, faded. Connell became, in effect, a politician without a party.

The bottom line to all this furor was that in 1998, Gray Davis, whose lack of political ethics had triggered the cronyism issue in the first place, was elected governor, although later recalled in the face of California's energy crisis. The Inheritance Tax Referee system survives to this day.

A ppendixes

A

CONTENTS OF A PROBATE FILE

Every county courthouse maintains an individual file for each probate case. The following are samples of just some of the many forms to look for when you begin investigating a probate file:

- Application and Order Appointing Inheritance Tax Referee (California only)
- Petition for Probate
- Proof of Publication
- Inventory and Appraisement and Attachment
- Notice of Death and of Petition to Administer Estate
- Order for Probate
- Clerk's Certificate of Posting or Mailing

NAME AND ADDRESS OF ATTORNEY	TELEPHONE NO.	FOR COURT USE ONLY

NAME OF COURT, OR BRANCH, MAILING AND STREET ADDRESS

ESTATE OF

☐ DECEDENT   ☐ INCOMPETENT   ☐ CONSERVATEE   ☐ MINOR

CASE NUMBER

APPLICATION AND ORDER APPOINTING INHERITANCE TAX REFEREE

It is requested that an Inheritance Tax Referee be appointed to appraise the assets of the above entitled estate consisting of the following approximate values, including Joint Tenancy Property:

1. CASH $ _____

2. REAL ESTATE $ _____

3. PERSONAL PROPERTY $ _____

REMARKS _____

_____

_____
Attorney

IT IS ORDERED that (name):

a disinterested person, is appointed Referee to appraise the above-entitled estate. When an Inheritance Tax Referee is appointed, such referee is authorized to fix the clear market value of the estate as of the date of death of the decedent, or as of the date of appointment if a conservatorship or guardianship, and to appraise all interests, inheritances, transfers, and property of the estate subject to the payment of inheritance tax under the laws of the State of California.

DATED: _____
Judge of the Superior Court

APPLICATION AND ORDER APPOINTING INHERITANCE TAX REFEREE

RP—5

229A   76A650Q(Rev. 11-77)—PS 1-78   PROB C 605

ATTORNEY OR PARTY WITHOUT ATTORNEY (NAME AND ADDRESS)   TELEPHONE NO   FOR COURT USE ONLY

ATTORNEY FOR (NAME)

SUPERIOR COURT OF CALIFORNIA, COUNTY OF

STREET ADDRESS

MAILING ADDRESS

CITY AND ZIP CODE

BRANCH NAME

ESTATE OF (NAME):

Decedent

PETITION FOR

- ☐ PROBATE OF WILL AND FOR LETTERS TESTAMENTARY
- ☐ PROBATE OF WILL AND FOR LETTERS OF ADMINISTRATION WITH WILL ANNEXED
- ☐ LETTERS OF ADMINISTRATION
- ☐ SPECIAL LETTERS OF ADMINISTRATION
- ☐ AUTHORIZATION TO ADMINISTER UNDER THE INDEPENDENT ADMINISTRATION OF ESTATES ACT

CASE NUMBER

HEARING DATE

DEPT   TIME

1   Attorney requests publication in   **METROPOLITAN NEWS (or its designee)**

_____ (Type or print name)   _____ (Signature of attorney)

2   Petitioner* (name of each):

    requests that

    a   ☐ decedent's will and codicils, if any, be admitted to probate.

    b   ☐ (name):

       be appointed (1) ☐ executor   (3) ☐ administrator

                   (2) ☐ administrator with will annexed   (4) ☐ special administrator

       and Letters issue upon qualification.

    c   ☐ authority be granted to administer under the Independent Administration of Estates Act.

    d   ☐ bond not be required for the reasons stated in attachment 2d

       ☐ bond be fixed at $ _____ to be furnished by an authorized surety company or as otherwise provided by law *(specify reasons if the amount is different from the minimum required by section 541 of the Probate Code).*

       ☐ deposits at *(specify institution):*

       in the amount of $ _____ be allowed. Receipts will be filed

3   a   Decedent died on (date):   at (place):

       ☐ a resident of the county named above

       ☐ a non-resident of California and left an estate in the county named above located at *(specify location permitting publication in the newspaper named in item 1):*

    b   Street address, city, and county of decedent's residence at time of death.

    c   Character and estimated value of the property of the estate

       Personal property: $_____

       Annual gross income from

          ☐ real property: $_____

          ☐ personal property: $_____

                Total: $_____

       Real property: $_____

    d   ☐ Will waives bond.

       ☐ All beneficiaries have waived bond and the will does not require a bond *(affix waiver as attachment 3d).*

       ☐ All heirs at law have waived bond *(affix waiver as attachment 3d).*

    e   ☐ Decedent died intestate.

       ☐ Copy of decedent's will dated: ☐ and codicil dated:

       is affixed as attachment 3e.

Form Approved by the Judicial Council of California Revised Effective January 1 1981 DE-110(81)   (Continued on reverse)   *All petitioners must sign the petition. Only one need sign the declaration.

PETITION FOR PROBATE

ESTATE OF (NAME):	CASE NUMBER:
Decedent	

PETITION FOR PROBATE

f. Appointment of personal representative

    (1) Appointment of executor or administrator with will annexed

        ☐ Proposed executor is named as executor in the will.

        ☐ No executor is named in the will.

        ☐ Proposed personal representative is a nominee *(affix nomination as attachment 3f(1)).*

        ☐ Other named executors will not act because of ☐ death ☐ declination ☐ other reasons *(specify in attachment 3f(1)).*

    (2) Appointment of administrator

        ☐ Petitioner is a nominee *(affix nomination as attachment 3f(2)).*

        ☐ Petitioner is related to the decedent as:

    (3) ☐ Appointment of special administrator requested *(specify grounds and requested powers in attachment 3f(3)).*

g. Proposed personal representative is a ☐ resident of California ☐ non-resident of California ☐ resident of the United States ☐ non-resident of the United States.

4. a. *(Complete in all cases.)* The decedent is survived by

    (1) ☐ spouse   ☐ no spouse.

    (2) ☐ parent   ☐ no parent.

    (3) ☐ child   ☐ no child.

    (4) ☐ issue of predeceased child ☐ no issue of predeceased child.

  b. No surviving child or issue of a predeceased child has been omitted from the list of heirs (item 6).

  c. *(Complete only if no spouse or issue survived the decedent.)* The decedent

    (1) ☐ had no predeceased spouse.

    (2) ☐ had a predeceased spouse whose heirs are named in the list of heirs (item 6).

    (3) ☐ had a predeceased spouse who had no heirs.

  d. *(Complete only if no parent or issue survived the decedent.)* The decedent is survived by

    (1) ☐ a brother or sister or issue of a predeceased brother or sister. None has been omitted from the list of heirs (item 6).

    (2) ☐ no brother or sister or issue of a predeceased brother or sister.

5. ☐ Decedent's will does not preclude independent administration of this estate under sections 591—591.7 of the Probate Code.

6. The names, residence or mailing addresses, relationships, and ages of heirs, devisees, predeceased devisees, legatees, and predeceased legatees so far as known to petitioner are ☐ listed below ☐ listed in attachment 6.

    NAME AND RELATIONSHIP   AGE   RESIDENCE OR MAILING ADDRESS

7. ☐ Number of pages attached:

Dated:. . . . .   _____

                                         (Signature of petitioner)

I declare under penalty of perjury under the laws of the State of California that the foregoing is true and correct and that this declaration is executed on (date):. . . . . at (place): . . . .

. . . .   _____

        (Type or print name)   (Signature of petitioner)

IN THE SUPERIOR COURT OF THE STATE OF CALIFORNIA
IN AND FOR THE COUNTY OF LOS ANGELES

Case No. ....

Hearing Date ....

Department ....

In the Matter of ....

(Space below for Filing Stamp only.)

PROOF OF PUBLICATION
(2015.5 C.C.P.)

STATE OF CALIFORNIA,
County of Los Angeles,   } ss.

I am a citizen of the United States and a resident of the County aforesaid; I am over the age of eighteen years, and not a party to or interested in the above entitled matter. I am the principal clerk of the printer of THE LOS ANGELES DAILY JOURNAL, a newspaper of general circulation, printed and published Daily, except Saturday and Sunday, in the City of Los Angeles, County of Los Angeles, and which newspaper has been adjudged a newspaper of general circulation by the Superior Court of the County of Los Angeles, State of California, under date of June 5, 1952, Case Number 599,382; that the notice, of which the annexed is a printed copy, has been published in each regular and entire issue of said newspaper and not in any supplement thereof on the following dates, to-wit:

Paste Clipping
of Notice
SECURELY
In This Space

all in the year 19____

I certify (or declare) under penalty of perjury that the foregoing is true and correct.

....
Signature

Date.., 19........

Executed at Los Angeles.

THE LOS ANGELES DAILY JOURNAL
210 South Spring Street, P.O. Box 54026
Los Angeles, California 90054
Telephone (213) 625-2141

PROOF OF PUBLICATION

NAME AND ADDRESS OF ATTORNEY	TELEPHONE NO	FOR COURT USE ONLY
ATTORNEY FOR:		

SUPERIOR COURT OF CALIFORNIA, COUNTY OF . . . .

ESTATE OF

☐ DECEDENT   ☐ CONSERVATEE   ☐ WARD

INVENTORY AND APPRAISEMENT*	☐ FINAL ☐ PARTIAL NO ☐ SUPPLEMENTAL ☐ REAPPRAISAL FOR SALE	CASE NUMBER:
		Date of Death or of Appointment of Guardian or Conservator

APPRAISALS

1. Total appraisal by representative (Attachment 1) . . . . $
2. Total appraisal by referee (Attachment 2) . . . . $

                                                  TOTAL: $

DECLARATION OF REPRESENTATIVE

3. Attachment 1 & 2 together with all prior inventories filed herein contain a true statement of ☐ all ☐ a portion of the estate that has come to my knowledge or possession, including particularly all money and just claims against me. I have truly, honestly and impartially appraised each item as set forth in Attachment 1 to the best of my ability.

I certify (declare) under penalty of perjury that the foregoing is true and correct and that this declaration is executed on (Date):   at (Place):   , California.

. . . .
(Type or print name of representative including title of corporate officer)   (Signature of representative)

STATEMENT OF ATTORNEY REGARDING BOND
(Complete if required by local court rule)

4. ☐ Bond is waived
5. ☐ Bond filed in the amount of: $ ☐ Sufficient   ☐ Insufficient

Date:
                                             (Signature of attorney for estate)

DECLARATION OF INHERITANCE TAX REFEREE

6. I have truly, honestly, and impartially appraised to the best of my ability each item set forth in Attachment 2.
7. A true account of my commission and expenses actually and necessarily incurred pursuant to my appointment is
    Statutory commission: $
    Expenses (Specify): $

                   Total: $

8. I certify (or declare) under penalty of perjury that the foregoing is true and correct and that this declaration was executed on (Date):   at (Place):   , California.

. . . .
         (Type or print name of referee)   (Signature of referee)

(Continued on Reverse Side)

200   * See reverse side for instructions before completing. The declaration must be signed in California (CCP 2015.5); affidavit required when signed outside California. No attachment permitted less than on a full page (California Rule of Court 201 (b)).

Form Approved by the
Judicial Council of California
Effective January 1, 1976   **INVENTORY & APPRAISEMENT**   761552H — PS 8-81   Prob C 481, 600–611,
RP007   784, 1550, 1901

ESTATE OF:

CASE NUMBER

ATTACHMENT NO:

(IN DECEDENTS' ESTATES, ATTACHMENTS MUST CONFORM TO PROBATE CODE 601
REGARDING COMMUNITY AND SEPARATE PROPERTY)

PAGE . . . . . OF . . . . . TOTAL PAGES
(ADD PAGES AS REQUIRED)

Item No.   Description   Appraised value
1. $

200A

Form Approved by the
Judicial Council of California
Effective January 1, 1976

INVENTORY AND APPRAISEMENT (ATTACHMENT)

Prob C 481,
600–605 784,
1550 1901
761350C-RP-34 — PS 10-8I

ATTORNEY OR PARTY WITHOUT ATTORNEY (Name and Address)	TELEPHONE NO	FOR COURT USE ONLY

ATTORNEY FOR (Name)

NAME AND ADDRESS OF COURT, OR BRANCH

SUPERIOR COURT OF CALIFORNIA, COUNTY OF

ESTATE OF

DECEDENT

NOTICE OF

CASE NUMBER

PETITION TO ADMINISTER ESTATE

1. To all heirs, beneficiaries, creditors, contingent creditors, and persons who may be otherwise interested in the will or estate of (specify all names by which decedent was known):

2. A petition has been filed by (name of petitioner):

   in the Superior Court of
   County requesting that (name):

   be appointed as personal representative to administer the estate of the decedent.

3. ☐ The petition requests authority to administer the estate under the Independent Administration of Estates Act.

4. ☐ A petition for community property determination pursuant to section 650 of the Probate Code is joined with the petition to administer the estate.

5. A hearing on the petition will be held

   on (date):   at (time):   in ☐ Dept.:   ☐ Div.:   ☐ Room:

   located at (address of court):

6. IF YOU OBJECT to the granting of the petition, you should either appear at the hearing and state your objections or file written objections with the court before the hearing. Your appearance may be in person or by your attorney.

7. IF YOU ARE A CREDITOR or a contingent creditor of the deceased, you must file your claim with the court or present it to the personal representative appointed by the court within four months from the date of first issuance of letters as provided in section 700 of the California Probate Code. The time for filing claims will not expire prior to four months from the date of the hearing noticed above.

8. YOU MAY EXAMINE the file kept by the court. If you are a person interested in the estate, you may file a request with the court to receive special notice of the filing of the inventory of estate assets and of the petitions, accounts and reports described in section 1200.5 of the California Probate Code.

9. ☐ Petitioner   ☐ Attorney for petitioner (name):

   (address):

   _____
   (Signature of ☐ petitioner ☐ attorney for petitioner)

10. This notice was mailed on (date): . . . . at (place): . . . ., California.

    (Continued on reverse)   **336**

NOTE: If this notice is published, print the caption, beginning with the words NOTICE OF DEATH, and do not print the information from the form above the caption. The caption and decedent's name must be printed in at least 8-point type and the text in at least 7-point type. Print the case number as part of the caption. Print items preceded by a box only if the box is checked. Do not print the instructions in parentheses, the paragraph numbers, the mailing information or the material on the reverse.

336

Form Approved by the
Judicial Council of California
Revised effective January 1, 1981

**NOTICE OF DEATH AND OF PETITION
TO ADMINISTER ESTATE**

76N585B (Rev. 1-81) 1-81
RP054

Prob C 327, 328, 333,
361, 441, 654,
1200

NAME AND ADDRESS OF ATTORNEY: TELEPHONE NO.:   FOR COURT USE ONLY:

ATTORNEY FOR:

Name and address of court, or branch:
SUPERIOR COURT OF CALIFORNIA, COUNTY OF

ESTATE OF:

DECEDENT

ORDER FOR PROBATE: CASE NUMBER:

☐ ORDER APPOINTING   ☐ EXECUTOR
                            ☐ ADMINISTRATOR WITH WILL ANNEXED
                            ☐ ADMINISTRATOR
                            ☐ SPECIAL ADMINISTRATOR
☐ ORDER AUTHORIZING INDEPENDENT ADMINISTRATION OF ESTATE

1. Date of hearing: ☐ Dept. ☐ Div. ☐ Room No.:   Judge:

   THE COURT FINDS:

2. a. All notices required by law have been given.
   b. Decedent died on (date):
      (1) ☐ a resident of the above-named county of the State of California.
      (2) ☐ a nonresident of California and left an estate in the above-named county.
3. ☐ The decedent's will dated:
      and each codicil dated:
      was admitted to probate by Minute Order on (date):

   IT IS ORDERED:

4. (name):
   is appointed
   a. ☐ Executor of the decedent's will   d. ☐ Special Administrator
   b. ☐ Administrator with will annexed   (1) ☐ with general powers
   c. ☐ Administrator   (2) ☐ with special powers as specified in Attachment 4d
                                                    (3) ☐ without notice of hearing

   and letters shall issue on qualification.
5. ☐ Authority is granted to administer estate under The Independent Administration of Estates Act.
6. Bond is
   a. ☐ not required.
   b. ☐ fixed at: $ to be furnished by an authorized surety company or as otherwise provided by law.
7. ☐ The inheritance tax referee appointed is (name):

Dated: . . . .   ------------------------------
                                                        Judge of the Superior Court
                                                        ☐ Signature follows last attachment.
8. Total number of pages attached:

No attachment permitted on less than a full page (California Rule of Court 201(b)).

Form Approved by the   760051A   Prob C 329, 351, 362
Judicial Council of California   RP 041 (12-77) PS 3-79   407, 409, 410
Effective July 1, 1977 **213A**   **ORDER FOR PROBATE**   461, 462, 465, 541
                                                                    591, 605, 1220-1224
                                                                    1240

CLERK'S CERTIFICATE OF ☐ POSTING ☐ MAILING

I certify that I am not a party to this cause and that a true copy of the foregoing Notice of Death and of Petition to Administer Estate

1. ☐ was posted at (address):

   on (date):

2. ☐ was mailed, first class, postage fully prepaid, in a sealed envelope addressed to each person whose name and address is given below and that the notice was mailed and this certificate was executed on (date): . . . . at (place): . . . ., California.

Clerk, by _____ , Deputy

PROOF OF SERVICE BY MAIL

I am over the age of 18 and not a party to this cause. I am a resident of or employed in the county where the mailing occurred. My residence or business address is:

I served the foregoing Notice of Death and of Petition to Administer Estate by enclosing a true copy in a sealed envelope addressed to each person whose name and address is given below and depositing the envelope in the United States mail with the postage fully prepaid.

(1) Date of deposit: (2) Place of deposit (city and state):

I declare under penalty of perjury that the foregoing is true and correct and that this declaration is executed on (date): . . . . at (place): . . . ., California.

. . . .   _____
(Type or print name)   (Signature of declarant)

NAME AND ADDRESS OF EACH PERSON TO WHOM NOTICE WAS MAILED

B

STATE-BY-STATE LEGISLATED FEE STRUCTURES FOR PROBATE EXECUTORS/ADMINISTRATORS OR PERSONAL REPRESENTATIVES

The following is a state-by-state breakdown of statutory (that is, state-legislated) fees to be charged by probate executors, administrators, or personal representatives (the terms for those individuals vary from state to state.) Unless otherwise indicated, percentages are based on an estate's gross value.

Note: "Reasonable compensation" or "No provision" means that the state has set no limits for fees.

Alabama	2.5% of all income, payments of debts, and personal property.
Alaska	Reasonable compensation.
Arizona	Reasonable compensation.
Arkansas	Personal property: 10% of first $1,000; 5% of next $4,000; 3 percent of balance. Real estate: Reasonable compensation.

California	4% of first $15,000; 3% of the next $85,000; 2% of the next $900,000; .5% of the next $15,000,000. Reasonable compensation determined by the court for the balance. Court may award higher fees.
Colorado	Reasonable compensation.
Connecticut	Reasonable compensation.
Delaware	Reasonable compensation.
District of Columbia	Reasonable compensation, with court approval.
Florida	An estate of $1 million or less, 3%; estates from $1 million to $5 million, 2.5%; estates from $5 million to $10 million, 2%; estates from $10 million and above, 1.5%.
Georgia	2.5% on cash; 10% of interest on money loaned; 3% on property distributed; 10% of income from real estate. Court may award higher fees.
Hawaii	4% of first $15,000; 3% of next $85,000; 2% of next $900,000; 1.5% of next $2 million; 1% on $3 million and higher; 7% of first $5,000 of estate's annual income; 5% of annual income greater than $5,000. Court may award higher fees.
Idaho	Reasonable compensation.
Illinois	Reasonable compensation.
Indiana	Reasonable compensation.
Iowa	6% of first $1,000; 4% of next $4,000; 2% for over $5,000. Court may award higher fees.
Kansas	Reasonable compensation.

Kentucky	5% of personal property and 5% of all income. Court may award higher fees.
Louisiana	2.5% of inventory value. Court may award higher fees.
Maine	Reasonable compensation.
Maryland	9% of first $20,000, and $1,800 plus 3.6 percent of value over $20,000.
Massachusetts	No set rate. Usually 2.5 to 3.5% of first $500,000 and 1% for over $500,000.
Michigan	Reasonable compensation.
Minnesota	Reasonable compensation.
Mississippi	Fees not to exceed 7% at court's discretion.
Missouri	5% on first $5,000; 4% on next $20,000; 3% on next $75,000; 2.75% on next $300,000; 2.5% on estates over $1 million. The court may award higher fees.
Montana	3% of first $40,000 of estate value; 2% on excess over $40,000. Personal representative minimum of $100.
Nebraska	Reasonable compensation.
Nevada	4% of first $15,000; 3% of next $85,000; 2% over $100,000. Court may award higher fees.
New Hampshire	No provision.
New Jersey	6% of estate value.
New Mexico	10% of first $3000; 5% of balance. Court sets real estate fees.

New York	For income and payments, 5% of first $100,000; 4% of next $200,000; 3% of next $700,000; 2.5% of next $4 million; 2% on over $5 million. Court may award higher fees.
North Carolina	5% of income and payments.
North Dakota	Reasonable compensation.
Ohio	4% of first $100,000; 3% of next $300,000; 2% on excess, plus 1% on real estate not sold and nonprobate property used in computing Ohio Estate Tax.
Oklahoma	5% on first $1,500; 4% on next $4,000; 2.5% on excess over $5000.
Oregon	7% on first $1,000; 4% on next $9,000; 3% on next $40,000; 2% above $50,000, plus 1% of taxable Oregon property excluding life insurance. Court may award higher fees.
Pennsylvania	Reasonable compensation.
Rhode Island	Reasonable compensation.
South Carolina	5% of appraised value of personal property, including income from estate. Court permits additional payments for extraordinary services, with minimum of $50.
South Dakota	5% of first $1,000; 4% of next $4,000; 2.5% over $5,000. Court sets fees on real estate sold and not sold.
Tennessee	Reasonable compensation.
Texas	5% of gross estate valuation.
Utah	Reasonable compensation.

Vermont	Necessary expenses.
Virginia	Reasonable compensation, usually 5%.
Washington	Reasonable compensation with court approval.
West Virginia	Reasonable compensation.
Wisconsin	2% of inventory, minus mortgages and liens.
Wyoming	10% of first $1,000; 5% of next $4,000; 3% of next $15,000; 2% on everything over $20,000.

C

STATE-BY-STATE LEGISLATED FEE STRUCTURES FOR PROBATE ATTORNEYS

The following is a state-by-state breakdown of statutory, legislated fees to be charged by probate attorneys. Unless otherwise indicated, percentages are based on an estate's gross value.

Note: "Reasonable compensation," "No provision," or "No statutory law" means that the state has set no limits for fees. Compared to the fee structure for personal representatives (Appendix B), there is little or no supervision of attorney's fees. Even if attorney's fees require approval from a local county probate judge, legal courtesy will likely result in a ruling in favor of the attorney—certainly not the estate.

Alabama	Set by the court, with a limit of $100 on sale of real estate. Note: Laws differ in each county.
Alaska	Reasonable compensation (usually with no court supervision).
Arizona	Reasonable compensation.
Arkansas	5% of the first $5,000 on real estate and personal property; 4% on the next $20,000; 3% on the next $75,000; 2.75% on the next $300,000; 2.5% on the next $600,000; 2% above $600,000. Court may award higher fees.
California	4% on the first $15,000; 3% on the next $85,000; 2% on the next $900,000; 1% on the next $900,000; .5% on the next $15 million. Reasonable compensation determined by the court for the balance. Court may award higher fees.
Colorado	Reasonable compensation.
Connecticut	Reasonable compensation.
Delaware	Reasonable compensation.
District of Columbia	Reasonable compensation with court approval.
Florida	Reasonable compensation with notice to personal representative and all heirs, divisees, legatees, and beneficiaries.
Georgia	Reasonable compensation.
Hawaii	4% of the first $15,000; 3% on the next $85,000; 2% on the next $900,000; 1.5% of the next $2 million; 1% over $4 million.

Idaho	Reasonable compensation.
Illinois	Reasonable compensation.
Indiana	Reasonable compensation.
Iowa	6% of first $1,000; 4% of next $4,000; 2% over $5,000. Court may award higher fees.
Kansas	Reasonable compensation.
Kentucky	Reasonable compensation.
Louisiana	No statutory law.
Maine	Reasonable compensation.
Maryland	Reasonable compensation.
Massachusetts	No provision.
Michigan	Reasonable compensation.
Minnesota	Reasonable compensation.
Mississippi	Reasonable compensation.
Missouri	5% of the first $5,000; 4% of the next $20,000; 3% of the next $75,000; 2.75% of the next $300,000; 2.5% of the next $600,000; 2% over $1 million. Court may award higher fees. If attorney is also the personal representative, only one set of fees should be paid (unenforceable).
Montana	4.5% of the first $40,000; 3% over $40,000. Court may award higher fees.
Nebraska	Reasonable compensation.
Nevada	Reasonable compensation.
New Hampshire	No provision.
New Jersey	Reasonable compensation.

New Mexico	10% of the first $3000; 5% of the balance. Court sets real estate fees.
New York	Reasonable compensation.
North Carolina	Reasonable compensation.
North Dakota	Reasonable compensation.
Ohio	Compensation differs for each county according to court rulings.
Oklahoma	Reasonable compensation.
Oregon	Reasonable compensation.
Pennsylvania	7% of the first $25,000; 6% of the next $25,000; 5% of the next $50,000; 4% of the next $100,000; 3% of the next $900,000; 2% of the next $1 million; 1.5% of the next $1 million; 1% of the next $1 million; .5% of the next $1 million, plus 3.5% for transferring joint accounts; 1% of assets outside the will up to $1 million, and .5% required fees on joint accounts and trust funds.
Rhode Island	Reasonable compensation.
South Carolina	Reasonable compensation.
South Dakota	No provision.
Tennessee	Reasonable compensation, usually 3 to 5%.
Texas	Reasonable compensation.
Utah	Reasonable compensation.
Vermont	No provision.
Virginia	No provision.
Washington	Reasonable compensation.

West Virginia	Reasonable compensation.
Wisconsin	Reasonable compensation.
Wyoming	10% of the first $1,000; 5% of the next $4,000; 3% of the next $15,000; 2% over $20,000.

D

PROBATE NOTICES FOR EVERY STATE (PLUS DISTRICT OF COLUMBIA)

The following pages contain samples of probate notices from each state. The probate notice, which is located in the newspaper where legal notices are printed, is called different things in different states:

- Notice of Administration
- Notice to Creditors
- Notice to Debtors and Creditors
- Notice of Letters Testamentary Granted
- Notice to Interested Persons
- Notice to Administer Estate of _____

In all cases these probate notices are not obituary notices. You would do well to familiarize yourself with the notices from the states in which you are mining probate, so you can spot them quickly and easily in the newspapers.

Notice that different states have varying time allotments for claims to be submitted after the notice has been published, and that in the majority of states, the probate notice is called Notice to Creditors.

ALABAMA

Case No. 117998
NOTICE TO CREDITORS
The State of Alabama, Jefferson County
Probate Court
Estate of: CHESTER H. COOPER,
Deceased.

Letters Testamentary upon the last will of said decedent, having been granted to the undersigned on the 4th day of November, 1985, by the Honorable O. H. Florence, Judge of the Probate Court of Jefferson County, Alabama, notice Is hereby given that all persons having claims against said Estate are required to file an Itemized and verified statement of such claim in the office of said Judge of Probate within six months from above date, or said claim will be barred and payment prohibited.
EVELYN T. COOPER, Executrix,
ALA, MS.- Nov. 9, 16, 23 1985

Case No. 117981
NOTICE TO CREDITORS
The State of Alabama, Jefferson County
Probate Court
Estate of: HAZEL D. HOWARD,
Deceased.

Letters Testamentary upon the last will of said decedent. having been granted to the undersigned on the 1st day of November, 1985, by the Honorable O. H. Florence, Judge of the Probate Court of Jefferson County, Alabama, notice is hereby given that all persons having claims against said Estate are required to file an Itemized and verified statement of such claim in the office of said Judge of Probate within six months from above date or said claim will be, barred and payment prohibited.
JERRY H. HOWARD, Executor. ALA.
MS.-Nov. 9, 16, 23, 1985

ALASKA

IN THE SUPERIOR COURT
FOR THE STATE OF ALASKA
THIRD JUDICIAL DISTRICT

INTHE MATTER OF THE ESTATE
OF DAVID EUGENE BLAKE,
Deceased.

Case No. 3AN-83-1277-P

NOTICE TO CREDITORS

NOTICE IS HEREBY GIVEN that the undersigned has been appointed personal representative of the above named estate. All persons having claims against the said deceased are required to present their claims within four months after the date of the first publication of the notice or said claims will be forever barred. Claims must either be presented to the personal representative of the estate, c/o Smith, Coe & Patterson, P.C., 733 West 4th Avenue, Suite 308, Anchorage, Alaska 99501, or filed with the Court.

DATED the 3rd day of July, 1985, at Anchorage, Alaska.

SMITH, COE & PATTERSON
Attorneys for Personal
Representative

/s/ Steven D. Smith

Pub: July 11, 18 & 25, 1985

ARIZONA

NO. P148509
NOTICE TO CREDITORS
IN THE SUPERIOR COURT OF THE STATE OF
ARIZONA IN AND FOR THE COUNTY OF MARICOPA

In the Matter of the Estate of MAUDE H. SHERRED,
Deceased.

NOTICE IS HEREBY GIVEN that the undersigned has been appointed Personal Representative of this estate. All persons having claims against the estate are required to present their claims within four months after the date of the first publication of this notice or the claims will be forever barred. Claims must be presented to the undersigned Personal Representative, c/o Ken. A. Blake. Fennemore. Craig, von Ammon, Udall & Powers, 1700 First Interstate Bank Plaza, 100 West Washington Street, Phoenix, Arizona 85003.
DATED: October 28, 1985.

/s/Gloria Isabelle Landon
GLORIA ISABELLE LANDON as
Personal Representative, of the
estate of Maude H. Sherred, deceased
Published: November 11,18,25, 1985.

ARKANSAS

NOTICE
IN THE PROBATE COURT OF PULASKI
COUNTY, ARKANSAS
IN THE MATTER OF THE ESTATE
OF
JOHN STEPHENS HILL, JR, deceased

No. 86-0004

Last known address of decedent: 7423
Dahlia, Little Rock, Arkansas. Date of death:
December 20, 1985.

The undersigned was appointed Administratrix of the estate of the above-named decedent on the 2nd day of January, 1988.

All persons having claims against the estate must exhibit them, duly verified, to the undersigned within six months from the date of the first publication of this notice, or they will be forever barred and precluded from any benefit in the estate.

This notice first published 15th day of January, 1986.

Sarah Lou Hill
(Administratrix)
HOWELL, PRICE, TRICE, BASHAM
& HOPE. P.A.
211 Spring

Little Rock, Ark. 72201

CALIFORNIA

NOTICE TO ADMINISTER
ESTATE OF
BLANCHE E. SMITH
NO. 138736

To all heirs, beneficiaries, creditors, contingent creditors, and persons who may be otherwise interested in the will or estate of BLANCHE E. SMITH.

A petition has been filed by: CECIL HALTERMAN In the Superior Court of San Diego County requesting that: CECIL HALTERMAN be appointed as personal representative to administer the estate of the decedent.

A hearing on the petition will be held on: SEP 26 1985 at: 9:00 A.M. In DEPT. 22 located at: 220 West Broadway, San Diego, California 92101

IF YOU OBJECT to the granting of the petition you should either appear at the hearing and state your objections or file written objections with the court before the hearing. Your appearance may be in person or by your attorney.

IF YOU ARE A CREDITOR or a contingent creditor of the deceased, you must file your claim with the court or present it to the personal representative appointed by the court within four months from the date of first issuance of letters as provided in section 700 of the California Probate Code. The time for filing claims will not expire prior to four months from the date of the hearing noticed above.

YOU MAY EXAMINE the file kept by the Court. If you are a person interested in the estate, you may serve upon the executor or administrator, or upon the attorney for the executor or administrator, and file with the court with proof of service, a written request stating that you desire special notice of the filing of an inventory and appraisement of estate assets or of the petitions or accounts mentioned In sections 1200 and 1200.5 of the California Probate Code.

Attorney for petitioner:
William M. Apgar
Suite. 300,
444 West C Street
San Diego, California 92101

Sept. 9. 10,16   27949

COLORADO

NOTICE TO CREDITORS
Case No. 85-PR-1264
Estate at John N. Cochran, also
Known as John Newton Cochran, Jr., and
John N. Cochran, Jr., Deceased. All persons having
claims against the above named estate are required
to present them to the undersigned or to the Probate
Court of the City and County of Denver, Colorado
on or before December 4, 1985, or said claims shall
be forever barred. .
ANN P. COCHRAN
Personal Representative
5715 Third Ave.
Denver, Colo. 80220
F 8/2/85-F 8/16/85
Published in The Daily Journal   841

841

CONNECTICUT

NOTICE TO CREDITORS
ESTATE OF WALTER F.
NOCH a/k/a WALTER NOCH,
deceased.
The Hon. Donald F. Auchter,
Judge of the Court of Probates,
District of Glastonbury, at a
hearing held on Nov. 13, 1985,
ordered that all claims must be
presented to the fiduciary on or
before Feb. 17, 1986, or be barred
as by law provided.

ALLENE M. SCAGLIA,
Clerk
The fiduciary is:
c/o Attorney John H. Goodrich, Jr.
29 Lafayette Street
Hartford, Conn. 06106

Court of Probate, District of

NOTICE OF HEARING
ESTATE OF JULIA C. RICHARDS,
Deceased.
Pursuant to an order of Hon. Michael
A. DeIlafera, Judge, dated Nov. 18,
1985, a hearing will be held on an
application praying for authority to sell
real estate, as in said application on file
more fully appears, at the Court of
Probate on Dec. 2, 1985, at 10:00 a.m.

Certified from Record,
DIANNE E. YUSINAS,
Asst. Clerk.

DELAWARE

NOTICE
In pursuance of an order of RALPH R.
SMITH, Registrar of Wills, in and for Kent
County, Delaware, dated January 25, A.D.
1994, notice is hereby given at the granting
Letters Testamentary on the estate of Annie R.
Abbott on the 25th day at January A.D. 1994.
All persons having claims against the said
Annie R. Abbott are required 10 exhibit the
same to such Executrix within six months after
the date of the granting of such Letters, or
abide by the law in that behalf, which provides
that such claims against the said estate not so
exhibited shall be forever barred.
RALPH R. SMITH
Registrar of Wills
Attorney For Estate
Gladvs V. Hawkins, Executrix
of the Estate of
Annie R. Abbott, Deceased.
Jan. 30, Feb. 6, U. 1994

DISTRICT OF COLUMBIA

SUPERIOR COURT OF THE
DISTRICT OF COLUMBIA
PROBATE DIVISION
Administration No 3145-BS
ERASMUS JEFFERSON, JR
Deceased
Dan R. Jennings. Attorney
866 Camelhead Street, Suite 825 .
Silver Springs, Maryland 20921
Notice of Appointment
Notice to Creditors and
Notice to Unknown Heirs
Mahalia Jefferson, whose address is
44521 Liddlesex Drive, Waldorf,
Maryland 20601, was appointed
Personal Representative of the estate
Of Erasmus Jefferson, Jr., who died on
May 15, 1996, with a Will. All
unknown heirs and heirs whose
whereabouts are unknown shall enter
their appearance in this proceeding.
Objections to such appointment
(or to the probate of the decedent's
Will) shall be filed with the Registrar
of Wills, D.C., 500 Indiana Avenue,
N.W., Washington, D.C. 20001 on or
before December 13, 1996.
Claims against the decedent shall be
presented to the undersigned with a
copy to the Registrar of Wills, or to
the Registrar of Wills with a copy to
the undersigned on or before Dec. 13,
1996 or be forever barred.
Persons believed to be heirs or legatees
of the decedent who do not receive a
copy of this Notice by mail within
25 days of its first publication shall
so inform the Registrar of Wills,
including name, address and relationship
DAMIEN D. HENDLEY
Personal Representative

TRUE TEST COPY:
Henry L. Rucker, Registrar of Wills
First Published:
June 13. 1996

FLORIDA

IN THE CIRCUIT COURT FOR
ORANGE COUNTY, FLORIDA
PROBATE DIVISION
File Number 95-8229
IN RE. ESTATE OF
CHARLES E CAMPBELL Deceased
NOTICE OF ADMINISTRATION
The administration of the estate of
CHARLES E. CAMPBELL. deceased, File
Number 95-8229, is pending in the Circuit
Court for Orange County. Florida, Probate
Division, the address of which is Orange
County Courthouse, Orlando, Florida. The
names and addresses of the personal repre-
sentative and the personal representative's .
Attorney are set forth below.
All interested persons are required to file
with this court, WITHIN THREE MONTHS
OF THE FIRST PUBLICATION OF THIS
NOTICE: (1) all claims against the estate and
(2) any objection by an interested person on
whom this notice was served that challenges
the validity of the will, the qualifications of the
personal representative, venue, or jurisdiction
of the court.
ALL CLAIMS AND OBJECTIONS NOT SO
FILED WILL BE FOREVER BARRED.
Publication of this Notice has begun on
October 16, 1995
Personal Representative:
TO. CLARA BELL
2822 East Livingston Street
Orlando. Florida 32806
Attorney for Personal
Representative:
/s/A. Fuller Moon
A. Fuller Moon
Bonesteel, Hurt, Moon & Love
1302 Robinson Street
Orlando. Florida 32801
Telephone: 407/898-6229
LS-721(J)   Oct.16,23rd 1995

GEORGIA

PUBLIC NOTICES

**NOTICE TO DEBTORS
AND CREDITORS**
All creditors of the estate
of MYRTLE J. MACK late
of Fulton County deceased,
are hereby notified to render
in their demands to the
undersigned according to law,
and all persons indebted to
said estate are required to
make immediate payment.

November 20, 1998.
LOUIS BEVENSONG
Temporary Administrator
826 Edgepond Cir., N.E.
Atlanta, GA 30304
246-7103
Sept 23 30 Oct 7 14 1998x-1

HAWAII

LEGAL NOTICE

FIRST CIRCUIT I
COURT NOTICE
AND NOTICE
TO CREDITORS
P. NO. 99-2603
ESTATE OF ROSCOE
HULBURT WEED-
MAN (also known as
ROSCOE HULBURT
WEEDMAN, SR. and
ROSCOE H. WEED-).
MAN}, Deceased
FILED a document
purporting to be the Last
Will and Testament of the
above named decedent,
together with a Petition
praying for probate
thereof and issuance of
Letters to HAWAIIAN
TRUST COMPANY, LTD.,
P. O. Box 3170, Hono-
lulu, Hawaii 96802.
Monday, December 27,
1999, at 9:00 A.M., before
the Presiding Judge, in
Probate, in his courtroom,
Kaahumanu Hale, Hono-
lulu, Hawaii, is appointed
the time and place for
proving said Will and
hearing all interested
persons. .
All creditors of the
above named estate are
hereby notified to present
their claims with proper
vouchers or duly authen-
ticated copies thereof,
even if the claim is
secured by mortgage
upon real estate, to said
nominee, at the address
shown above, within four
months from the date of
the first publication of
this notice or they will be
forever barred.
DATED: Honolulu,
Hawaii; NOV. 13, 1999.
H. SETO
Clerk
JOHN A. LOCKWOOD,
ESQ.
P. O. Box 131
Honolulu, Hawaii 96810
Attorney for Petitioner
(Hon. Adv.: Nov. 20, 27;
Dec. 4, 1985)
(A-57498)

IDAHO

NOTICE TO CREDITORS

CASE NO. 3P-12634
IN THE DISTRICT COURT OF THE
FOURTH JUDICIAL DISTRICT OF THE
STATE OF IDAHO IN AND FOR THE
COUNTY OF ADA
In the matter of the estate of:
JOSE.PH FRANKLINFLANNERY,
Deceased.

Notice is hereby given that the
undersigned has been appointed Personal
Representative of the above named estate.
All persons having claims against the said
deceased are required to present their claims
within four (4) months after the date of the
first publication of this notice, *or* said claims
will be forever barred. Claims must be
presented to Violet Hulk, Personal
Representative of the estate, c/o Howling,
Hulky, Landgrove & Renoir, Post Office Box
2527, Boisese, Idaho 83701, or filed with the
Court.

Dated this 19th day of December,
1998
VIOLET **HULKY**
c./o Howling, Hulky
Landgrove & Renoir
Post Office Box 2527
Boise, Idaho 83701
Pub. Dec 30. 1998; Jan. 6.13. 1999   9953

ILLINOIS

IN THE CIRCUIT COURT OF
COOK COUNTY. ILLINOIS,
COUNTY DEPARTMENT,
PROBATE DIVISION.
ESTATE OF SALLIE W. BALDWIN,
DECEASED. NO. 95P-6334, DOCKET
919, PAGE 165.
Notice Is given of the death of Sallie W.
Baldwin. Letters of office were issued on
August 15. 1995. to Anice Luckett. 60 East
37th Street, Chicago, Illinois, as independent
administrator, whose attorney of record is
Daniel J. Suber, 127 North Dearborn.
Chicago. Illinois.
The estate will be administered without
court supervision, unless under section 28-.4
of the Probate Act, any interested person
terminates independent administration at any
time by mailing or delivering a petition to
terminate to the clerk.
Claims against the estate may be filed in the
office of the clerk in Room 1202, Richard J.
Daley Center, Chicago, Illinois, or with the
representative or both, within 6 months from
the date of issuance of letter and any claim not
filed within the period is barred.
Copies of a claim flied with the clerk must be
mailed or delivered to the representative and
to the attorney within 10 days after it has been
filed.   Aug-21-28-4
534121

INDIANA

LARRY J. WALLACE
Attorney
NOTICE OF
ADMINISTRATION
In the Marion Superior Court
Probate Division
In the Matter of the Estate of Jo
Anne Wright, deceased.
Estate Docket:E95-1670
Notice is hereby given that Robert
D. Wiggles was on the 23rd day of
October. 1995, appointed personal
representative of the estate of Jo
Anne Wright, deceased.
All persons having claims against
said estate, whether or not now
due, must file the same in said
Court within five (5) months from
the date of the first publication of
this notice or said claim will be
forever barred.
Dated at Indianapolis. Indiana, this
23rd day of October, 1995.
BERNARD J.
GOLDMAN, JR.
Clerk. Marion Superior
Court, Probate Division
95-8304-10:28-11:4

IOWA

NOTICE OF PROBATE OF WILL, OF APPOINTMENT OF EXECUTOR, AND NOTICE TO CREDITORS

The Iowa District Court
Polk County

Probate No. 47-21-452

In the Estate of

Perry Neal Dristine, deceased.

To all persons interested in the estate of Perry Neal Dristine, who died on or about November 26, 1994:

You are hereby notified that on the 31st day of October, 1995, the last will and testament of Perry Neal Dristine, deceased, bearing date of the 17th day of November 1971, and the First Codicil to Last Will and Testament, were admitted to probate in the above named Court and that Ida Jo Dristine was duly appointed executrix of the estate.

Notice is further given that any action to set aside the will must be brought in the district court of said county within four months from the date of the second publication of this notice, or thereafter be forever barred.

Notice is further given that all persons indebted to the estate are requested to make immediate payment to the undersigned and creditors having claims against said estate shall file them with the clerk of the above named district court as provided by law, duly authenticated, for allowance, and unless so filed within four months from the second publication of this notice (unless otherwise allowed or paid) a claim is thereafter forever barred.

Dated this 31st day of October 1995.

Ida Jo Dristine
Executrix of Esate
4225 Country Club
Des Moines, IA 50323

Howard B. Roundhouse
Attorney for Executrix
300 Liberty Building
Des Moines, IA 50312
Date of second publication : Nov 18, 1995

KANSAS

(First published in The Daily Record, Nov. 1 1985) 15 3t
JONES ESTATE
IN THE EIGHTEENTH JUDICIAL DISTRICT
DISTRICT COURT, SEDGWICK COUNTY, KANSAS
PROBATE DEPARTMENT
IN THE MATTER OF THE ESTATE
OF
WILLIAM A. (TEX) JONES, SR.,
aka W.R. JONES, aka W.R. (TEX) JONES,
Deceased.
Pursuant to Chapter 59 of
Kansas Statutes Annotated.
NOTICE OF HEARING
Case No. 83 P 1141
THE STATE OF KANSAS TO ALL PERSONS CONCERNED:

You are hereby notified that a Petition has been filed in the Court by Jack Douglass, duly appointed, qualified and and acting Executor of the Estate of William R. (Tex) Jones, Sr., aka W.A Jones, aka W.R. (Tex) Jones, deceased, praying that his acts be approved; that his account be settled and allowed, that the Will be construed and the estate be assigned to the persons entitled thereto; that fees and expenses be allowed; that the costs be determined and ordered paid; that the administration of the estate be closed; that the Executor be discharged and that he be released from further liability.

You are required to file your written defenses thereto on or before the 25th day of November, 1998, at 10:00 A.M., of said day, in said Court, In the City of Wichita, Sedgwick County, Kansas, at which time and place said cause will be heard. Should you fail therein, judgment and decree will be entered in due course upon the Petition

KENTUCKY

NOTICE IS HEREBY GIVEN THAT BY THE PROPER ORDER OF THE JEFFERSON DISTRICT COURT NO. 15, THE FOLLOWING WERE APPOINTED AND QUALIFIED AS FIDUCIARIES FOR THE ESTATES LISTED BELOW. ALL PERSONS HAVING CLAIMS AGAINST SAID ESTATES SHALL PRESENT THEM VERIFIED ACCORDING TO LAW BY NOT LATER THAN 6 MONTHS FROM THE DATE OF APPOINTMENT UNDER K.R.S.424.303

TRUSTEES

10-3-95, Carrie C. Hawley, 2112 Bucket Road, Louisville, KY; John Douglas Nunn, Trustee, 304 Kings Chase, Camden, SC; Atty and Process Agent William Peedon, 650 Starks Bldg., Louisville, KY.

10-4-95, Ed White, Jr., 1311 Mined Rd. Louisville, KY; Mack Meiner, Trustee, 2233 Berrytown Rd., Anchorage, KY; Atty Woosley N. Cave, 400 Taylor Bldg., Louisville, KY

10-8-95, Mary Jo Quacker, Trustee, 289 Hollowdale St., Louisville, KY; Francine Greenwell, Trustee, 3243 Wistful Vista Dr., Louisville, KY; Attys Arthur H. Wilding and Arthur J. Hyde.

10-16-95, Lyman D. Dawson, 2116 Bank Rd., Louisville, KY, First Ky. Trust Co., Trustee. P.O. Box 36571, Louisville, KY; Atty Steven A. Watkins. 1220 One Riverfront Plaza, Louisville. KY.

10-23-95, Marie L. Richards, Decd., 800 S. Fourth St., Louisville, KY; Citizens Fidelity Bank & Trust Co., Trustee, Citizens Plaza, Louisville, KY; Atty John J. Ford, 901 Ky Home Life Bldg, Louisville, KY

10-25-95, Robert E. Adams, Jr., 402 Rolling Lane, Louisville, KY, First Ky Trust Co., Trustee, P.O. Box 36010, Louisville, KY; Atty J.P. Hancock, 576 Starks Bldg., Louisville, KY.

A COPY ATTEST
PAULIE MILLER, CLERK
JEFFERSON DISTRICT
COURT NO. 15
BY /s/ Betty Baker, D.C.

LOUISIANA

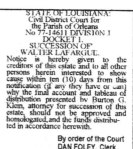

STATE OF LOUISIANA:
Civil District Court for
the Parish of Orleans
No 77-1461 DIVISION I
DOCKET 1.
SUCCESSION OF
WALTER LAFARGUE.
Notice is hereby given to the creditors of this estate and to all other persons herein interested to show cause within ten (10) days from this notification (if any they have or can) why the final account and tableau of distribution presented by Burton G. Klein, attorney for succession of this estate, should not be approved and homologated, and the funds distributed in accordance herewith.

By order of the Court
DAN FOLEY, Clerk
Attorney, Alvarez T. Ferrouillet, Jr.
Publication: T.P. - S.1., September 26, 1995

MARYLAND

STATE OF MARYLAND
NOTICE OF APPOINTMENT
AND
NOTICE TO CREDITORS
TO ALL PERSONS INTERESTED IN THE ESTATE OF (A.24221)
MATTHEW S. CLAVA

This is to give notice that the undersigned, NICHOLAS V. BROCCOLI, whose address is 4930 Belair Rd., Baltimore, Md. 21206 was, on April 15, 1996, appointed personal representative of the estate of Matthew S. Clava who died on April 11, 1995 with a Will.

All persons having any objection to the appointment or to the probate of the Will of the decedent shall file the same with the Registrar of Wills for Baltimore City, Civil Courts Building, Baltimore, Md. 21202 on or before six months from the date of the appointment.

All persons having claims against the decedent must present a verified, written statement of the claim to the undersigned or file said claim with the Registrar of Wills for Baltimore City and deliver or mail a copy of the statement to the undersigned Personal Representative on or before six months from the date of appointment.

Any claim not filed on or before that date or any extension provided by law, is unenforceable thereafter.

NICHOLAS V. BROCCOLI,
Personal Representative,
MARY W. CONAWAY,
Registrar of Wills for Baltimore City
ap16,23,30

MAINE

STATE OF MAINE
PROBATE COURT
Penobscot, ss.
97 Hammond Street
Bangor, Maine 04401-4996
NOTICE TO CREDITORS
18.A MRSA Sec. 2-801
The following Personal Representa-. tives have been appointed in the estates noted. The first publication date of this notice is November 9, 1995.

If you are a creditor of an estate listed below, you must present your claim within four months of the first publication date of this Notice to Creditors or be forever barred.

You may present your claim by filing a written statement of your claim on a proper form with the Registrar of Probate of this Court or by delivering or mailing to the Personal Representative listed below at the address published by his name. A written statement of the claim indicating the basis therefor, the name and address of the claimant and the amount claimed or in such other manner as the law may provide. See 18-A MRSA 3-804.

ESTATE OF MAURICE L.KELLY, JR., late of Bangor. Deceased. Mary M. Kelly, 151 Third Street, Bangor, Maine 04401 appointed Personal Representative.
ESTATE OF JENNIE MAE McGUNCH, late of Milford, deceased. Sherwood P. McGunch, 185 Main Street, Milford. Maine 04461 appointed Personal Representative
ESTATE OF NORA J. LANDER, late of Newport, deceased. Martha L. Maynard, 10 High Street, Newport, Maine 04953, appointed Personal Representative.
ESTATE OF HELEN B. CLARK, late of Newport, deceased. George P. Piddle, 46 High Street, Newport. Maine 04953 and David B. Snark, 74 Main Street, Newport, Maine 04953 appointed Personal Representatives.
ESTATE OF MARY FLORENCE RUSH, also known as MARY FLORENCE W. RUSH, late of Milknockup, deceased. Harry A. M. Rush. Jr., 40 Elm Street, East Milknockup, Maine 04430 appointed Personal Representative. November 1, 1995.
Susan Blossom,
Register of Probate
Nov, 9,16, 1995

MASSACHUSETTS

COMMONWEALTH OF MASSACHUSETTS
THE TRIAL COURT
THE PROBATE AND FAMILY COURT
Norfolk Division   Docket No. 98P2169.T1

Estate of ROSE O'GRADY

late of BROOKLINE

In the County of NORFOLK

NOTICE

A petition has been presented in the above-captioned matter praying that the last will of said decedent be proved and allowed and that LILLIAN O'GRADY of BROOKLINE in the County of NORFOLK be appointed executrix named in the will without surety on the bond.

If you desire to object to the allowance of said petition, you or your attorney should file a written appearance in said Court at Dedham on or before 10:00 in the forenoon on October 30, 1998.

In addition you should file a written statement of objections to the petition, giving the specific grounds therefore. within thirty (30) days after the return day for such other time as the Court, on motion with notice to the petitioner, may allow in accordance with Probate Rule 2A.

Witness, Robert M. Ford, Esquire. First Justice of said Court at Dedham. the first day of October in the year of our Lord one thousand nine hundred and ninety eight.
Thomas Patrick Hughes
Register of Probate
10/10

MICHIGAN

File No. 779,412
STATE OF MICHIGAN – The Probate Court for the County of Wayne.
Estate of: **MARTIN Q. BEAURING**, Deceased. Decedent's date of death: August 9, 1995, Social Security No. 378-07-0610A.
Last known address: 9150 Cadieux Street, Detroit, Michigan. TAKE NOTICE:
Creditors of the Deceased are notified that all claims against the Estate must be presented to Robert L. Baggins, Personal Representative, at 45262 Pierre, Mt. Clemens, Michigan 48044, and copies of the claims must be filed with the Court on or before November 1, 1995. Notice is further given that the Estate will be thereafter assigned to persons appearing of record entitled thereto.
Dated: August 19, 1995.
ROBERT L. BAGGINS
Petitioner
45262 Pierre
ML Clemens, Michigan 48044

MINNESOTA

FILE NO. P4-98-46376

ORDER AND NOTICE OF
HEARING ON PETITION FOR
FORMAL PROBATE OF WILL
AND APPOINTMENT OF
PERSONAL
REPRESENTATIVE IN
SUPERVISED
ADMINISTRATION AND
NOTICE TO CREDITORS

STATE OF MINNESOTA
COUNTY OF HENNEPIN

FOURTH JUDICIAL DISTRICT

DISTRICT COURT PROBATE
COURT DIVISION
en re: Estate of
RONALD S. PUCHENBECKER
Deceased.

TO ALL INTERESTED PERSONS
AND CREDITORS:
It is Ordered and Notice is hereby
given that on Monday, the 9th day of December,
1998, at ten o'clock A.M., a hearing will be held
In the above named Court at C-4, Hennepin
County Government Center, Minneapolis,
Minnesota, for the formal probate of an
instrument dated July 4, 1976 purporting to be
the last will of the above named decedent, and
for the appointment of Frances G. Puchenbecker,
whose address is 9432 West River Road,
Brooklyn Park, Minnesota 55444, as personal
representative of the estate of the above named
decedent In supervised administration, and that
any objections thereto must be filed with the
Court. That, if proper, and no objections are
filed, said personal representative will be
appointed to administer the estate, to collect all
assets, pay all legal debts, claims, taxes and
expenses, and sell real and personal property,
and do all necessary acts for the estate. Upon
completion of the administration, the
representative shall file a final account for
allowance thereof and shall distribute the estate
to the persons thereunto entitled as ordered by
the Court, and close the estate.
Notice is further given that ALL
CREDITORS having claims against said
estate are required to present the same to
said personal representative or to the Clerk
of Probate Court within four months after
the date of this notice or said claims will be
barred.
Dated November 8, 1998
HON. ELVIN J.
PATTERSON,
District Judge,
Probate Court
Division.
MARY MAE
POPPINJAY,
Clerk of Probate
Court.
(COURT SEAL)
Talle, Trimble and Oilhead
(Herman L. Talle)
Attorneys
316 East Main Street
Anoka, Minnesota 552 01
(November 14.,21, 1998
57302

MISSISSIPPI

NOTICE TO CREDITORS
OF
MABEL FLOSSY CLIFTER
PROBATE NO 7980
NOTICE is hereby given that
Letters Testamentary of the
Last Will and Testament of
Mabel Flossy Clifter, deceased,
were granted to the
undersigned by the Chancery
Court of Hines County, Missis-
sippi on the 22nd day of
November, 1992, and all
persons having claims against
said estate are hereby notified
and required to have the same
probated and registered by the
Clerk of said Court as required
by law within ninety (90) days
from date of the first
publication of this notice.
Failure to do so will forever bar
such claims.
WITNESS my signature this
22nd day of November, 1992.
Emmett Wart. Sr.

EMMETT WART, SR.

EXECUTOR
DOUGLAS E. HASSLE
POST OFFICE DRAWER 666
VICKSBURG, MISSISSIPPI
39182
TELEPHONE: 601-637-5683
ATTORNEY FOR EXECUTOR
December 2. 9. 16, 23. 1992

MISSOURI

IN THE CIRCUIT COURT OF
JACKSON COUNTY, MISSOURI
PROBATE DIVISION
At Kansas City
IN THE ESTATE OF
JOHN P. DOSTER
Deceased

ESTATE NUMBER 154298

NOTICE OF LETTERS
TESTAMENTARY GRANTED
(Supervised Administration)
(Sec. 473.003. RSMo.)

TO ALL PERSONS INTER-
ESTED IN THE ESTATE OF
JOHN P. DOSTER, decedent:

On the 2nd day of April, 1999, the
last will of the decedent having been
admitted to probate, ALLEN H.
DOSTER, was appointed the personal
representative of the estate of John A.
Doster, decedent, by the probate
division of the circuit court of Jackson
County, Missouri. The business address
of the personal representative is 919
West 78th, Street, Kansas City, MO.
64114 whose telephone number is 816-
523-7836 and whose attorney is
KEVIN R. KLINGER, whose business
address is 4120 Pennsylvania, No. 2-B,
Kansas City, Missouri 64111 and
whose telephone number is 816-931-
8802.

All creditors of said decedent are
notified to file claims in court within
six months from the date of the first
publication of this notice or be forever
barred.

Receipt of this notice by mail should
not be construed by the recipient to
indicate that he necessarily has a
beneficial interest in the estate. The
nature and extent of any person's
interest, if any, can be determined from
the files and records of this estate in the
probate division of the circuit court of
Jackson County, Missouri.

Date of first publication is April 4,
1999.

MARGARET L. SAUER
Division Clerk
(SEAL)
By LATICIA IRWIN
Deputy Division Clerk
Published April 4, 11, 18-, 25,
1999
P.199-204-209. 214 --Thursday
(P18032)

MONTANA

IN THE DISTRICT COURT OF
THE SECOND JUDICIAL
DISTRICT OF THE STATE OF
MONTANA IN AND FOR THE
COUNTY OF SILVER BOW
In the matter of the estate of
Marguerite I. Shead. Deceased. No.
94-P-211.

NOTICE TO CREDITORS
NOTICE IS HEREBY GIVEN
that the undersigned has been
appointed Personal Representative
of the above named estate. All
persons having claims against the
said deceased are required to
present their claims within four (4)
months after the date of the first
publication of this notice, or said
claims will be forever barred.

Claims must either be mailed to
Edward P. Podd, the Personal
Representative. return receipt
requested. in care of GORE,
ROTT & WILDER, P.C., attys of
record for the Personal
Representative, at 8229 Harrison
Dr., Butte, Montana 59703-2822.
or filed with the Clerk of the
above-entitled Court.

DATED this 4th day of Decem-
ber, 1994.
/s/Edward P. Podd
Personal Representative
2229 Mead Avenue
Butte Montana 59712
GORE, ROTT &
WILDER, P.C.
Attorneys for
Personal Representative
8229 Harrison Drive
Butte. Montana 59703-2822

NEBRASKA

MARX, CLARE, HOPKINS,
ROTH, CUDGEL, OFFNER & WHAPSOM
Attorneys
2047 Perry Street
Suite 7B
NOTICE
In the County Court of Douglas County,
Nebraska
Book 135, Page 412
In the Matter of the Estate of Paul
Henders, Deceased.

Notice is hereby given that on December 17, 1998, in the County Court of Douglas County, Nebraska, Margaret F. Henders, whose address is 2038 North 54th Street, Omaha, Nebraska 68104, has been appointed as the Personal Representative of this estate. Creditors of this estate must file their claims with this Court on or before February 18, 1999, or be forever barred.

JOHN R. DOUGHERTY,
Deputy Clerk of the
County Court

w12-18.31

NEVADA

IN THE EIGHTH JUDICIAL DISTRICT COURT
OF THE STATE OF NEVADA IN AND FOR THE
COUNTY OF COWETA

CASE NO. P32045

IN THE MATTER OF THE ESTATE OF
SARA KATHERINE BOVINA ROE, DECEASED.
NOTICE TO CREDITORS
{ 90 } Days Notice
Notice is hereby given the that the undersigned has been duly appointed and qualified by the above entitled Court on the 10th day of June, 1997, as Executrix of the estate of SARA KATHERINE BOVINA ROE, deceased.

All creditors having claims against said estate are required to file the same with the proper vouchers attached, with the Clerk of the Court within 90 days after the first publication of this notice.
Dated June 10th A.D. 1997
a/ Marla Dietrich Roe

JEFFREY A. BIRD, LTD.
Attorney(s) for the Estate
23 Tamber Lane, Suite 711
Las Vegas, Nevada 89230

Published in *Nevada Legal News*
June 20,27 1997, July 3, 1997

NEW HAMPSHIRE

LEGAL PROBATE NOTICE
THE STATE OF NEW HAMPSHIRE

Hillsborough, SS   Court of Probate

REGULAR TERMS OF COURT

January 15 Nashua   **January 22 Manchester**   **January 29 Nashua**

To all persons interested in the estates and other matters (the originals are on file in said Court) hereinafter named and listed.

You are hereby cited to appear at Court to be held in said County, and be heard thereon and object if you see cause.

AT MANCHESTER
ON THE FIFTH (5th) DAY OF FEBRUARY NEXT
ACCOUNTS

ACORACE, Dominic, late of Manchester, deceased. First and Final Account filed by Anno E. Acorace and Arthur G. Greene, Executors.

ADDENTON, Annie S., late of Manchester, deceased. Twenty-fourth Account filed by Merchants National Bank, Trustee for the benefit of Scholarship Fund.

BERNHARD, Amalie, late of Manchester, deceased. First and Final Account filed by Bernice Krauzer, Administratrix with will annexed.

BLOOD, Blanche Noel, of Manchester, Second Account filed by Pauline R. Lemay, Conservator

BONDI, Anthony Michael, late of Manchester, deceased. First and Final Account filed by Solly Ja Bondi, Executrix.

COLBY, Henry S., late of GOFFSTOWN, deceased. Fifth Account filed by Merchants National Bank and James Tracy Colby, Jr., Trustees for the benefit of Mary M. Colby et. al.

NEW JERSEY

NOTICE TO CREDITORS
Camden N J . October 11. 1999

Estate of WALTER RILEY aka Walter A. Riley deceased

Pursuant to the order of EUGENE FELDMAN, Surrogate of the County of Camden, this day made on the application of the undersigned, Walter A. Riley, III. Executor of said deceased, notice is hereby given to the creditors of said deceased to exhibit to the subscriber, under oath or affirmation, their claims and demands against the estate of said deceased, within six months from this date, or they will be forever barred from prosecuting or recovering the same against the subscriber.

Walter A. Riley, III
Executor

10'24,99   Prt s Fee 5864

NEW MEXICO

SECOND JUDICIAL DISTRICT COUNTY OF BERNALILLO STATE OF NEW MEXICO
No. PB-98-481

IN THE MATTER OF THE ESTATE OF DESIDERIO JOSE MARIA SAIS, Deceased.

NOTICE TO CREDITORS

NOTICE IS HEREBY GIVEN that the undersigned has been appointed Personal Representative of this estate. All persons having claim against this estate are required to present their claims within two months after the date of this Notice or the claims will be forever barred. Claims must be presented either to the undersigned Personal Representative in care of the Law Offices of Lorenzo Chavez and Martin Chavez, 1010 United New Mexico Bank at Albuquerque Building, 200 Lomas Boulevard, N.W, Albuquerque, New Mexico, 87102, or filed with the Bernalillo County District Court, Post Office Box 488, Albuquerque, New Mexico, 87103.

DATE: Nov. 8, 1998

/s/ Lupita Sais
LUPITA SAIS
Personal Representative
4236 Brockmont, N.E.
Albuquerque, NM 87108
LORENZO A. CHAVEZ
MARTIN J. CHAVEZ
By: /s/ Gerald A. Hanrahan
Gerald A. Hanrahan, Attorney
for Personal Representative
Suite 1010
United New Mexico Bank at
Albuquerque Building
200 Lomas Blvd. N.W.
Albuquerque, NM 87102
Telephone: (505) 243-6716
HCS Nov. 15, 22. 1998.

NEW YORK

**CITATION FOR
PROBATE OF WILL
Estate or Mildred J. Netsch
Deceased
File No. 85-4912mc**

Surrogate's Court, Erie County, New York. Joseph S. Mattina, Surrogate.

The people of the State of New York, To George Metz, Leo Metz, Joseph Metz, Raymond Metz, Mary Zimmerman, Bradley Metz, Arlene Metz Smitn, Walter Guoelman, Hon. Robert S. Abrams Attorney General of the State of New York, and to any and all persons who are, or who claim to be heirs at law next of kin, distributees of Mildred J. Netsch, deceased, if any such there be, all of whom and all of whose names, ages, places of residence, and Post Office addresses are unknown to Petitioner, and cannot after due diligence used, be ascertained.

A petition having been duly filed by Jack I. Morris of the Town of Orchard Park, New York.

You Are Hereby Cited To Show Cause before the Surrogate Court, Erie County, At County Hall in the city of Buffalo, in said County of Erie on November 19, 1995 at 2:00 P.M. why a decree should not be made in the Estate of Mildred J. Netsch, late of the City of Buffalo, in the County of Erie, admitting to probate as Last Will and Testament, a written document dated November 29, 1978

Dated, Attested and Sealed, September 25 1985.

(Seal)   GEORGE F. DANGLER
Chief Clerk

This citation is served upon you as required by law and specifically for the reason hereinafter set forth. You are not obliged to appear in person. If you fail to appear it will be assumed that you do not object to the relief requested. You have a right to have an attorney-at-law appear for you. The Attorney for the petitioner, upon written request, will furnish you with a copy of the Will if you do not receive one with this citation.

Attorney: MORRIS and BRAY, 1299 Union Road, West Seneca, New York 14224 (116) 674-9100.
oct.7,14,21,28

NORTH CAROLINA

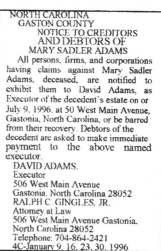

NORTH CAROLINA
GASTON COUNTY
NOTICE TO CREDITORS
AND DEBTORS OF
MARY SADLER ADAMS

All persons, firms, and corporations having claims against Mary Sadler Adams, deceased, are notified to exhibit them to David Adams, as Executor of the decedent's estate on or July 9, 1996, at 50 West Main Avenue, Gastonia, North Carolina, or be barred from their recovery. Debtors of the decedent are asked to make immediate payment to the above named executor.

DAVID ADAMS,
Executor
506 West Main Avenue
Gastonia, North Carolina 28052
RALPH C. GINGLES, JR.
Attomey at Law
506 West Main Avenue Gastonia,
North Carolina 28052
Telephone: 704-864-2421
4C-January 9, 16, 23, 30, 1996

NORTH DAKOTA

IN THE COUNTY COURT OF CASS COUNTY,
STATE OF NORTH DAKOTA
In the Matter of the Estate of Dannelle S. Merchello,
Deceased
NOTICE TO CREDITORS
NOTICE IS HEREBY GIVEN that the undersigned has been
Appointed personal representative of the above estate. All
persons having claims against the said deceased are required
to present their claims within three months of the first publica-
tion or be forever barred. Claims must either be presented to
Lynnette I. Marchello, personal representative of the estate, at
424 12th Street North #3, Fargo, North Dakota 58102, or filed
with the Court
        Dated this 23rd day of October, 1995.
                        Lynnette I. Marchello
                        424 12th Street North 1/3
                        Fargo, North Dakota 58102
Bruce D. Johnson
GACKLE, JOHNSON & BUGGERTY
101 Roberta Street
P.O. Box 314
Fargo, North Dakota 58107
(701)235-641 I
Attorney for Personal Representative
First publication on the 4th day of November, 1995

(November 4, 11, 1995)   6903

OHIO

Notice of Appointment of Fiduciary

On October 22, 1995, In the Hamilton County
Probate Court, Case No.855010, Jeanette C.
MacSnuffle, 3920 Middleton Court, Cincinnati,
Ohio 45220, was appointed executrix of the
estate *of* Bruce G. MacSnuffle, deceased, late of
3920 Middleton Court, Cincinnati, Ohio 45223.
        MELVIN G. RUEGER,
                Probate Judge
Cincinnati. Ohio. October 24, 1995.
                                oct 24-31 nov 7

OKLAHOMA

                194238
        Published in the Tulsa Daily
        Business Journal & Legal Record
        December 20 & 27, 2001

IN THE DISTRICT COURT IN AND
    FOR TULSA COUNTY, STATE
    OF OKLAHOMA
IN THE MATTER OF THE
        ESTATE OF: EDMUNDO
SPARVILLIANO,
                        Deceased.
        No. P-01-2930
    NOTICE TO CREDITORS
All persons having claims against
Edmundo Sparvilliano, deceased, are
required to present the same, with the
necessary supporting documents, to the
undersigned personal representative
Alonzo D. Schott, c/o Tonstan Lee
Balling, Attorney at Law, 6209 Hakira
Bldg., Tulsa, Oklahoma 74201, within
two months of the date of the first
publication hereof, or the same will be
forever barred.
        Dated December 20, 2001
                /s/ Alonzo D. Schott

Tonstan Lee Balling
6209 Hakira Bldg.
Tulsa, OK 74201

OREGON

Estate **FRANKIE L. DOFFMAN**
    Notice to Interested Persons
        (No. 95-023-8618)
In the Circuit Court of the State of Oregon for the
County of Zipporah, Probate Department.
    In the Matter of the Estate of Frankie L.
                        Doffman, Deceased.
Notice is hereby given that Phyllis Coarse
and Frank Holyman have been appointed as the
personal representatives of .the above estate.
All persons having claims against the estate are
required to present them.to the undersigned
personal representatives in care of the undersigned
attorneys at; 700 N. Hayden Island Drive, Suite
300, Portland, Oregon 97217 within four months
after the date of first publication of this here notice,
as stated below, or they may be barred.
All persons whose rights may be affected by the
proceedings in this estate may obtain additional
information from the records of the Court, the
personal representatives or the attorneys for the
personal representatives.
        Dated and first published June 13. 1995.
                PHYLLIS COARSE,
                Personal representative
                8002 NE Hwy 99, #61 Vancouver,
                WA 98665 FRANKIE L.
                DOFFMAN, Personal
                representative
                2914 E. 14th Court Vancouver, WA
                98661
McCLASKEY, GREIG & TROUTWINE,
Attorneys for Personal Representatives
700 N Hayden Island Drive
SUite 300
Portland. Oregon 97217
                            P6821.3Th

PENNSYLVANIA

ESTATE NOTICES

Letters have been granted on the estate of each of the following decedents to the personal representative named, who request all persons having claims against the estate of the decedent to make known the same in writing to him or his attorney, and all persons indebted to the decedent to make payment to him without delay:

Silthole, Geraldine, a/k/a Gerry Silthole, deceased, of Pgh., PA. No. 4580 of 1995. Ethelyn Paulauskas, Extrx., 13305 Second St., East Madeira Beach. FL 33708; CARL HUDSON SHELLY, Atty. 1000 Law & Finance Bldg., Pgh., PA 15219. 3 W 376-301

Geyer, Charles E., deceased, of Pgh., PA. No. 4592 of 1995. Margaret J. Smith, Admrx., 3425 Delaware St., 2nd Fl., Pgh., PA 15212; LINDSEY D. ALTON. Atty. 5th Flr., 600 Grant St., Pgh., PA 15219.   3 W 829-130

Solido, Arthur L., deceased, of Plum Boro, PA. No. 4410 of 1995. Carol Pekarek, Extrix, 255 Center New Texas Rd., Pgh., PA 15239; JOHN L. CHAFFO, Atty, 403 Frick Bldg., Pgh., PA 15219.   3 W 188-313

Thompson, Esther E., deceased, of Allison Park. PA. No. 4601 of 1995. June L. Schad and Charles Schad, Extrs., 9750 Katherine Dr. Allison Park. PA 15101; DAVID M CHARLES. Atty. 1508 Frick Bldg., Pgh. PA 15219.   3 W 189-203

RHODE ISLAND

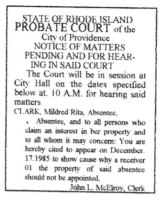

STATE OF RHODE ISLAND
PROBATE COURT of the
City of Providence
NOTICE OF MATTERS
PENDING AND FOR HEAR-
ING IN SAID COURT
The Court will be in session at City Hall on the dates specified below at. 10 A.M. for hearing said matters
CLARK, Mildred Rita, Absentee.

. Absentee, and to all persons who claim an interest in her property and to all whom it may concern: You are hereby cited to appear on December. 17.1985 to show cause why a receiver 01 the property of said absentee should not be appointed,

        John L. McElroy, Clerk

SOUTH CAROLINA

975 | Probate Notice

CREDITORS NOTICE
ESTATE OF DEBORAH F. ANDERSON. Deceased.   All persons having claims against the Estate of Deborah F. Anderson, deceased, will present them duly attested, and all persons indebted to said Estate will make payment to the undersigned c/o Patrick F. Stringer, Esq., Attorney and Counselor-at-Law, P.O. Box 2066, Charleston, South Carolina 29411.
Lorraine Winchester, Administratix

SOUTH DAKOTA

NOTICE OF HEARING
PETITION FOR PROBATE OF
WILL AND
NOTICE TO CREDITORS
IN CIRCUIT COURT
SIXTH JUDICIAL CIRCUIT
STATE OF SOUTH DAKOTA)
                    :ss
COUNTY OF HUGHES   )
IN THE MATTER OF   )
OF THE ESTATE OF   )
LEON R. CROW,   )
)

    Deceased.)
THE STATE OF SOUTH
DAKOTA SENDS GREETINGS
TO: RICHARD JULIAN CROW,
HEWITT WILLIS CROW,
MARY LENORE CAYOU,
HARVEY MARSHALL CROW,
CHARLES ARTHUR CROW,
AND LEON CHARLES CROW,
THE HEIRS, DEVISEES, AND
LEGATEES, AND TO THE
EXECUTOR NAMED IN THE
WILL OF THE DECEASED,
AND TO ALL CREDITORS OF
SAID DECEASED, AND TO
ALL TO WHOM THESE
PRESENTS MAY COME:
    Notice is hereby given that
Charles Arthur Crow, by and
through his attorney, Bernard E.
Duffy, Pierre, South, Dakota, has
filed in this court a Petition for the
admission to probate of the Last
Will of Leon R. Crow, deceased,
and for the issuance of Letters
Testamentary to Charles Arthur
Crow, Pierre, South Dakota,
under: the Independent
Administration of Estates Act,
SDCL ~18A, (Ch 176, Laws of
1976), and that Monday, the 23rd
day of December, 1985, at the
hour of 11:00 o'clock a.m., at the
courthouse in the courtroom in the
City of Pierre, Hughes County,
South Dakota, has been set as the
time and .place when and where
Said Petition will be heard, and all
persons interested may appear and
be heard upon the granting of said
Petition, and may, if they desire,
contest the said Will.
The names of the heirs, devisees,
and executor of the Will as shown
by the Petition, are stated above,
and said Petition is referred to for
further particulars.

    NOTICE TO CREDITORS
    Notice is also given that all
persons having claims against the
said estate are hereby notified to
file the same with the Clerk of the
above court within two (2) months
from the date of the first
publication of this Notice, or be
forever barred.
        Dated this 27th day of
November, 1985.
                BY THE COURT

TENNESSEE

NOTICE TO CREDITORS.
NO. 76203
    ESTATE OF JIMMY DALE MAJORS
(DECEASED)
    Notice is hereby given that on the 28th day
of October, 1999, Letters Administration in
respect of the estate of Jimmy Dale Majors,
deceased, were issued to the undersigned
by the Probate Court of Davidson County,
Tennessee.
    All persons resident and nonresident,
having claims, matured or unmatured, against
his estate are required to file same with the
Clerk of the above named Court within six (6)
months from the date of the first publication of
this notice, otherwise their claims will be
forever barred.
    This 31st day of October, 1999.
    Billie Jean Tune, Public Administratrix of the
Estate of Jimmy Dale Majors, (Deceased)
12th Flr., First American Center, Nashville,
TN 37238.
    Insertion Dates: October 31, November 7,
1999.
    AD NO. 8990

TEXAS

9/4

NOTICE TO CREDITORS

Notice is hereby given that original Letters Testamentary for the Estate of CHARLES W. CLINE. Deceased. were issued on August 26, 1995, in Docket No. 85.3109.P, pending in Probate Court #1 of Dallas County, Texas, to CHARLES D. CLINE.

The address of the Executor is as follows:

CHARLES D. CLINE, 5440 Wales, Fort Worth, Texas 76133

All persons having claims against this Estate which is currently being administered are required to present them within the time and in the manner prescribed by law.

DATED the 28th day of August, 1995.

CHARLES D. CLINE, independent Executor of the Estate of CHARLES W. CLINE, Deceased

By THOMAS J. ODOREAL
State Bar #17482200
ODOREAL & AROMANO. Attorneys
Two Energy Square, Suite 368
Dallas, Texas 75206 691-0611
Attorney for the Estate

9/4

UTAH

NOTICE TO CREDITORS AND ANNOUNCEMENT OF APPOINTMENT
Probate No. P82-873
IN THE DISTRICT COURT, PROBATE DIVISION IN AND FOR SALT LAKE COUNTY, STATE OF UTAH

In the Matter of the Estate of LLOYD H. BLACK, Deceased.

Elaine Eatchel whose address is 4278 Mackay Drive, Salt Lake City, Utah, .has been appointed Personal Representative of the estate of the above named decedent. Creditors of the estate are hereby notified to present their claims to the' above Personal Representative or to the Clerk of the Court within three months after the date of the first publication of this notice or be forever barred.

DATED this 23rd day of Octo ber.1995.

ESTATE OF LLOYD H. BLACK
/s/ ELAINE EATCHEL
Elaine Eatchel
Personal Representative

Dwight L. King, Attorney
2121 South State Street, #205
Salt Lake City, Utah 84115

Date of first publication October 25, 1995.   *(11/8/95)*

VERMONT

IN RE THE ESTATE OF
KATIE H. JONES
             PROBATE COURT
             DOCKET NO. 24540
STATE OF VERMONT
DISTRICT OF
WASHINGTON, 55.

NOTICE TO CREDITORS

To the creditors of the estate of Katie H. Jones late of Waltsfield. Vermont, I have been appointed a personal representative of the above named estate. All creditors having claims against the estate must present their claims in writing within 4 months of the date of the first publication of this notice. The claim must be presented to me at the address listed below with a copy filed with the registrar of the Probate Court. The claim will be forever barred if it is not presented as described above within the four-month deadline.

Signed: Charles J. Adams
Address: Adams, Darby
                & Louddon
12 North Main Street
Waterbury. Vt. 05675
Telephone: (802)246-7342

Dated, October 30, 1995
Date of First Publication:
November 9, 1985 Address of
Probate Court
Probate Court
Washington District
P. O. Box 589
Montpelier, VT. 05602
Nov. 9. 16

VIRGINIA

VIRGINIA:
     IN THE CIRCUIT
     . COURT OF
     ARLINGTON COUNTY
          Re: Estate of Fiora
     Luella Dover, Deceased
          Will No. 16835
SHOW CAUSE ORDER
IT APPEARING that a report of the accounts of Griffin T. Garnett, Jr., Executor of the Estate of Fiora Luella Dover, deceased, and of the debts and demands against the estate, has filed in the Clerk's Office. and that six (6) months have elapsed since the qualification, on motion of the Executor;

IT IS ORDERED that the creditors of. and all other interested in the Estate do show cause, if any they can, on the 22nd day of June, 1985, before this Court against the payment and delivery of the remainder of the estate to the legatees without requiring refunding bonds.

IT IS FURTHER ORDERED that the foregoing portion of this order be published once a week for two (2) successive weeks in the Northern Virginia Sun, a newspaper published in the County of Arlington, Virginia, ENTERED this 23rd day of May, 1995.

/s/ PAUL. D. BROWN
                              Judge

WASHINGTON

NOTICE TO CREDITORS
Estate of
KALLEM H. RISBERG
SUPERIOR COURT OF WASH-
INGTON FOR KING COUNTY
Estate of Kallem H. Risberg Deceased. Probate No. 95-6-01952-7.
Notice to Creditors, (RCW 11.40.020)
The undersigned has been appointed and
has qualified as personal representative
(PR) of the estate of the above named
deceased. Each person having a claim
against the deceased must serve the claim
on the undersigned PR or on the attorney
of record at the address stated below and
must file an executed copy of the claim
with the clerk of the court within four
months after the date of first publication
of this notice or within four months
after the date of filing of a copy of this
notice with the clerk of the court,
whichever is the later, or the claim will
be barred, except under those provisions
included in RCW 11.40.020.

Date of filing copy of notice to creditors,
June 25, 1995,

Date of first publication, June 26,
1995.

PR: ADELA S. KNUTSON,

Address: 1012 Seattle Tower,
Seattle, WA 98101.

JOHN D, MrLAUCHLAN Attorney
for the Estate. Address:

1012 Seattle Tower, Seattle, Washington 98101. Telephone: 624-8822

(8995)

WEST VIRGINIA

LEGAL NOTICE

NOTICE

NOTICE
To the Creditors and Beneficiaries
of the Estates of:
GLADYS SNYDER
MAE McCLELLAN
NOVA LEE KING
MAGGIE L. BAYS
All persons having claims against
the estates of the said GLADYS
SNYDER, MAE McCLELLAN, NOVA
LEE KING, or MAGGIE L. BAYS,
deceased, whether due or not, are notified
to exhibit same, with the voucher thereof,
legally verified, to the undersigned, at
Suite 240 Frederick Building, Hunting-
ton, West Virginia 25701, on or before
the 1st day of May, 1996; otherwise they
may by law be excluded from all benefit
of said estates. All beneficiaries of said
estates may appear on or before said day
to examine said claims and otherwise
protect their interests.
GIVEN under my hand this
1st day of January, 1996.
DAVID M. BAKER
Fiduciary Commissioner,
County of Cabell
State of West Virginia
.LH.16   1-6.13.96

WISCONSIN

INFORMAL ADMINISTRATION:
ORDER SETTING TIME AND
NOTICE TO CRE0lTORS
File No. 517-435
STATE OF WISCONSIN - CIRCUIT
COURT - MILWAUKEE COUNTY-
PROBATE JURISDICTION, In the
Matter of the Estate of JULIA D. BAKER.
Deceased.

An application for Informal Adminstration
of the estate of Julia D. Baker, Milwaukee
County, Wisconsin, post office address 1807
S. 8th Street, Apt. 1. Milwaukee, Wisconsin,
having been filed;

It Is Ordered That:

All creditor's claims must be filed
on or before February 25. 1986, or be barred.

Dated November 25. 1985.
ROSEMARY THORNTON.
12-9-3M   Probate Registrar.
JAMES L. WALT, Attorney.
845 N. 11th Street.
Milwaukee. WI 53233.

WYOMING

STATE OF WYOMING   )
)88.

COUNTY OF LARAMIE
                    IN THE DISTRICT COURT
                    FIRST JUDICIAL DISTRICT
                    Docket 31 No. 232
IN THE MATTER OF THE ESTATE   )

                of   )
)
)
CAROLE L. REES, deceased.   )
                    NOTICE OF PROBATE
TO ALL PERSONS INTERESTED IN SAID ESTATE:

You are hereby notified that on the 21th day of August, 1985, the Last Will and Testament of decedent was admitted to probate by the above named Court, and that J.E. Preece, aka Ted Preece, aka John E. Preece of Cheyenne, Wyoming, was appointed Personal Representative thereof. Any action to set aside said Will shall be filed in said Court within three (3) months from the date of the first publication or this Notice, or thereafter be forever barred.

Notice is further given that all persons indebted to the decedent or to her Estate are requested to make immediate payment to the J.E. Preece, aka Ted Preece, aka John E. Preece, Personal Representative, at 222 West 5th Avenue, Cheyenne, Wyoming 82001.

Creditors having claims against the decedent or the Estate are required to file them in duplicate with the necessary vouchers, in the office of the Clerk of said Court, on or before (3) three months after the date of the first publication of this Notice, and if such claims are not so filed, unless otherwise allowed or paid, they will be forever barred.

DATED this 19th day of December, 1985.
J.E. Preece, aka Ted Preece
aka John E. Preece
Personal Representative
December 23,30,1985, January 6,1986

SAMPLE NOTICES—PUBLIC AND PRIVATE SALES

Sale of Real Property at Private Sale

NOTICE OF SALE OF REAL
PROPERTY AT
PRIVATE SALE
NO. P640923

In the Superior Court of the State of California, for the County of Los Angeles.

In the Matter of the Estate of ERNEST A. HERNANDEZ, Deceased.

Notice is hereby given that the undersigned will sell at Private sale to the highest and best bidding subject to confirmation of sold Superior Court, on or after the 6th day of September 1994, at the office of Ernest V. Shockley, 205 South Broadway, Los Angeles 90012. County of Los Angeles, State of California, all the right, title and interest of said deceased at the time of death and all the right, title and interest that the estate of said deceased has acquired by operation of law or otherwise other than or in addition to that of said deceased at the time of death, in and to all the certain real property situated in the City of Los Angeles, County of Los Angeles, State of California, particularly described as follows, to-wit:

Lot 51 in Block 19, Workman Hollenbeck Tract 0004, as per map recorded in Book 5, Pages 426 and 427 of Maps, in the office of the County Recorder of said county.

More commonly known as: 1917 Second Street, Los Angeles, California 90033.

Terms of sale cash in lawful money of the United States on confirmation of sale, or part cash and balance evidenced by note secured by Mortgage or Trust Deed on the property so sold. Ten per cent of amount bid to be deposited with bid.

Bids or offers to be in writing and will be received at the aforesaid office at any time after the first publication hereof and before date of sale.

Dated this 25th day of August, 1994.

MARTHA HERNANDEZ

Executrix of the estate of said Decedent.

Ernest V. Shockley, Attorney-at-Law, 205 South Broadway, Los Angeles, California 90012.

(CR21373) Aug. 26, 27, Sept. 2

Daily Commerce

NOTICE OF SALE OF REAL PROPERTY AT PUBLIC AUCTION

#23-58263-G

No. 664-359

Superior Court of the State of California for the County of Los Angeles

In the Matter of the Estate of JOSEPH CLARK, aka JOE CLARK, JR., Conservatee.

Notice is hereby given that the undersigned, Gordon W. Treharne, Public Guardian, as Conservator of the estate of Joseph Clark, Conservatee, will sell at Public Auction on February 15, 1984, at 12:15 P.M. on the premises as hereinafter described, to the highest and best bidder upon the terms and conditions hereinafter mentioned, subject to the confirmation by the Superior Court, all the right, title and interest of said conservatee at the time of the appointment, and all the right, title and interest that the estate of said conservatee has by operation of law or otherwise acquired other than, or in addition to, that of said conservatee at the time of appointment in and to all of that certain real property described as follows, to-wit:

ATTACHMENT

The land referred to herein is situated in the State of California, County of Los Angeles, City of Los Angeles, and is described as follows:

UNDIVIDED ONE-HALF INTEREST in and to:

Lot 18 of Firth's Boulevard Tract as shown on Book 5, Page 112 of Maps, in the office of the County Recorder of Los Angeles County, California, EXCEPTING THEREFROM the Northerly 50 feet of said lot.

SUBJECT TO a Oil and Gas Lease. Lessor; Joe Clark Jr., and Estella Faye Clark, as owner of said land and by other persons as owners of other lands in the community area. Lessee; Western Gulf Oil Company, a Delaware Corporation, recorded in Official Records, Book 56480, Page 228, expressly without right of surface entry.

SUBJECT TO a Oil and Gas Lease. Lessor; Sammy Warren, an unmarried man. Lessee; American Petrofina Exploration Company, recorded in Official Records, In Book M 3143, Page 168, expressly without right of surface entry.

Commonly known as 9229 Firth Boulevard, Los Angeles, California.

SAID REAL PROPERTY AND IMPROVEMENTS THEREON ARE SOLD IN AN "AS IS PHYSICAL CONDITION, NO TERMITE CLEARANCE."

APPRAISAL: $70,000.00

Single Family Residence	Four Bedroom
Rental Income	Vacant
Taxes 1982-83	$402.70
Lot size - approximately	100'x175'

The first twenty five hundred ($2,500.00) dollars or 10% deposit must be in the form of a Cashiers Check.

Subject to current taxes, conditions, covenants, restrictions, reservations, easements, rights and rights of way of record.

The sale will be made on the following terms: Cash in lawful money of the United States upon the confirmation of sale. Deposit of ten percent in cash upon acceptance of bid.

Policy of Title and one-half of escrow fee at expense of seller and one-half of escrow fee at expense of the purchaser.

A thirty-day escrow shall be opened by the seller at sellers choice.

Taxes, rent, fire insurance and interest on encumbrances, if any, shall be pro-rated to the close of escrow.

The undersigned reserves the right to reject any and all bids, and to postpone the sale from time to time in accordance with the provisions of Section 783 of the Probate Code.

Dated: January 11, 1984.

GORDON W. TREHARNE, blic Administrator, as Administrator of the estate of said Conservatee

KENNEDY/WILSON, INC. (213) 393-5302

(G45855 Thurs) Jan 26 Feb 2, 9

NOTICE OF SALE OF REAL PROPERTY AT PUBLIC AUCTION

#36-01781-D

No. 655-029

Superior Court of the State of California for the County of Los Angeles

In the Matter of the Estate of MARY FONG, aka ESTHER MARIE LINKOFF, aka MARIE LINKOFF, Deceased.

Notice is hereby given that the undersigned, Gordon W. Treharne, Public Administrator, as Administrator of the estate of Mary Fong, aka Esther Marie Linkoff, Deceased, will sell at Public Auction on February 15, 1984, at 10:00 A.M. on the premises as hereinafter described, to the highest and best bidder upon the terms and conditions hereinafter mentioned, subject to confirmation by the Superior Court, all the right, title and interest of said decedent at the time of the death, and all the right, title and interest that the estate of said decedent has by operation of law or otherwise acquired other than, or in addition to, that of said decedent at the time of death in and to all of that certain real property described as follows, to-wit:

The land referred to herein is situated in the State of California, County of Los Angeles, City of Los Angeles, and is described as follows:

Lot 11, Block 28 Angelino Heights Tract as per map recorded in Book 10, Pages 63 to 66 Miscellaneous Records, in the office of the County Recorder of said County.

Commonly known as 1220 West Sunset Boulevard, Los Angeles, California.

SAID REAL PROPERTY AND IMPROVEMENTS THEREON ARE SOLD IN AN "AS IS PHYSICAL CONDITION, NO TERMITE CLEARANCE."

APPRAISAL: Pending

Lot	Unimproved
Rental Income	None
Taxes 1982-83	$442.08
Lot size - approximately	50.43'x173.65'

The first twenty five hundred ($2,500.00) dollars or 10% deposit must be in the form of a Cashiers Check.

Subject to current taxes, conditions, covenants, restrictions, reservations, easements, rights and rights of way of record.

The sale will be made on the following terms: Cash in lawful money of the United States upon the confirmation of sale. Deposit of ten per cent in cash upon acceptance of bid.

Policy of title and one-half of escrow fee at expense of seller and one-half of escrow fee at expense of the purchaser.

A thirty-day escrow shall be opened by the seller at sellers choice.

Taxes, rent, fire insurance and interest on encumbrances, if any, shall be pro-rated to the close of escrow.

The undersigned reserves the right to reject any and all bids, and to postpone the sale from time to time in accordance with the provisions of Section 783 of the Probate Code.

Dated: January 18, 1984

GORDON W. TREHARNE, Public Administrator, as Administrator of the estate of said Decedent

KENNEDY/WILSON, INC. (213) 393-5302

(G45854 Thurs) Jan 26 Feb 2, 9

Daily Commerce

NOTICE OF SALE OF REAL PROPERTY AT PUBLIC AUCTION

#98-95310-G

No. 666-591

Superior Court of the State of California for the County of Los Angeles

In the Matter of the Estate of CLARICE WYNNE, aka CLARICE R. WYNN, Conservatee.

Notice is hereby given that the undersigned, Gordon W. Treharne, Public Guardian, as Conservator of the estate of Clarice R. Wynn, Conservatee, will sell at Public Auction on February 15, 1984, at 11:15 A.M. on the premises as hereinafter described, to the highest and best bidder upon the terms and conditions hereinafter mentioned, subject to the confirmation by the Superior Court, all the right, title and interest of said conservatee at the time of the appointment, and all the right, title and interest that the estate of said conservatee has by operation of law or otherwise acquired other than, or in addition to, that of said conservatee at the time of appointment in and to all of that certain real property described as follows, to-wit:

The land referred to herein is situated in the State of California, County of Los Angeles, and is described as follows:

Lot 3 except the Northerly 25.27 feet thereof, measured along the Westerly line thereof, in Block 25 of Athens Tract as per map recorded in Book 8, Page 167 of Maps, in the office of the County Recorder of said County. EXCEPT the West 20 feet thereof, conveyed to the County of Los Angeles for street purposes.

Commonly known as 12220 Athens Way, Los Angeles, California.

SAID REAL PROPERTY AND IMPROVEMENTS THEREON ARE SOLD IN AN "AS IS PHYSICAL CONDITION. NO TERMITE CLEARANCE."

APPRAISAL: Pending

Single Family Residence	Two Bedroom
Rental Income	Vacant
Taxes 1982-83	$205.58
Lot size - approximately	75.27'x155.72' irregular

The first twenty five hundred ($2,500.00) dollars or 10% deposit must be in the form of a Cashiers Check.

Subject to current taxes, conditions, covenants, restrictions, reservations, easements, rights and rights of way of record.

The sale will be made on the following terms: Cash in lawful

NOTICE OF SALE OF REAL PROPERTY AT PUBLIC AUCTION

#43-75378-D

No. 655-318

Superior Court of the State of California for the County of Los Angeles

In the Matter of the Estate of ELSBETH GUNTHER, Deceased.

Notice is hereby given that the undersigned, Gordon W. Treharne, Public Administrator, as Administrator of the estate of Elsbeth Gunther, Deceased, will sell at Public Auction on February 15, 1984, at 4:30 P.M. on the premises as hereinafter described, to the highest and best bidder upon the terms and conditions hereinafter mentioned, subject to confirmation by the Superior Court, all the right, title and interest of said decedent at the time of the death, and all the right, title and interest that the estate of said decedent has by operation of law or otherwise acquired other than, or in addition to, that of said decedent at the time of death in and to all of that certain real property described as follows, to-wit:

The land referred to herein is situated in the State of California, County of Los Angeles, City of Unincorporated area, and is described as follows:

Lot 20, Block 6 of Tract No. 4301, as per map recorded in Book 50, Pages 98 and 99 of Maps, in the office of the County Recorder of said County.

SUBJECT TO a Oil and Gas Lease dated June 21, 1956. Karl Gunther and Elsbeth Gunther as Lessor, and Aeco Corporation, as Lessee, recorded December 4, 1956 in Official Records, Book 53030, Page 102, as Instrument No. 4298. Expressly without right of surface entry.

Commonly known as 1355 South Sunol Drive, Los Angeles, California.

SAID REAL PROPERTY AND IMPROVEMENTS THEREON ARE SOLD IN AN "AS IS PHYSICAL CONDITION. NO TERMITE CLEARANCE."

APPRAISAL: $55,000

Single Family Residence	One Bedroom
Rental Income	Occupied
Taxes 1979-80	$106.64
Lot size - approximately	40'x135'

Subject to current taxes, conditions, covenants, restrictions, reservations, easements, rights and rights of way of record.

The sale will be made on the following terms: Cash in lawful money of the United States upon the confirmation of sale. Deposit of ten percent in cash upon acceptance of bid.

Policy of title and one-half of escrow fee at expense of seller and one-half of escrow fee at expense of the purchaser.

A thirty-day escrow shall be opened by the seller at sellers choice.

Taxes, rent, fire insurance and interest on encumbrances, if any, shall be pro-rated to the close of escrow.

The undersigned reserves the right to reject any and all bids, and to postpone the sale from time to time in accordance with the provisions of Section 783 of the Probate Code.

The first twenty five hundred ($2,500.00) dollars or 10% deposit must be in the form of a Cashiers Check.

Dated: January 17, 1984

GORDON W. TREHARNE,

Public Administrator, as Administrator of the estate of said Decedent

KENNEDY/WILSON, INC. (213) 393-5302

(G45840 Thurs) Jan 26 Feb 2, 9

F

SAMPLE WORKING CASE SHEET

DATE DOWN

—   —

DATE OF PUBLICATION

Paste Notice Here

WORKING CASE SHEET # ___ P ___

EXECUTOR OR ADMINISTRATOR:	
ADDRESS ST.:	
CITY ZIP.:	
TEL. #:	RELATIONSHIP:
DECEDANT:	TG:
SITUS:	
CITY ZIP.:	PRESONAL RESID. ☐ Yes ☐ No
A.P.N. #:	LAST SOLD: $
LEGAL:	TEL. #: #YRS. +
AMENITIES:	PROP. VIEWED: ☐ Yes ☐ No

A.P.N. # (OTHER)s	ZONE	SQ.FT	YR.BT	BR/BA	DT.SLD	TAX VALUE	TAXES
SAME AS ABOVE APN							

DATE FILED OR APPRAISED:	ITA: Real= $
APPRAISERS NAME:	Personal= $
ADDRESS ST.:	
CITY ZIP.:	TEL. #:

HEIRS NAME'(S)	RELATION	%	ADDRESS ST. / CITY ZIP.	TEL. #

<<<<<<< COMPARABLE SALES >>>>>>>

ADDRESS & STREET	ZONE	YR.BT	BR/BA	SQ.FT	DT.RECD	SALES PRICE

COURT CONFIRMATION HEARING

☐ WITHOUT NOTICE   ☐ WITH NOTICE

DATE ___ / TIME ___ : LOCI ___

...TORNEY'S NAME & Tel.# ___

AVERAGE COMPS. $ ___   QUICK SALE EST. $ ___

RETAIL GUESSTIMATE $ ___ LESS ENCUMBERENCES $ ___

POSSIBLE I.R.R. = ___ % " GROSS PROFIT $ ___

☐ GO? ☐ NO GO? ☐ WHY? ___

MAX. BID PRICE : $ ___

© OMNIVEST CO. LTD.   " Not incl. fix up

G

SAMPLE PROBATE CASE MASTER NUMERICAL LIST

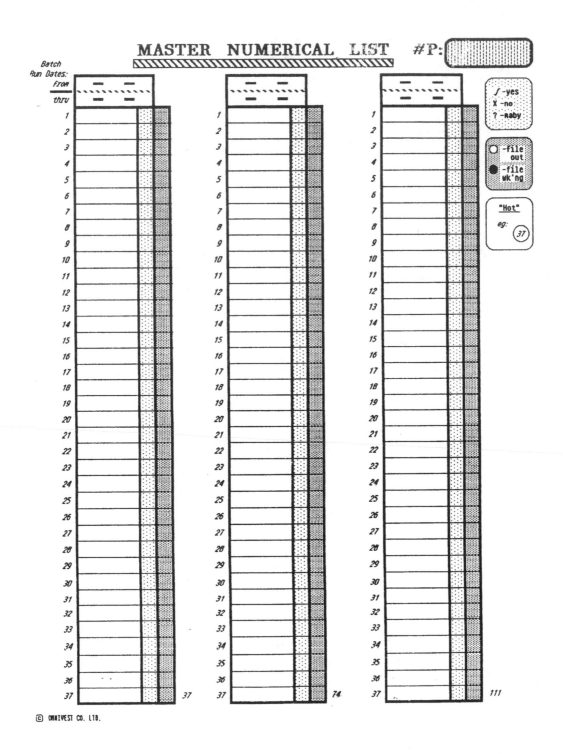

H

SAMPLE PROPERTY REPAIR
EXPENSE SURVEY

Property Repair Expense Survey

MAJOR

1. Plumbing...$_____
2. Electrical...$_____
3. Roofing...$_____
4. Structural..$_____
5. Foundation...$_____
6. Other eg. _____......$_____

                 Sub Total.........$_____

MINOR

1. Front / Rear Yard Work.............................$_____
2. Walkways / Driveways...............................$_____
3. Landscaping...$_____
4. Front Door / Entrance...............................$_____
5. Exterior paint / Trim................................$_____
6. Windows / Screens / Shutters ....$_____
7. Lighting / Door Chimes.............................$_____
8. Interior / Exterior Painting.........................$_____
9. Wall Coverings / Ceilings...........................$_____
10. Window Coverings...................................$_____
11. Floor Coverings.....................................$_____
12. Tiles / Counter Tops...............................$_____
13. Cabinets..$_____
14. Toilets / Showers & Tubs / Sinks..................$_____
15. Faucets / Fixtures..................................$_____
16. Appliances..$_____
17. Decorations & Plants...............................$_____
18. Miscellaneous eg: _____......$_____

                 Sub-total.........$_____

Features Affecting Future Property Value

A. The Surrounding Neighborhood: Good___   Fair___   Poor___
B. General Appearance for location: Good___   Fair___   Poor___
C. Floor Plan Acceptance: Good___   Fair___   Poor___
D. Closet / Storage Space: Good___   Fair___   Poor___
E. Garage Space / Access / Condition: Good___   Fair___   Poor___
F. Other:_____;   Good___   Fair___   Poor___

          Features: Cost Factor +/−.....$_____

          GRAND TOTAL.....$_____

*SELLER*_____ *DATE*_____

STATE TAXES AND PROBATE TAX DUE REQUIREMENTS

State	Income Tax	Gift Tax	Inheritance Tax	Estate Tax	Tax Due Requirement
Alabama	Y	N	N	N	Within 9 mos. of date of death
Alaska	N	N	N	N	Report within 2 mos. of date of death; tax within 15 mos. of date of death
Arizona	Y	N	N	N	Within 9 mos. of date of death
Arkansas	Y	N	N	N	Within 9 mos. of date of death
California	Y	N	N	N	Within 9 mos. of date of death
Colorado	Y	N	N	N	Within 9 mos. of date of death
Connecticut	Y	N	Y	N	Within 9 mos. of date of death

State	Income Tax	Gift Tax	Inheritance Tax	Estate Tax	Tax Due Requirement
Delaware	Y	Y	Y	N	Within 9 mos. of date of death
District of Columbia	Y	N	N	N	Within 10 mos. of date of death
Florida	N	N	N	N	Report within 2 mos. of date of death or appointment of personal rep
Georgia	Y	N	N	N	Within 9 mos. of date of death
Hawaii	Y	N	N	N	Within 9 mos. of date of death
Idaho	Y	N	N	N	Within 9 mos. of date of death
Illinois	Y	N	N	N	Within 9 mos. of date of death
Indiana	Y	N	Y	N	Within 10 mos. of date of death
Iowa	Y	N	Y	N	Within 9 mos. of date of death
Kansas	Y	N	Y	N	Within 9 mos. of date of death
Kentucky	Y	N	Y	N	Within 18 mos. of date of death; 5% discount if paid within 9 mos.
Louisiana	Y	Y	Y	N	Within 9 mos. of date of death
Maine	Y	N	N	N	Within 9 mos. of date of death
Maryland	Y	N	Y	N	Within 9 mos. of date of death

State	Income Tax	Gift Tax	Inheritance Tax	Estate Tax	Tax Due Requirement
Massachusetts	Y	N	N	Y	Within 9 mos. of date of death
Michigan	Y	N	Y	N	Within 9 mos. of date of death
Minnesota	Y	N	N	N	Within 9 mos. of date of death
Mississippi	Y	N	N	N	Notice within 2 mos. of date of death; tax within 9 mos. of date of death
Missouri	Y	N	N	N	Within 9 mos. of date of death
Montana	Y	N	Y	N	Within 9 mos. of date of death
Nebraska	Y	N	Y	N	Within 10 mos. of date of death
Nevada	N	N	N	N	Not applicable
New Hampshire	Y	N	Y	N	Within 12 mos. of date of death
New Jersey	Y	N	Y	N	Within 8 mos. of date of death
New Mexico	Y	N	N	N	Within 9 mos. of date of death
New York	Y	Y	N	Y	Within 9 mos. of date of death; interest on tax accrues from 6 mos. after date of death
North Carolina	Y	Y	Y	N	Within 9 mos. of date of death
North Dakota	Y	N	N	N	Within 9 mos. of date of death

State	Income Tax	Gift Tax	Inheritance Tax	Estate Tax	Tax Due Requirement
Ohio	Y	N	N	Y	Within 9 mos. of date of death
Oregon	Y	N	N	N	Within 9 mos. of date of death
Pennsylvania	Y	N	Y	N	Tax within 9 mos. of date of death; 5% discount if paid within 3 mos. of date of death
Rhode Island	Y	N	N	N	Within 10 mos. of date of death
South Carolina	Y	Y	N	Y	Within 9 mos. of date of death
South Dakota	N	N	Y	N	Within 9 mos. of date of death
Tennessee	N	Y	Y	N	Within 9 mos. of date of death
Texas	N	N	Y	N	Within 9 mos. of date of death
Utah	Y	N	N	N	Within 9 mos. of date of death
Vermont	Y	N	N	N	Within 9 mos. of date of death
Virginia	Y	N	N	N	Within 9 mos. of date of death
Washington	N	N	N	N	Not applicable
West Virginia	Y	N	N	N	Within 9 mos. of date of death
Wisconsin	Y	N	N	N	Within 12 mos. of date of death
Wyoming	N	N	N	N	Not applicable

J

CELEBRITY PROBATE CASES

Legendary bankers, a famous accountant, a prominent stockbroker, entertainers, industrialists, and even a president of the United States—all died thinking their heirs would enjoy the benefits of a generous inheritance. Yet, using the probate courts, hoards of lawyers descended on all these estates and became the real heirs. The following list reflects the approximate percentages of estate value lost by the heirs of 36 prominent Americans, people whose fame and celebrity didn't prevent the legal pilferage of their assets after their deaths.

	Estate Value	Cost of Settlement	Percent of Estate Value
Marilyn Monroe	$ 819,176	$ 718,176	88
Nat King Cole	1,876,648	1,577,740	84
Harold Gould	67,535,386	52,549,682	78
Elvis Presley	10,165,434	7,374,635	73
J.P. Morgan	17,121,482	11,893,691	69
John D. Rockefeller, Sr.	29,900,000	17,200,000	64
Marian Davies	5,519,009	3,311,781	60
Dixie Crosby	1,332,571	781,953	59
Mary Duke Biddle	60,600,000	35,730,803	58
Frederick Vanderbilt	78,838,530	42,846,112	56
Alwin C. Ernst, CPA	12,642,431	7,124,112	56
Andrew Jergens	5,891,781	3,343,323	56
Joseph Schenk	1,801,179	998,172	55
Alfred N. Steele	1,155,829	633,195	54
William Frawley	92,446	46,000	49
William Boeing	22,386,158	10,589,748	47
Myford Irvine	13,445,552	6,012,585	45
Henry J. Kaiser, Sr.	5,97772	2,488,364	44
Ludwig Van Der Rohe	793,044	342,724	43
Joseph M. Cuhady	1,582,453	670,443	42
W.C. Fields	884,680	327,331	37
Cecil B. DeMille	4,043,607	1,396,064	35
Earle Stanley Gardner	1,795,092	636,705	35

	Estate Value	Cost of Settlement	Percent of Estate Value
Hedda Hopper	$ 472,661	$ 165,982	35
Ernest T. Weir	10,581,318	3,678,913	34
Rick Nelson	744,400	238,200	31
William F. "Bull" Halsey	624,965	198,322	31
George S. Patton, Jr.	844,364	266,825	31
Al Jolson	4,385,143	1,349,066	31
Gary Cooper	4,948,985	1,520,454	31
Walt Disney	23,004,851	6,811,943	30
Clark Gable	2,806,528	1,101,038	30
Franklin D. Roosevelt	1,900,000	575,000	30
Humphrey Bogart	910,146	274,284	30
James D. Zellerbach	5,925,223	1,822,085	30
Fred Allen	1,062,697	281,777	26
Dean Witter	7,451,055	1,830,717	25
Harry M. Warner	8,946,618	2,308,717	25
Orville Wright	1,023,904	251,643	24
Nelson Eddy	472,715	109,990	23
Dwight D. Eisenhower	2,905,857	671,429	23
Paul Muni	1,198,998	264,136	22
James B. Black	1,172,199	264,136	22
Louis B. Mayer	8,173,397	1,558,702	19
William Bendix	592,629	61,614	10

JUDICIAL FLOWCHART
FOR EVERY STATE
(PLUS DISTRICT OF COLUMBIA)

WHERE THE PROBATE COURT FITS INTO
YOUR STATE LEGAL SYSTEM

ALABAMA COURT STRUCTURE

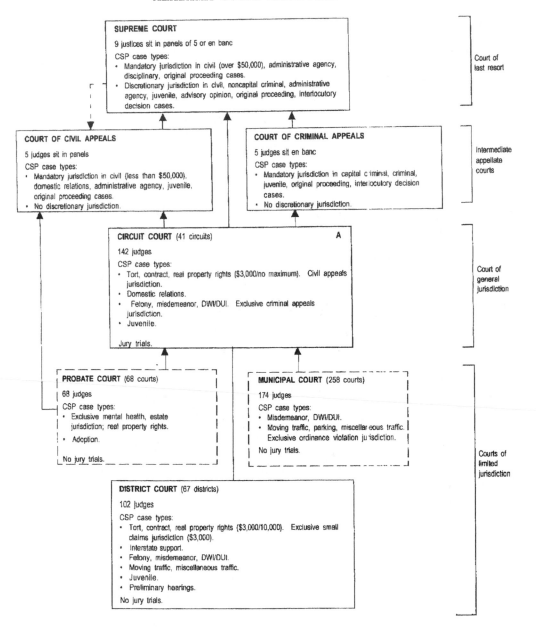

SUPREME COURT

9 justices sit in panels of 5 or en banc

CSP case types:
- Mandatory jurisdiction in civil (over $50,000), administrative agency, disciplinary, original proceeding cases.
- Discretionary jurisdiction in civil, noncapital criminal, administrative agency, juvenile, advisory opinion, original proceeding, interlocutory decision cases.

Court of last resort

COURT OF CIVIL APPEALS

5 judges sit in panels

CSP case types:
- Mandatory jurisdiction in civil (less than $50,000), domestic relations, administrative agency, juvenile, original proceeding cases.
- No discretionary jurisdiction.

COURT OF CRIMINAL APPEALS

5 judges sit en banc

CSP case types:
- Mandatory jurisdiction in capital criminal, criminal, juvenile, original proceeding, interlocutory decision cases.
- No discretionary jurisdiction.

Intermediate appellate courts

CIRCUIT COURT (41 circuits)   A

142 judges

CSP case types:
- Tort, contract, real property rights ($3,000/no maximum). Civil appeals jurisdiction.
- Domestic relations.
- Felony, misdemeanor, DWI/DUI. Exclusive criminal appeals jurisdiction.
- Juvenile.

Jury trials.

Court of general jurisdiction

PROBATE COURT (68 courts)

68 judges

CSP case types:
- Exclusive mental health, estate jurisdiction; real property rights.
- Adoption.

No jury trials.

MUNICIPAL COURT (258 courts)

174 judges

CSP case types:
- Misdemeanor, DWI/DUI.
- Moving traffic, parking, miscellaneous traffic. Exclusive ordinance violation jurisdiction.

No jury trials.

DISTRICT COURT (67 districts)

102 judges

CSP case types:
- Tort, contract, real property rights ($3,000/10,000). Exclusive small claims jurisdiction ($3,000).
- Interstate support.
- Felony, misdemeanor, DWI/DUI.
- Moving traffic, miscellaneous traffic.
- Juvenile.
- Preliminary hearings.

No jury trials.

Courts of limited jurisdiction

ALASKA COURT STRUCTURE.

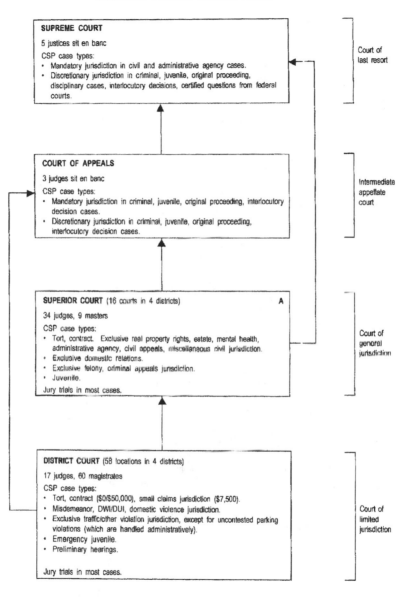

SUPREME COURT

5 justices sit en banc

CSP case types:
- Mandatory jurisdiction in civil and administrative agency cases.
- Discretionary jurisdiction in criminal, juvenile, original proceeding, disciplinary cases, interlocutory decisions, certified questions from federal courts.

Court of
last resort

COURT OF APPEALS

3 judges sit en banc

CSP case types:
- Mandatory jurisdiction in criminal, juvenile, original proceeding, interlocutory decision cases.
- Discretionary jurisdiction in criminal, juvenile, original proceeding, interlocutory decision cases.

Intermediate
appellate
court

SUPERIOR COURT (16 courts in 4 districts)   A

34 judges, 9 masters

CSP case types:
- Tort, contract. Exclusive real property rights, estate, mental health, administrative agency, civil appeals, miscellaneous civil jurisdiction.
- Exclusive domestic relations.
- Exclusive felony, criminal appeals jurisdiction.
- Juvenile.

Jury trials in most cases.

Court of
general
jurisdiction

DISTRICT COURT (58 locations in 4 districts)

17 judges, 60 magistrates

CSP case types:
- Tort, contract ($0/$50,000), small claims jurisdiction ($7,500).
- Misdemeanor, DWI/DUI, domestic violence jurisdiction.
- Exclusive traffic/other violation jurisdiction, except for uncontested parking violations (which are handled administratively).
- Emergency juvenile.
- Preliminary hearings.

Jury trials in most cases.

Court of
limited
jurisdiction

ARIZONA COURT STRUCTURE

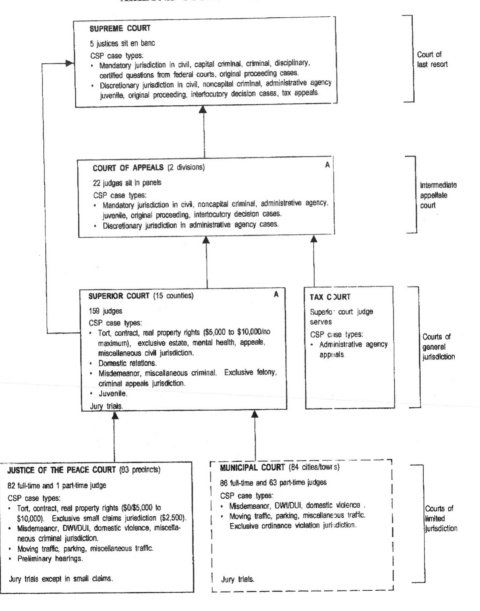

SUPREME COURT

5 justices sit en banc

CSP case types:
- Mandatory jurisdiction in civil, capital criminal, criminal, disciplinary, certified questions from federal courts, original proceeding cases.
- Discretionary jurisdiction in civil, noncapital criminal, administrative agency juvenile, original proceeding, interlocutory decision cases, tax appeals.

Court of last resort

COURT OF APPEALS (2 divisions)   A

22 judges sit in panels

CSP case types:
- Mandatory jurisdiction in civil, noncapital criminal, administrative agency, juvenile, original proceeding, interlocutory decision cases.
- Discretionary jurisdiction in administrative agency cases.

Intermediate appellate court

SUPERIOR COURT (15 counties)   A

159 judges

CSP case types:
- Tort, contract, real property rights ($5,000 to $10,000/no maximum), exclusive estate, mental health, appeals, miscellaneous civil jurisdiction.
- Domestic relations.
- Misdemeanor, miscellaneous criminal. Exclusive felony, criminal appeals jurisdiction.
- Juvenile.

Jury trials.

TAX COURT

Superior court judge serves

CSP case types:
- Administrative agency appeals.

Courts of general jurisdiction

JUSTICE OF THE PEACE COURT (83 precincts)

82 full-time and 1 part-time judge

CSP case types:
- Tort, contract, real property rights ($0/$5,000 to $10,000). Exclusive small claims jurisdiction ($2,500).
- Misdemeanor, DWI/DUI, domestic violence, miscellaneous criminal jurisdiction.
- Moving traffic, parking, miscellaneous traffic.
- Preliminary hearings.

Jury trials except in small claims.

MUNICIPAL COURT (84 cities/towns)

86 full-time and 63 part-time judges

CSP case types:
- Misdemeanor, DWI/DUI, domestic violence.
- Moving traffic, parking, miscellaneous traffic. Exclusive ordinance violation jurisdiction.

Jury trials.

Courts of limited jurisdiction

ARKANSAS COURT STRUCTURE.

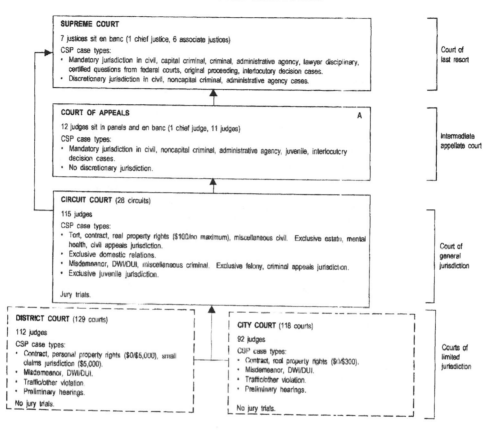

SUPREME COURT

7 justices sit en banc (1 chief justice, 6 associate justices)

CSP case types:
- Mandatory jurisdiction in civil, capital criminal, criminal, administrative agency, lawyer disciplinary, certified questions from federal courts, original proceeding, interlocutory decision cases.
- Discretionary jurisdiction in civil, noncapital criminal, administrative agency cases.

Court of last resort

COURT OF APPEALS   A

12 judges sit in panels and en banc (1 chief judge, 11 judges)

CSP case types:
- Mandatory jurisdiction in civil, noncapital criminal, administrative agency, juvenile, interlocutory decision cases.
- No discretionary jurisdiction.

Intermediate appellate court

CIRCUIT COURT (28 circuits)

115 judges

CSP case types:
- Tort, contract, real property rights ($100/no maximum), miscellaneous civil. Exclusive estate, mental health, civil appeals jurisdiction.
- Exclusive domestic relations.
- Misdemeanor, DWI/DUI, miscellaneous criminal. Exclusive felony, criminal appeals jurisdiction.
- Exclusive juvenile jurisdiction.

Jury trials.

Court of general jurisdiction

DISTRICT COURT (129 courts)

112 judges

CSP case types:
- Contract, personal property rights ($0/$5,000), small claims jurisdiction ($5,000).
- Misdemeanor, DWI/DUI.
- Traffic/other violation.
- Preliminary hearings.

No jury trials.

CITY COURT (118 courts)

92 judges

CSP case types:
- Contract, real property rights ($0/$300).
- Misdemeanor, DWI/DUI.
- Traffic/other violation.
- Preliminary hearings.

No jury trials.

Courts of limited jurisdiction

Note: In 2001, Arkansas combined the Chancery and Probate Court with the Circuit Court and reduced the number of limited jurisdiction courts from six to two by combining the County, Police, Common Pleas, and Justice of the Peace Courts into the Municipal Court which was renamed and is now the District Court.

CALIFORNIA COURT STRUCTURE.

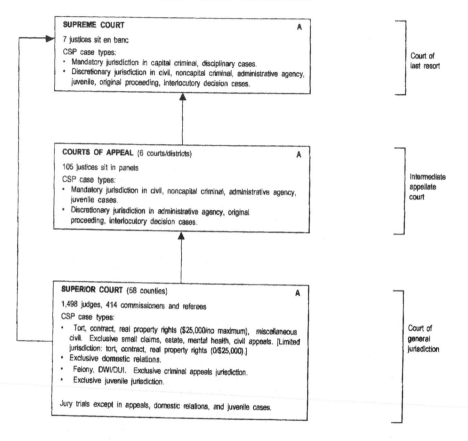

SUPREME COURT   A

7 justices sit en banc

CSP case types:
- Mandatory jurisdiction in capital criminal, disciplinary cases.
- Discretionary jurisdiction in civil, noncapital criminal, administrative agency, juvenile, original proceeding, interlocutory decision cases.

Court of last resort

COURTS OF APPEAL (6 courts/districts)   A

105 justices sit in panels

CSP case types:
- Mandatory jurisdiction in civil, noncapital criminal, administrative agency, juvenile cases.
- Discretionary jurisdiction in administrative agency, original proceeding, interlocutory decision cases.

Intermediate appellate court

SUPERIOR COURT (58 counties)   A

1,498 judges, 414 commissioners and referees

CSP case types:
- Tort, contract, real property rights ($25,000/no maximum), miscellaneous civil. Exclusive small claims, estate, mental health, civil appeals. [Limited jurisdiction: tort, contract, real property rights (0/$25,000).]
- Exclusive domestic relations.
- Felony, DWI/DUI. Exclusive criminal appeals jurisdiction.
- Exclusive juvenile jurisdiction.

Jury trials except in appeals, domestic relations, and juvenile cases.

Court of general jurisdiction

Note: All trial courts were unified as of 7/1/00.

COLORADO COURT STRUCTURE

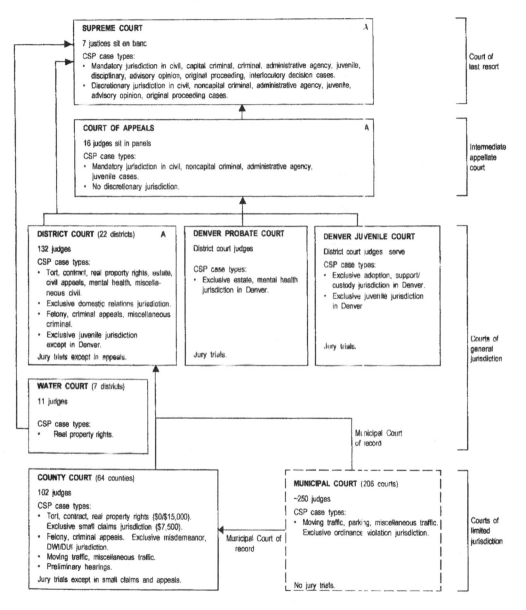

SUPREME COURT A

7 justices sit en banc

CSP case types:
- Mandatory jurisdiction in civil, capital criminal, criminal, administrative agency, juvenile, disciplinary, advisory opinion, original proceeding, interlocutory decision cases.
- Discretionary jurisdiction in civil, noncapital criminal, administrative agency, juvenile, advisory opinion, original proceeding cases.

Court of last resort

COURT OF APPEALS A

16 judges sit in panels

CSP case types:
- Mandatory jurisdiction in civil, noncapital criminal, administrative agency, juvenile cases.
- No discretionary jurisdiction.

Intermediate appellate court

DISTRICT COURT (22 districts) A

132 judges

CSP case types:
- Tort, contract, real property rights, estate, civil appeals, mental health, miscellaneous civil.
- Exclusive domestic relations jurisdiction.
- Felony, criminal appeals, miscellaneous criminal.
- Exclusive juvenile jurisdiction except in Denver.

Jury trials except in appeals.

DENVER PROBATE COURT

District court judges

CSP case types:
- Exclusive estate, mental health jurisdiction in Denver.

Jury trials.

DENVER JUVENILE COURT

District court judges serve

CSP case types:
- Exclusive adoption, support/custody jurisdiction in Denver.
- Exclusive juvenile jurisdiction in Denver

Jury trials.

Courts of general jurisdiction

WATER COURT (7 districts)

11 judges

CSP case types:
- Real property rights.

Municipal Court of record

COUNTY COURT (64 counties)

102 judges

CSP case types:
- Tort, contract, real property rights ($0/$15,000). Exclusive small claims jurisdiction ($7,500).
- Felony, criminal appeals. Exclusive misdemeanor, DWI/DUI jurisdiction.
- Moving traffic, miscellaneous traffic.
- Preliminary hearings.

Jury trials except in small claims and appeals.

Municipal Court of record

MUNICIPAL COURT (206 courts)

~250 judges

CSP case types:
- Moving traffic, parking, miscellaneous traffic. Exclusive ordinance violation jurisdiction.

No jury trials.

Courts of limited jurisdiction

CONNECTICUT COURT STRUCTURE

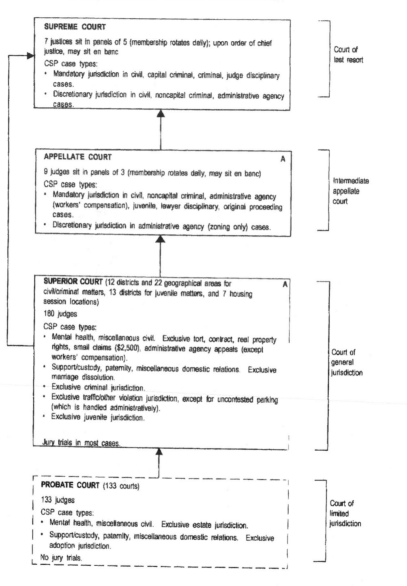

SUPREME COURT

7 justices sit in panels of 5 (membership rotates daily); upon order of chief justice, may sit en banc

CSP case types:

- Mandatory jurisdiction in civil, capital criminal, criminal, judge disciplinary cases.
- Discretionary jurisdiction in civil, noncapital criminal, administrative agency cases.

Court of last resort

APPELLATE COURT   A

9 judges sit in panels of 3 (membership rotates daily, may sit en banc)

CSP case types:

- Mandatory jurisdiction in civil, noncapital criminal, administrative agency (workers' compensation), juvenile, lawyer disciplinary, original proceeding cases.
- Discretionary jurisdiction in administrative agency (zoning only) cases.

Intermediate appellate court

SUPERIOR COURT (12 districts and 22 geographical areas for civil/criminal matters, 13 districts for juvenile matters, and 7 housing session locations)   A

180 judges

CSP case types:

- Mental health, miscellaneous civil. Exclusive tort, contract, real property rights, small claims ($2,500), administrative agency appeals (except workers' compensation).
- Support/custody, paternity, miscellaneous domestic relations. Exclusive marriage dissolution.
- Exclusive criminal jurisdiction.
- Exclusive traffic/other violation jurisdiction, except for uncontested parking (which is handled administratively).
- Exclusive juvenile jurisdiction.

Jury trials in most cases.

Court of general jurisdiction

PROBATE COURT (133 courts)

133 judges

CSP case types:

- Mental health, miscellaneous civil. Exclusive estate jurisdiction.
- Support/custody, paternity, miscellaneous domestic relations. Exclusive adoption jurisdiction.

No jury trials.

Court of limited jurisdiction

DELAWARE COURT STRUCTURE

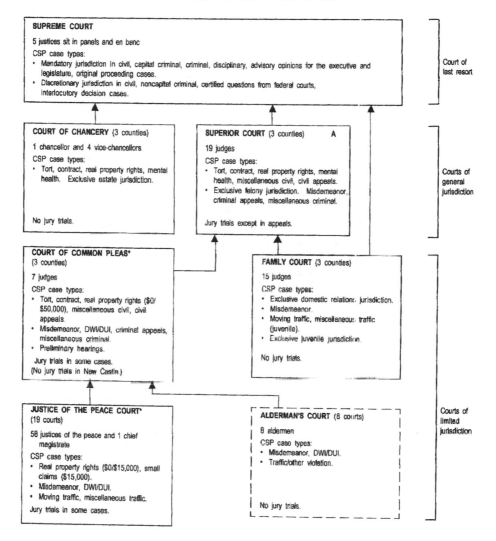

SUPREME COURT

5 justices sit in panels and en banc

CSP case types:
- Mandatory jurisdiction in civil, capital criminal, criminal, disciplinary, advisory opinions for the executive and legislature, original proceeding cases.
- Discretionary jurisdiction in civil, noncapital criminal, certified questions from federal courts, interlocutory decision cases.

Court of last resort

COURT OF CHANCERY (3 counties)

1 chancellor and 4 vice-chancellors

CSP case types:
- Tort, contract, real property rights, mental health. Exclusive estate jurisdiction.

No jury trials.

SUPERIOR COURT (3 counties)   A

19 judges

CSP case types:
- Tort, contract, real property rights, mental health, miscellaneous civil, civil appeals.
- Exclusive felony jurisdiction. Misdemeanor, criminal appeals, miscellaneous criminal.

Jury trials except in appeals.

Courts of general jurisdiction

COURT OF COMMON PLEAS* (3 counties)

7 judges

CSP case types:
- Tort, contract, real property rights ($0/ $50,000), miscellaneous civil, civil appeals.
- Misdemeanor, DWI/DUI, criminal appeals, miscellaneous criminal.
- Preliminary hearings.

Jury trials in some cases. (No jury trials in New Castle.)

FAMILY COURT (3 counties)

15 judges

CSP case types:
- Exclusive domestic relations jurisdiction.
- Misdemeanor.
- Moving traffic, miscellaneous traffic (juvenile).
- Exclusive juvenile jurisdiction.

No jury trials.

JUSTICE OF THE PEACE COURT* (19 courts)

58 justices of the peace and 1 chief magistrate

CSP case types:
- Real property rights ($0/$15,000), small claims ($15,000).
- Misdemeanor, DWI/DUI.
- Moving traffic, miscellaneous traffic.

Jury trials in some cases.

ALDERMAN'S COURT (8 courts)

8 aldermen

CSP case types:
- Misdemeanor, DWI/DUI.
- Traffic/other violation.

No jury trials.

Courts of limited jurisdiction

* The Municipal Court of Wilmington was eliminated effective May 1, 1998, and a new Justice of the Peace Court was created in Wilmington.

DISTRICT OF COLUMBIA COURT STRUCTURE.

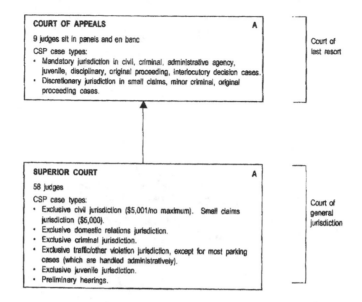

COURT OF APPEALS   **A**

9 judges sit in panels and en banc

CSP case types:
- Mandatory jurisdiction in civil, criminal, administrative agency, juvenile, disciplinary, original proceeding, interlocutory decision cases.
- Discretionary jurisdiction in small claims, minor criminal, original proceeding cases.

Court of last resort

SUPERIOR COURT   **A**

58 judges

CSP case types:
- Exclusive civil jurisdiction ($5,001/no maximum). Small claims jurisdiction ($5,000).
- Exclusive domestic relations jurisdiction.
- Exclusive criminal jurisdiction.
- Exclusive traffic/other violation jurisdiction, except for most parking cases (which are handled administratively).
- Exclusive juvenile jurisdiction.
- Preliminary hearings.

Court of general jurisdiction

FLORIDA COURT STRUCTURE

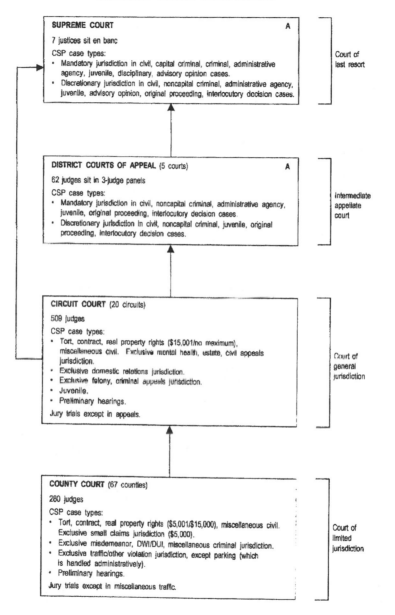

SUPREME COURT   A

7 justices sit en banc

CSP case types:
- Mandatory jurisdiction in civil, capital criminal, criminal, administrative agency, juvenile, disciplinary, advisory opinion cases.
- Discretionary jurisdiction in civil, noncapital criminal, administrative agency, juvenile, advisory opinion, original proceeding, interlocutory decision cases.

Court of last resort

DISTRICT COURTS OF APPEAL (5 courts)   A

62 judges sit in 3-judge panels

CSP case types:
- Mandatory jurisdiction in civil, noncapital criminal, administrative agency, juvenile, original proceeding, interlocutory decision cases.
- Discretionary jurisdiction in civil, noncapital criminal, juvenile, original proceeding, interlocutory decision cases.

Intermediate appellate court

CIRCUIT COURT (20 circuits)

509 judges

CSP case types:
- Tort, contract, real property rights ($15,001/no maximum), miscellaneous civil. Exclusive mental health, estate, civil appeals jurisdiction.
- Exclusive domestic relations jurisdiction.
- Exclusive felony, criminal appeals jurisdiction.
- Juvenile.
- Preliminary hearings.

Jury trials except in appeals.

Court of general jurisdiction

COUNTY COURT (67 counties)

280 judges

CSP case types:
- Tort, contract, real property rights ($5,001/$15,000), miscellaneous civil. Exclusive small claims jurisdiction ($5,000).
- Exclusive misdemeanor, DWI/DUI, miscellaneous criminal jurisdiction.
- Exclusive traffic/other violation jurisdiction, except parking (which is handled administratively).
- Preliminary hearings.

Jury trials except in miscellaneous traffic.

Court of limited jurisdiction

GEORGIA COURT STRUCTURE

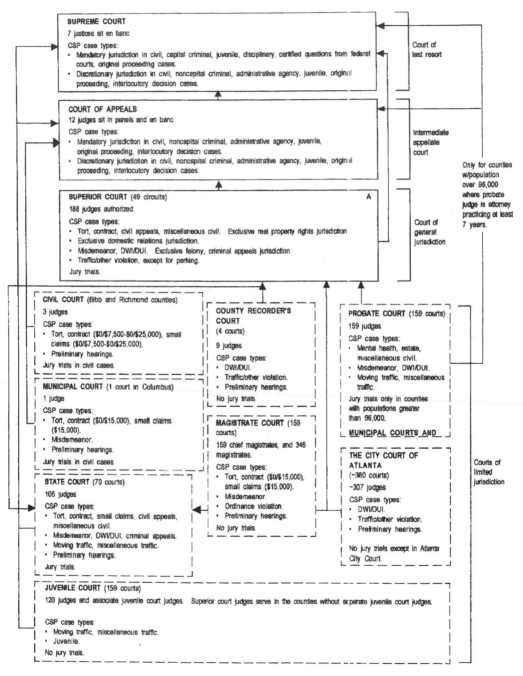

SUPREME COURT

7 justices sit en banc

CSP case types:

- Mandatory jurisdiction in civil, capital criminal, juvenile, disciplinary, certified questions from federal courts, original proceeding cases.
- Discretionary jurisdiction in civil, noncapital criminal, administrative agency, juvenile, original proceeding, interlocutory decision cases.

Court of last resort

COURT OF APPEALS

12 judges sit in panels and en banc

CSP case types:

- Mandatory jurisdiction in civil, noncapital criminal, administrative agency, juvenile, original proceeding, interlocutory decision cases.
- Discretionary jurisdiction in civil, noncapital criminal, administrative agency, juvenile, original proceeding, interlocutory decision cases.

Intermediate appellate court

SUPERIOR COURT (49 circuits)   A

188 judges authorized

CSP case types:

- Tort, contract, civil appeals, miscellaneous civil. Exclusive real property rights jurisdiction
- Exclusive domestic relations jurisdiction.
- Misdemeanor, DWI/DUI. Exclusive felony, criminal appeals jurisdiction.
- Traffic/other violation, except for parking.

Jury trials.

Court of general jurisdiction

Only for counties w/population over 96,000 where probate judge is attorney practicing at least 7 years.

CIVIL COURT (Bibb and Richmond counties)

3 judges

CSP case types:

- Tort, contract ($0/$7,500-$0/$25,000), small claims ($0/$7,500-$0/$25,000).
- Preliminary hearings.

Jury trials in civil cases.

MUNICIPAL COURT (1 court in Columbus)

1 judge

CSP case types:

- Tort, contract ($0/$15,000), small claims ($15,000).
- Misdemeanor.
- Preliminary hearings.

Jury trials in civil cases.

STATE COURT (70 courts)

105 judges

CSP case types:

- Tort, contract, small claims, civil appeals, miscellaneous civil.
- Misdemeanor, DWI/DUI, criminal appeals.
- Moving traffic, miscellaneous traffic.
- Preliminary hearings.

Jury trials.

COUNTY RECORDER'S COURT

(4 courts)

9 judges

CSP case types:

- DWI/DUI.
- Traffic/other violation.
- Preliminary hearings.

No jury trials.

MAGISTRATE COURT (159 courts)

159 chief magistrates, and 346 magistrates.

CSP case types:

- Tort, contract ($0/$15,000), small claims ($15,000).
- Misdemeanor.
- Ordinance violation.
- Preliminary hearings.

No jury trials.

PROBATE COURT (159 courts)

159 judges

CSP case types:

- Mental health, estate, miscellaneous civil.
- Misdemeanor, DWI/DUI.
- Moving traffic, miscellaneous traffic.

Jury trials only in counties with populations greater than 96,000.

MUNICIPAL COURTS AND

THE CITY COURT OF ATLANTA

(~380 courts)

~307 judges

CSP case types:

- DWI/DUI.
- Traffic/other violation.
- Preliminary hearings.

No jury trials except in Atlanta City Court.

Courts of limited jurisdiction

JUVENILE COURT (159 courts)

120 judges and associate juvenile court judges. Superior court judges serve in the counties without separate juvenile court judges.

CSP case types:

- Moving traffic, miscellaneous traffic.
- Juvenile.

No jury trials.

HAWAII COURT STRUCTURE

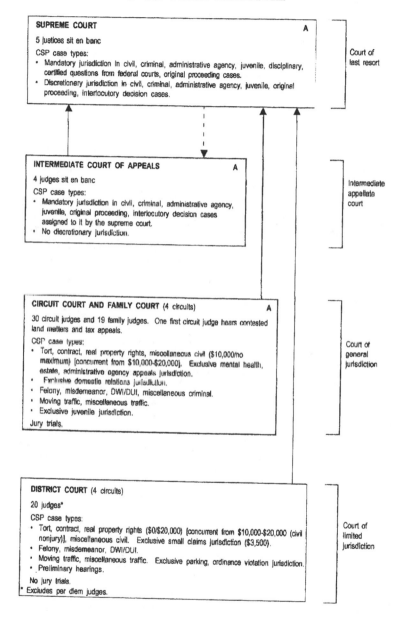

SUPREME COURT   **A**

5 justices sit en banc

CSP case types:
- Mandatory jurisdiction in civil, criminal, administrative agency, juvenile, disciplinary, certified questions from federal courts, original proceeding cases.
- Discretionary jurisdiction in civil, criminal, administrative agency, juvenile, original proceeding, interlocutory decision cases.

Court of last resort

INTERMEDIATE COURT OF APPEALS   **A**

4 judges sit en banc

CSP case types:
- Mandatory jurisdiction in civil, criminal, administrative agency, juvenile, original proceeding, interlocutory decision cases assigned to it by the supreme court.
- No discretionary jurisdiction.

Intermediate appellate court

CIRCUIT COURT AND FAMILY COURT (4 circuits)   **A**

30 circuit judges and 19 family judges. One first circuit judge hears contested land matters and tax appeals.

CSP case types:
- Tort, contract, real property rights, miscellaneous civil ($10,000/no maximum) [concurrent from $10,000-$20,000]. Exclusive mental health, estate, administrative agency appeals jurisdiction.
- Exclusive domestic relations jurisdiction.
- Felony, misdemeanor, DWI/DUI, miscellaneous criminal.
- Moving traffic, miscellaneous traffic.
- Exclusive juvenile jurisdiction.

Jury trials.

Court of general jurisdiction

DISTRICT COURT (4 circuits)

20 judges*

CSP case types:
- Tort, contract, real property rights ($0/$20,000) [concurrent from $10,000-$20,000 (civil nonjury)], miscellaneous civil. Exclusive small claims jurisdiction ($3,500).
- Felony, misdemeanor, DWI/DUI.
- Moving traffic, miscellaneous traffic. Exclusive parking, ordinance violation jurisdiction.
- Preliminary hearings.

No jury trials.
* Excludes per diem judges.

Court of limited jurisdiction

— Indicates assignment of cases.

IDAHO COURT STRUCTURE.

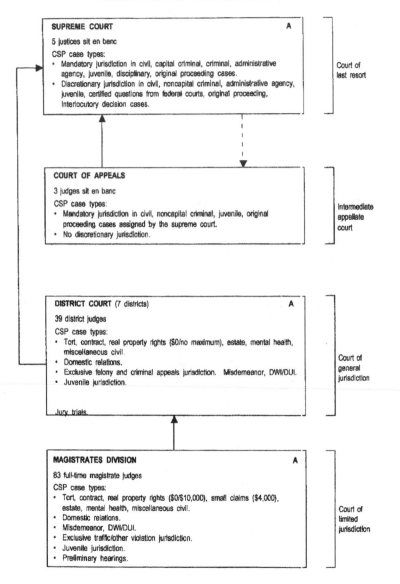

SUPREME COURT   A

5 justices sit en banc

CSP case types:
- Mandatory jurisdiction in civil, capital criminal, criminal, administrative agency, juvenile, disciplinary, original proceeding cases.
- Discretionary jurisdiction in civil, noncapital criminal, administrative agency, juvenile, certified questions from federal courts, original proceeding, interlocutory decision cases.

Court of last resort

COURT OF APPEALS

3 judges sit en banc

CSP case types:
- Mandatory jurisdiction in civil, noncapital criminal, juvenile, original proceeding cases assigned by the supreme court.
- No discretionary jurisdiction.

Intermediate appellate court

DISTRICT COURT (7 districts)   A

39 district judges

CSP case types:
- Tort, contract, real property rights ($0/no maximum), estate, mental health, miscellaneous civil.
- Domestic relations.
- Exclusive felony and criminal appeals jurisdiction. Misdemeanor, DWI/DUI.
- Juvenile jurisdiction.

Jury trials.

Court of general jurisdiction

MAGISTRATES DIVISION   A

83 full-time magistrate judges

CSP case types:
- Tort, contract, real property rights ($0/$10,000), small claims ($4,000), estate, mental health, miscellaneous civil.
- Domestic relations.
- Misdemeanor, DWI/DUI.
- Exclusive traffic/other violation jurisdiction.
- Juvenile jurisdiction.
- Preliminary hearings.

Court of limited jurisdiction

— —   Indicates assignment of cases.

Note: The Magistrates Division of the District Court functions as a limited jurisdiction court.

ILLINOIS COURT STRUCTURE

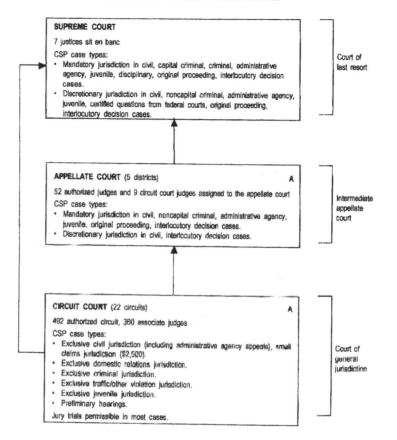

SUPREME COURT

7 justices sit en banc

CSP case types:
- Mandatory jurisdiction in civil, capital criminal, criminal, administrative agency, juvenile, disciplinary, original proceeding, interlocutory decision cases.
- Discretionary jurisdiction in civil, noncapital criminal, administrative agency, juvenile, certified questions from federal courts, original proceeding, interlocutory decision cases.

Court of last resort

APPELLATE COURT (5 districts)   A

52 authorized judges and 9 circuit court judges assigned to the appellate court

CSP case types:
- Mandatory jurisdiction in civil, noncapital criminal, administrative agency, juvenile, original proceeding, interlocutory decision cases.
- Discretionary jurisdiction in civil, interlocutory decision cases.

Intermediate appellate court

CIRCUIT COURT (22 circuits)   A

492 authorized circuit, 360 associate judges

CSP case types:
- Exclusive civil jurisdiction (including administrative agency appeals), small claims jurisdiction ($2,500).
- Exclusive domestic relations jurisdiction.
- Exclusive criminal jurisdiction.
- Exclusive traffic/other violation jurisdiction.
- Exclusive juvenile jurisdiction.
- Preliminary hearings.

Jury trials permissible in most cases.

Court of general jurisdiction

INDIANA COURT STRUCTURE.

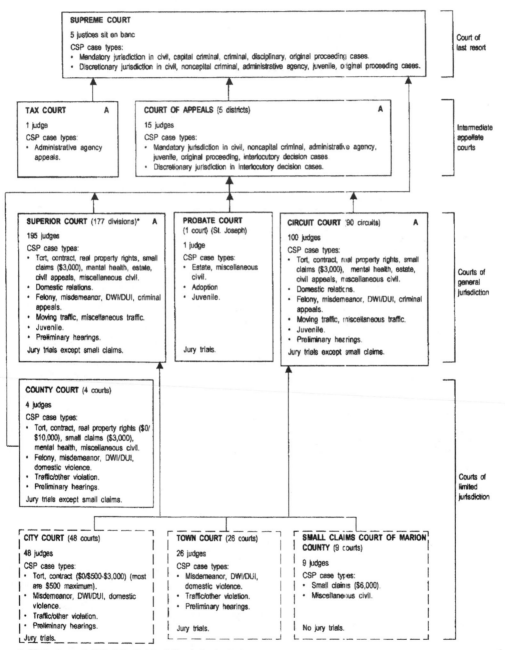

SUPREME COURT

5 justices sit en banc

CSP case types:
- Mandatory jurisdiction in civil, capital criminal, criminal, disciplinary, original proceeding cases.
- Discretionary jurisdiction in civil, noncapital criminal, administrative agency, juvenile, original proceeding cases.

Court of last resort

TAX COURT   A

1 judge

CSP case types:
- Administrative agency appeals.

COURT OF APPEALS (5 districts)   A

15 judges

CSP case types:
- Mandatory jurisdiction in civil, noncapital criminal, administrative agency, juvenile, original proceeding, interlocutory decision cases.
- Discretionary jurisdiction in interlocutory decision cases.

Intermediate appellate courts

SUPERIOR COURT (177 divisions)*   A

195 judges

CSP case types:
- Tort, contract, real property rights, small claims ($3,000), mental health, estate, civil appeals, miscellaneous civil.
- Domestic relations.
- Felony, misdemeanor, DWI/DUI, criminal appeals.
- Moving traffic, miscellaneous traffic.
- Juvenile.
- Preliminary hearings.

Jury trials except small claims.

PROBATE COURT
(1 court) (St. Joseph)

1 judge

CSP case types:
- Estate, miscellaneous civil.
- Adoption
- Juvenile.

Jury trials.

CIRCUIT COURT (90 circuits)   A

100 judges

CSP case types:
- Tort, contract, real property rights, small claims ($3,000), mental health, estate, civil appeals, miscellaneous civil.
- Domestic relations.
- Felony, misdemeanor, DWI/DUI, criminal appeals.
- Moving traffic, miscellaneous traffic.
- Juvenile.
- Preliminary hearings.

Jury trials except small claims.

Courts of general jurisdiction

COUNTY COURT (4 courts)

4 judges

CSP case types:
- Tort, contract, real property rights ($0/$10,000), small claims ($3,000), mental health, miscellaneous civil.
- Felony, misdemeanor, DWI/DUI, domestic violence.
- Traffic/other violation.
- Preliminary hearings.

Jury trials except small claims.

CITY COURT (48 courts)

48 judges

CSP case types:
- Tort, contract ($0/$500-$3,000) (most are $500 maximum).
- Misdemeanor, DWI/DUI, domestic violence.
- Traffic/other violation.
- Preliminary hearings.

Jury trials.

TOWN COURT (26 courts)

26 judges

CSP case types:
- Misdemeanor, DWI/DUI, domestic violence.
- Traffic/other violation.
- Preliminary hearings.

Jury trials.

SMALL CLAIMS COURT OF MARION COUNTY (9 courts)

9 judges

CSP case types:
- Small claims ($6,000).
- Miscellaneous civil.

No jury trials.

Courts of limited jurisdiction

* Effective January 1, 1996, all Municipal Courts became Superior Courts.

IOWA COURT STRUCTURE

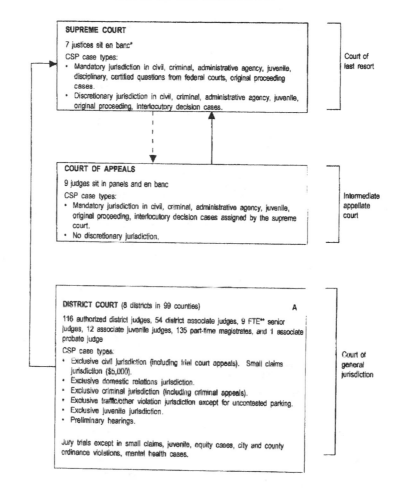

SUPREME COURT

7 justices sit en banc*

CSP case types:

- Mandatory jurisdiction in civil, criminal, administrative agency, juvenile, disciplinary, certified questions from federal courts, original proceeding cases.
- Discretionary jurisdiction in civil, criminal, administrative agency, juvenile, original proceeding, interlocutory decision cases.

Court of last resort

COURT OF APPEALS

9 judges sit in panels and en banc

CSP case types:

- Mandatory jurisdiction in civil, criminal, administrative agency, juvenile, original proceeding, interlocutory decision cases assigned by the supreme court.
- No discretionary jurisdiction.

Intermediate appellate court

DISTRICT COURT (8 districts in 99 counties)   **A**

116 authorized district judges, 54 district associate judges, 9 FTE** senior judges, 12 associate juvenile judges, 135 part-time magistrates, and 1 associate probate judge

CSP case types:

- Exclusive civil jurisdiction (including trial court appeals). Small claims jurisdiction ($5,000).
- Exclusive domestic relations jurisdiction.
- Exclusive criminal jurisdiction (including criminal appeals).
- Exclusive traffic/other violation jurisdiction except for uncontested parking.
- Exclusive juvenile jurisdiction.
- Preliminary hearings.

Jury trials except in small claims, juvenile, equity cases, city and county ordinance violations, mental health cases.

Court of general jurisdiction

---

* As of January, 2000 the court no longer sits in panels; it decides en banc.

** Includes 37 senior judges who work 1/4 time (13 weeks/year).

– – Indicates assignment of cases.

KANSAS COURT STRUCTURE

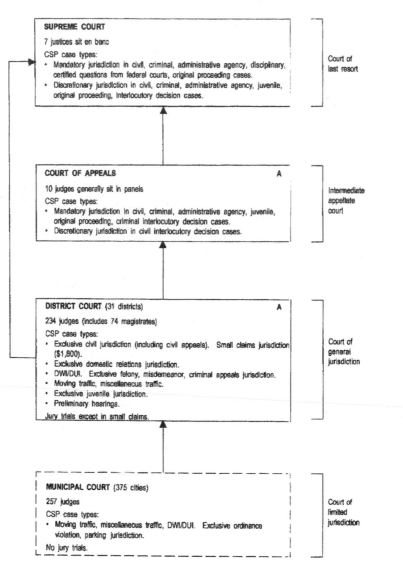

SUPREME COURT

7 justices sit en banc

CSP case types:
- Mandatory jurisdiction in civil, criminal, administrative agency, disciplinary, certified questions from federal courts, original proceeding cases.
- Discretionary jurisdiction in civil, criminal, administrative agency, juvenile, original proceeding, interlocutory decision cases.

Court of last resort

COURT OF APPEALS   A

10 judges generally sit in panels

CSP case types:
- Mandatory jurisdiction in civil, criminal, administrative agency, juvenile, original proceeding, criminal interlocutory decision cases.
- Discretionary jurisdiction in civil interlocutory decision cases.

Intermediate appellate court

DISTRICT COURT (31 districts)   A

234 judges (includes 74 magistrates)

CSP case types:
- Exclusive civil jurisdiction (including civil appeals). Small claims jurisdiction ($1,800).
- Exclusive domestic relations jurisdiction.
- DWI/DUI. Exclusive felony, misdemeanor, criminal appeals jurisdiction.
- Moving traffic, miscellaneous traffic.
- Exclusive juvenile jurisdiction.
- Preliminary hearings.

Jury trials except in small claims.

Court of general jurisdiction

MUNICIPAL COURT (375 cities)

257 judges

CSP case types:
- Moving traffic, miscellaneous traffic, DWI/DUI. Exclusive ordinance violation, parking jurisdiction.

No jury trials.

Court of limited jurisdiction

KENTUCKY COURT STRUCTURE

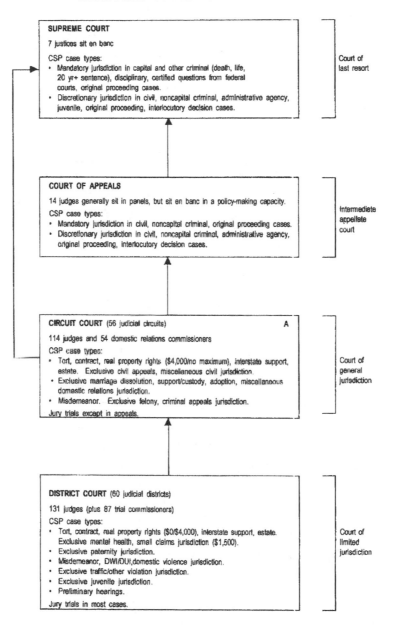

SUPREME COURT

7 justices sit en banc

CSP case types:
- Mandatory jurisdiction in capital and other criminal (death, life, 20 yr+ sentence), disciplinary, certified questions from federal courts, original proceeding cases.
- Discretionary jurisdiction in civil, noncapital criminal, administrative agency, juvenile, original proceeding, interlocutory decision cases.

Court of last resort

COURT OF APPEALS

14 judges generally sit in panels, but sit en banc in a policy-making capacity.

CSP case types:
- Mandatory jurisdiction in civil, noncapital criminal, original proceeding cases.
- Discretionary jurisdiction in civil, noncapital criminal, administrative agency, original proceeding, interlocutory decision cases.

Intermediate appellate court

CIRCUIT COURT (56 judicial circuits)   A

114 judges and 54 domestic relations commissioners

CSP case types:
- Tort, contract, real property rights ($4,000/no maximum), interstate support, estate. Exclusive civil appeals, miscellaneous civil jurisdiction.
- Exclusive marriage dissolution, support/custody, adoption, miscellaneous domestic relations jurisdiction.
- Misdemeanor. Exclusive felony, criminal appeals jurisdiction.

Jury trials except in appeals.

Court of general jurisdiction

DISTRICT COURT (60 judicial districts)

131 judges (plus 87 trial commissioners)

CSP case types:
- Tort, contract, real property rights ($0/$4,000), interstate support, estate. Exclusive mental health, small claims jurisdiction ($1,500).
- Exclusive paternity jurisdiction.
- Misdemeanor, DWI/DUI, domestic violence jurisdiction.
- Exclusive traffic/other violation jurisdiction.
- Exclusive juvenile jurisdiction.
- Preliminary hearings.

Jury trials in most cases.

Court of limited jurisdiction

LOUISIANA COURT STRUCTURE

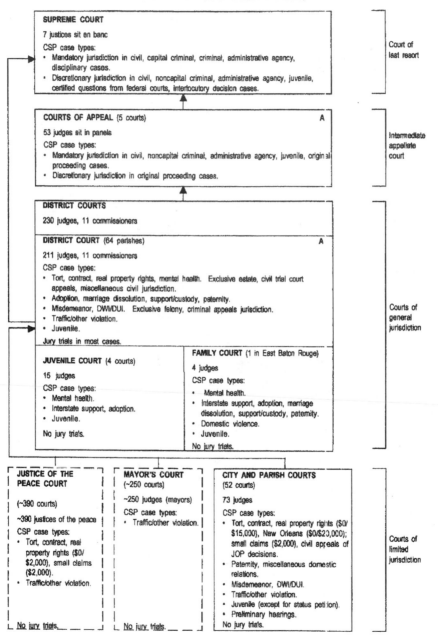

SUPREME COURT

7 justices sit en banc
CSP case types:
- Mandatory jurisdiction in civil, capital criminal, criminal, administrative agency, disciplinary cases.
- Discretionary jurisdiction in civil, noncapital criminal, administrative agency, juvenile, certified questions from federal courts, interlocutory decision cases.

Court of last resort

COURTS OF APPEAL (5 courts)   A

53 judges sit in panels
CSP case types:
- Mandatory jurisdiction in civil, noncapital criminal, administrative agency, juvenile, original proceeding cases.
- Discretionary jurisdiction in original proceeding cases.

Intermediate appellate court

DISTRICT COURTS

230 judges, 11 commissioners

DISTRICT COURT (64 parishes)   A

211 judges, 11 commissioners
CSP case types:
- Tort, contract, real property rights, mental health. Exclusive estate, civil trial court appeals, miscellaneous civil jurisdiction.
- Adoption, marriage dissolution, support/custody, paternity.
- Misdemeanor, DWI/DUI. Exclusive felony, criminal appeals jurisdiction.
- Traffic/other violation.
- Juvenile.

Jury trials in most cases.

JUVENILE COURT (4 courts)

15 judges
CSP case types:
- Mental health.
- Interstate support, adoption.
- Juvenile.

No jury trials.

FAMILY COURT (1 in East Baton Rouge)

4 judges
CSP case types:
- Mental health.
- Interstate support, adoption, marriage dissolution, support/custody, paternity.
- Domestic violence.
- Juvenile.

No jury trials.

Courts of general jurisdiction

JUSTICE OF THE PEACE COURT

(~390 courts)

~390 justices of the peace
CSP case types:
- Tort, contract, real property rights ($0/$2,000), small claims ($2,000).
- Traffic/other violation.

No jury trials.

MAYOR'S COURT (~250 courts)

~250 judges (mayors)
CSP case types:
- Traffic/other violation.

No jury trials.

CITY AND PARISH COURTS (52 courts)

73 judges
CSP case types:
- Tort, contract, real property rights ($0/$15,000), New Orleans ($0/$20,000); small claims ($2,000), civil appeals of JOP decisions.
- Paternity, miscellaneous domestic relations.
- Misdemeanor, DWI/DUI.
- Traffic/other violation.
- Juvenile (except for status petition).
- Preliminary hearings.

No jury trials.

Courts of limited jurisdiction

MAINE COURT STRUCTURE.

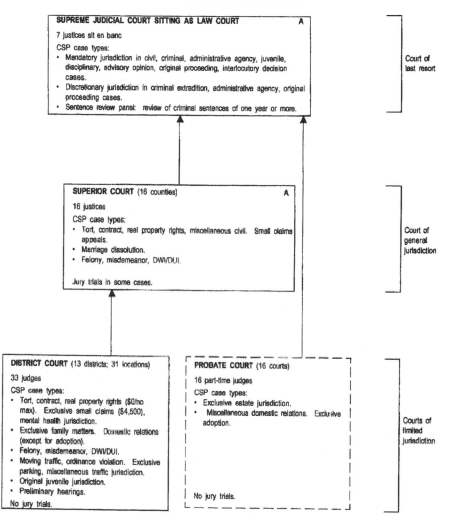

SUPREME JUDICIAL COURT SITTING AS LAW COURT   A

7 justices sit en banc

CSP case types:
- Mandatory jurisdiction in civil, criminal, administrative agency, juvenile, disciplinary, advisory opinion, original proceeding, interlocutory decision cases.
- Discretionary jurisdiction in criminal extradition, administrative agency, original proceeding cases.
- Sentence review panel: review of criminal sentences of one year or more.

Court of last resort

SUPERIOR COURT (16 counties)   A

16 justices

CSP case types:
- Tort, contract, real property rights, miscellaneous civil. Small claims appeals.
- Marriage dissolution.
- Felony, misdemeanor, DWI/DUI.

Jury trials in some cases.

Court of general jurisdiction

DISTRICT COURT (13 districts; 31 locations)

33 judges

CSP case types:
- Tort, contract, real property rights ($0/no max). Exclusive small claims ($4,500), mental health jurisdiction.
- Exclusive family matters. Domestic relations (except for adoption).
- Felony, misdemeanor, DWI/DUI.
- Moving traffic, ordinance violation. Exclusive parking, miscellaneous traffic jurisdiction.
- Original juvenile jurisdiction.
- Preliminary hearings.

No jury trials.

PROBATE COURT (16 courts)

16 part-time judges

CSP case types:
- Exclusive estate jurisdiction.
- Miscellaneous domestic relations. Exclusive adoption.

No jury trials.

Courts of limited jurisdiction

*The Administrative Court was eliminated effective March 15, 2001, with the caseload absorbed by District Court.

MARYLAND COURT STRUCTURE

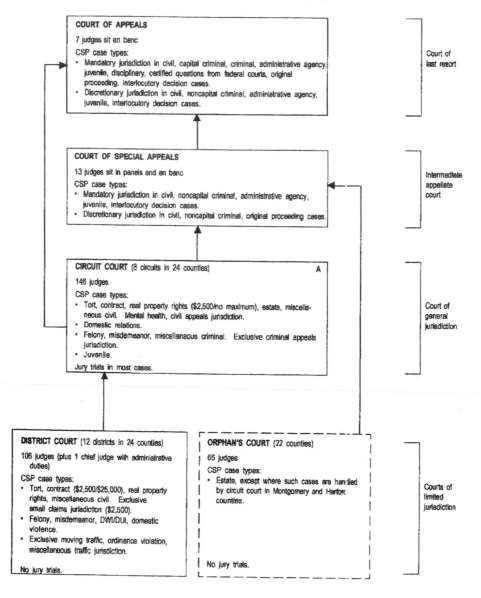

COURT OF APPEALS

7 judges sit en banc

CSP case types:
- Mandatory jurisdiction in civil, capital criminal, criminal, administrative agency, juvenile, disciplinary, certified questions from federal courts, original proceeding, interlocutory decision cases.
- Discretionary jurisdiction in civil, noncapital criminal, administrative agency, juvenile, interlocutory decision cases.

Court of last resort

COURT OF SPECIAL APPEALS

13 judges sit in panels and en banc

CSP case types:
- Mandatory jurisdiction in civil, noncapital criminal, administrative agency, juvenile, interlocutory decision cases.
- Discretionary jurisdiction in civil, noncapital criminal, original proceeding cases.

Intermediate appellate court

CIRCUIT COURT (8 circuits in 24 counties)   A

146 judges

CSP case types:
- Tort, contract, real property rights ($2,500/no maximum), estate, miscellaneous civil. Mental health, civil appeals jurisdiction.
- Domestic relations.
- Felony, misdemeanor, miscellaneous criminal. Exclusive criminal appeals jurisdiction.
- Juvenile.

Jury trials in most cases.

Court of general jurisdiction

DISTRICT COURT (12 districts in 24 counties)

106 judges (plus 1 chief judge with administrative duties)

CSP case types:
- Tort, contract ($2,500/$25,000), real property rights, miscellaneous civil. Exclusive small claims jurisdiction ($2,500).
- Felony, misdemeanor, DWI/DUI, domestic violence.
- Exclusive moving traffic, ordinance violation, miscellaneous traffic jurisdiction.

No jury trials.

ORPHAN'S COURT (22 counties)

66 judges

CSP case types:
- Estate, except where such cases are handled by circuit court in Montgomery and Harford counties.

No jury trials.

Courts of limited jurisdiction

MASSACHUSETTS COURT STRUCTURE

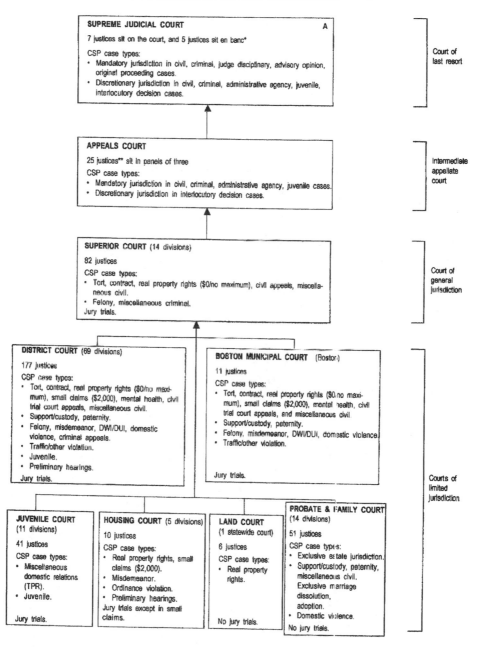

SUPREME JUDICIAL COURT   A

7 justices sit on the court, and 5 justices sit en banc*

CSP case types:
- Mandatory jurisdiction in civil, criminal, judge disciplinary, advisory opinion, original proceeding cases.
- Discretionary jurisdiction in civil, criminal, administrative agency, juvenile, interlocutory decision cases.

Court of last resort

APPEALS COURT

25 justices** sit in panels of three

CSP case types:
- Mandatory jurisdiction in civil, criminal, administrative agency, juvenile cases.
- Discretionary jurisdiction in interlocutory decision cases.

Intermediate appellate court

SUPERIOR COURT (14 divisions)

82 justices

CSP case types:
- Tort, contract, real property rights ($0/no maximum), civil appeals, miscellaneous civil.
- Felony, miscellaneous criminal.

Jury trials.

Court of general jurisdiction

DISTRICT COURT (69 divisions)

177 justices

CSP case types:
- Tort, contract, real property rights ($0/no maximum), small claims ($2,000), mental health, civil trial court appeals, miscellaneous civil.
- Support/custody, paternity.
- Felony, misdemeanor, DWI/DUI, domestic violence, criminal appeals.
- Traffic/other violation.
- Juvenile.
- Preliminary hearings.

Jury trials.

BOSTON MUNICIPAL COURT (Boston)

11 justices

CSP case types:
- Tort, contract, real property rights ($0/no maximum), small claims ($2,000), mental health, civil trial court appeals, and miscellaneous civil.
- Support/custody, paternity.
- Felony, misdemeanor, DWI/DUI, domestic violence.
- Traffic/other violation.

Jury trials.

Courts of limited jurisdiction

JUVENILE COURT (11 divisions)

41 justices

CSP case types:
- Miscellaneous domestic relations (TPR).
- Juvenile.

Jury trials.

HOUSING COURT (5 divisions)

10 justices

CSP case types:
- Real property rights, small claims ($2,000).
- Misdemeanor.
- Ordinance violation.
- Preliminary hearings.

Jury trials except in small claims.

LAND COURT (1 statewide court)

6 justices

CSP case types:
- Real property rights.

No jury trials.

PROBATE & FAMILY COURT (14 divisions)

51 justices

CSP case types:
- Exclusive estate jurisdiction.
- Support/custody, paternity, miscellaneous civil. Exclusive marriage dissolution, adoption.
- Domestic violence.

No jury trials.

* The justices also sit individually in the "single justice" side of the court, on a rotating basis.

MICHIGAN COURT STRUCTURE

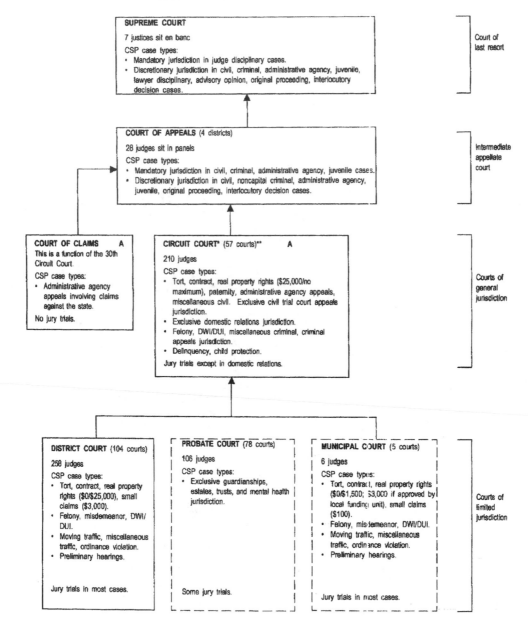

SUPREME COURT

7 justices sit en banc

CSP case types:
- Mandatory jurisdiction in judge disciplinary cases.
- Discretionary jurisdiction in civil, criminal, administrative agency, juvenile, lawyer disciplinary, advisory opinion, original proceeding, interlocutory decision cases.

Court of last resort

COURT OF APPEALS (4 districts)

28 judges sit in panels

CSP case types:
- Mandatory jurisdiction in civil, criminal, administrative agency, juvenile cases.
- Discretionary jurisdiction in civil, noncapital criminal, administrative agency, juvenile, original proceeding, interlocutory decision cases.

Intermediate appellate court

COURT OF CLAIMS   A

This is a function of the 30th Circuit Court.

CSP case types:
- Administrative agency appeals involving claims against the state.

No jury trials.

CIRCUIT COURT* (57 courts)**   A

210 judges

CSP case types:
- Tort, contract, real property rights ($25,000/no maximum), paternity, administrative agency appeals, miscellaneous civil. Exclusive civil trial court appeals jurisdiction.
- Exclusive domestic relations jurisdiction.
- Felony, DWI/DUI, miscellaneous criminal, criminal appeals jurisdiction.
- Delinquency, child protection.

Jury trials except in domestic relations.

Courts of general jurisdiction

DISTRICT COURT (104 courts)

258 judges

CSP case types:
- Tort, contract, real property rights ($0/$25,000), small claims ($3,000).
- Felony, misdemeanor, DWI/DUI.
- Moving traffic, miscellaneous traffic, ordinance violation.
- Preliminary hearings.

Jury trials in most cases.

PROBATE COURT (78 courts)

106 judges

CSP case types:
- Exclusive guardianships, estates, trusts, and mental health jurisdiction.

Some jury trials.

MUNICIPAL COURT (5 courts)

6 judges

CSP case types:
- Tort, contract, real property rights ($0/$1,500; $3,000 if approved by local funding unit), small claims ($100).
- Felony, misdemeanor, DWI/DUI.
- Moving traffic, miscellaneous traffic, ordinance violation.
- Preliminary hearings.

Jury trials in most cases.

Courts of limited jurisdiction

* The Recorder's Court of Detroit merged with the Circuit Court effective October 1, 1997.

** A Family Division of Circuit Court became operational on January 1, 1998.

MINNESOTA COURT STRUCTURE

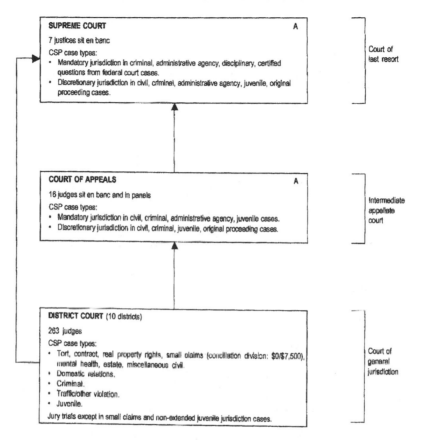

SUPREME COURT   A

7 justices sit en banc

CSP case types:
- Mandatory jurisdiction in criminal, administrative agency, disciplinary, certified questions from federal court cases.
- Discretionary jurisdiction in civil, criminal, administrative agency, juvenile, original proceeding cases.

Court of last resort

COURT OF APPEALS   A

16 judges sit en banc and in panels

CSP case types:
- Mandatory jurisdiction in civil, criminal, administrative agency, juvenile cases.
- Discretionary jurisdiction in civil, criminal, juvenile, original proceeding cases.

Intermediate appellate court

DISTRICT COURT (10 districts)

263 judges

CSP case types:
- Tort, contract, real property rights, small claims (conciliation division: $0/$7,500), mental health, estate, miscellaneous civil.
- Domestic relations.
- Criminal.
- Traffic/other violation.
- Juvenile.

Jury trials except in small claims and non-extended juvenile jurisdiction cases.

Court of general jurisdiction

MISSOURI COURT STRUCTURE

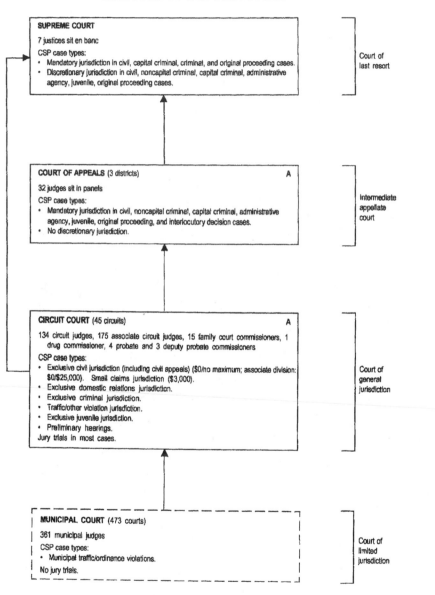

SUPREME COURT

7 justices sit en banc

CSP case types:
- Mandatory jurisdiction in civil, capital criminal, criminal, and original proceeding cases.
- Discretionary jurisdiction in civil, noncapital criminal, capital criminal, administrative agency, juvenile, original proceeding cases.

Court of last resort

COURT OF APPEALS (3 districts)   **A**

32 judges sit in panels

CSP case types:
- Mandatory jurisdiction in civil, noncapital criminal, capital criminal, administrative agency, juvenile, original proceeding, and interlocutory decision cases.
- No discretionary jurisdiction.

Intermediate appellate court

CIRCUIT COURT (45 circuits)   **A**

134 circuit judges, 175 associate circuit judges, 15 family court commissioners, 1 drug commissioner, 4 probate and 3 deputy probate commissioners

CSP case types:
- Exclusive civil jurisdiction (including civil appeals) ($0/no maximum; associate division: $0/$25,000). Small claims jurisdiction ($3,000).
- Exclusive domestic relations jurisdiction.
- Exclusive criminal jurisdiction.
- Traffic/other violation jurisdiction.
- Exclusive juvenile jurisdiction.
- Preliminary hearings.

Jury trials in most cases.

Court of general jurisdiction

MUNICIPAL COURT (473 courts)

361 municipal judges

CSP case types:
- Municipal traffic/ordinance violations.

No jury trials.

Court of limited jurisdiction

MISSISSIPPI COURT STRUCTURE

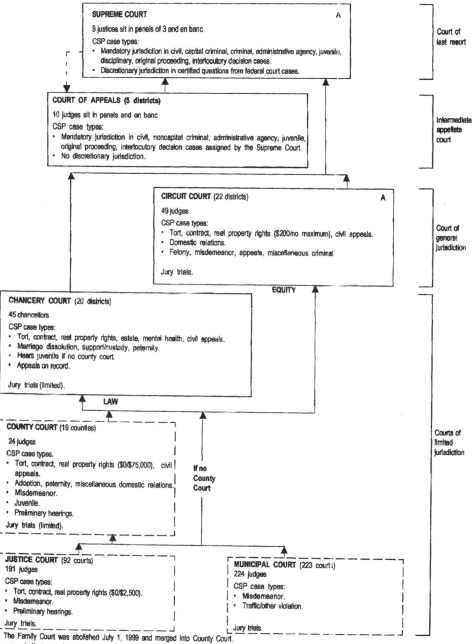

SUPREME COURT A

9 justices sit in panels of 3 and en banc

CSP case types:

- Mandatory jurisdiction in civil, capital criminal, criminal, administrative agency, juvenile, disciplinary, original proceeding, interlocutory decision cases.
- Discretionary jurisdiction in certified questions from federal court cases.

Court of last resort

COURT OF APPEALS (5 districts)

10 judges sit in panels and en banc

CSP case types:

- Mandatory jurisdiction in civil, noncapital criminal, administrative agency, juvenile, original proceeding, interlocutory decision cases assigned by the Supreme Court.
- No discretionary jurisdiction.

Intermediate appellate court

CIRCUIT COURT (22 districts) A

49 judges

CSP case types:

- Tort, contract, real property rights ($200/no maximum), civil appeals.
- Domestic relations.
- Felony, misdemeanor, appeals, miscellaneous criminal

Jury trials.

Court of general jurisdiction

EQUITY

CHANCERY COURT (20 districts)

45 chancellors

CSP case types:

- Tort, contract, real property rights, estate, mental health, civil appeals.
- Marriage dissolution, support/custody, paternity.
- Hears juvenile if no county court.
- Appeals on record.

Jury trials (limited).

LAW

Courts of limited jurisdiction

COUNTY COURT (19 counties)

24 judges

CSP case types:

- Tort, contract, real property rights ($0/$75,000), civil appeals.
- Adoption, paternity, miscellaneous domestic relations.
- Misdemeanor.
- Juvenile.
- Preliminary hearings.

Jury trials (limited).

If no County Court

JUSTICE COURT (92 courts)

191 judges

CSP case types:

- Tort, contract, real property rights ($0/$2,500).
- Misdemeanor.
- Preliminary hearings.

Jury trials.

MUNICIPAL COURT (223 courts)

224 judges

CSP case types:

- Misdemeanor.
- Traffic/other violation.

Jury trials.

* The Family Court was abolished July 1, 1999 and merged into County Court.

- - Indicates assignment of cases.

MONTANA COURT STRUCTURE

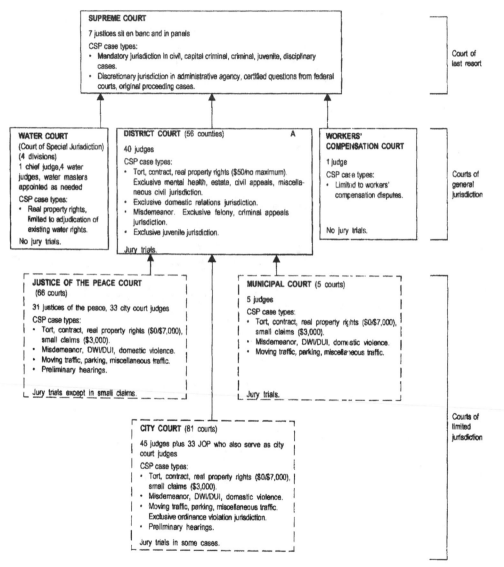

SUPREME COURT

7 justices sit en banc and in panels

CSP case types:
- Mandatory jurisdiction in civil, capital criminal, criminal, juvenile, disciplinary cases.
- Discretionary jurisdiction in administrative agency, certified questions from federal courts, original proceeding cases.

Court of last resort

WATER COURT
(Court of Special Jurisdiction)
(4 divisions)
1 chief judge, 4 water judges, water masters appointed as needed

CSP case types:
- Real property rights, limited to adjudication of existing water rights.

No jury trials.

DISTRICT COURT (56 counties)   A

40 judges

CSP case types:
- Tort, contract, real property rights ($50/no maximum). Exclusive mental health, estate, civil appeals, miscellaneous civil jurisdiction.
- Exclusive domestic relations jurisdiction.
- Misdemeanor. Exclusive felony, criminal appeals jurisdiction.
- Exclusive juvenile jurisdiction.

Jury trials.

WORKERS' COMPENSATION COURT

1 judge

CSP case types:
- Limited to workers' compensation disputes.

No jury trials.

Courts of general jurisdiction

JUSTICE OF THE PEACE COURT
(66 courts)

31 justices of the peace, 33 city court judges

CSP case types:
- Tort, contract, real property rights ($0/$7,000), small claims ($3,000).
- Misdemeanor, DWI/DUI, domestic violence.
- Moving traffic, parking, miscellaneous traffic.
- Preliminary hearings.

Jury trials except in small claims.

MUNICIPAL COURT (5 courts)

5 judges

CSP case types:
- Tort, contract, real property rights ($0/$7,000), small claims ($3,000).
- Misdemeanor, DWI/DUI, domestic violence.
- Moving traffic, parking, miscellaneous traffic.

Jury trials.

CITY COURT (81 courts)

45 judges plus 33 JOP who also serve as city court judges

CSP case types:
- Tort, contract, real property rights ($0/$7,000), small claims ($3,000).
- Misdemeanor, DWI/DUI, domestic violence.
- Moving traffic, parking, miscellaneous traffic. Exclusive ordinance violation jurisdiction.
- Preliminary hearings.

Jury trials in some cases.

Courts of limited jurisdiction

NEBRASKA COURT STRUCTURE

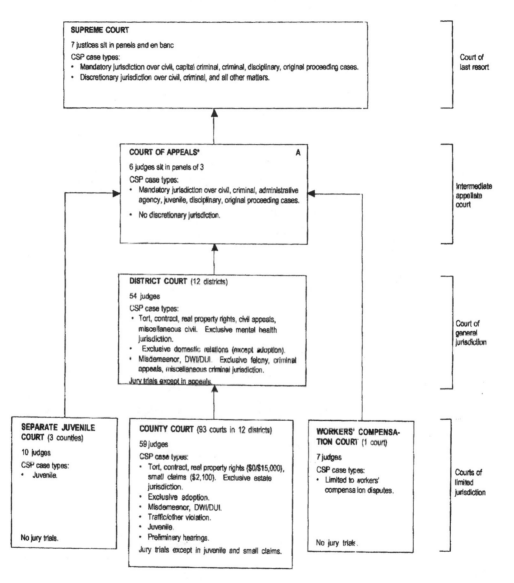

SUPREME COURT

7 justices sit in panels and en banc

CSP case types:
- Mandatory jurisdiction over civil, capital criminal, criminal, disciplinary, original proceeding cases.
- Discretionary jurisdiction over civil, criminal, and all other matters.

Court of last resort

COURT OF APPEALS*   A

6 judges sit in panels of 3

CSP case types:
- Mandatory jurisdiction over civil, criminal, administrative agency, juvenile, disciplinary, original proceeding cases.
- No discretionary jurisdiction.

Intermediate appellate court

DISTRICT COURT (12 districts)

54 judges

CSP case types:
- Tort, contract, real property rights, civil appeals, miscellaneous civil. Exclusive mental health jurisdiction.
- Exclusive domestic relations (except adoption).
- Misdemeanor, DWI/DUI. Exclusive felony, criminal appeals, miscellaneous criminal jurisdiction.

Jury trials except in appeals.

Court of general jurisdiction

SEPARATE JUVENILE COURT (3 counties)

10 judges

CSP case types:
- Juvenile.

No jury trials.

COUNTY COURT (93 courts in 12 districts)

59 judges

CSP case types:
- Tort, contract, real property rights ($0/$15,000), small claims ($2,100). Exclusive estate jurisdiction.
- Exclusive adoption.
- Misdemeanor, DWI/DUI.
- Traffic/other violation.
- Juvenile.
- Preliminary hearings.

Jury trials except in juvenile and small claims.

WORKERS' COMPENSA- TION COURT (1 court)

7 judges

CSP case types:
- Limited to workers' compensation disputes.

No jury trials.

Courts of limited jurisdiction

* The Nebraska Court of Appeals was established September 6, 1991.

NEVADA COURT STRUCTURE

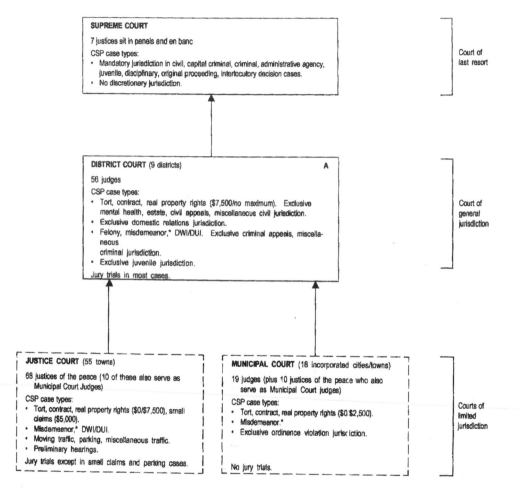

SUPREME COURT

7 justices sit in panels and en banc

CSP case types:
- Mandatory jurisdiction in civil, capital criminal, criminal, administrative agency, juvenile, disciplinary, original proceeding, interlocutory decision cases.
- No discretionary jurisdiction.

Court of last resort

DISTRICT COURT (9 districts)   **A**

56 judges

CSP case types:
- Tort, contract, real property rights ($7,500/no maximum). Exclusive mental health, estate, civil appeals, miscellaneous civil jurisdiction.
- Exclusive domestic relations jurisdiction.
- Felony, misdemeanor,* DWI/DUI. Exclusive criminal appeals, miscellaneous criminal jurisdiction.
- Exclusive juvenile jurisdiction.

Jury trials in most cases.

Court of general jurisdiction

JUSTICE COURT (55 towns)

68 justices of the peace (10 of these also serve as Municipal Court Judges)

CSP case types:
- Tort, contract, real property rights ($0/$7,500), small claims ($5,000).
- Misdemeanor,* DWI/DUI.
- Moving traffic, parking, miscellaneous traffic.
- Preliminary hearings.

Jury trials except in small claims and parking cases.

MUNICIPAL COURT (18 incorporated cities/towns)

19 judges (plus 10 justices of the peace who also serve as Municipal Court judges)

CSP case types:
- Tort, contract, real property rights ($0-$2,500).
- Misdemeanor.*
- Exclusive ordinance violation jurisdiction.

No jury trials.

Courts of limited jurisdiction

* District Court hears gross misdemeanor cases; Justice & Municipal Courts hear misdemeanors with fines under $1,000 and/or sentence of less than six months.

NEW HAMPSHIRE COURT STRUCTURE

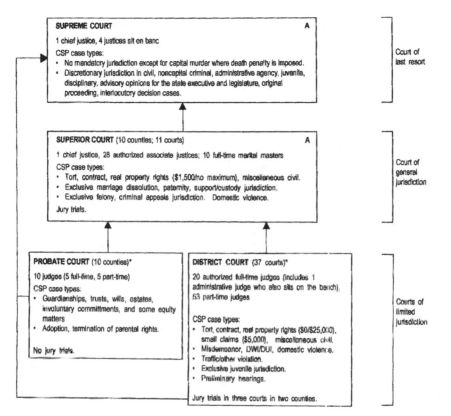

SUPREME COURT   A

1 chief justice, 4 justices sit en banc

CSP case types:
- No mandatory jurisdiction except for capital murder where death penalty is imposed.
- Discretionary jurisdiction in civil, noncapital criminal, administrative agency, juvenile, disciplinary, advisory opinions for the state executive and legislature, original proceeding, interlocutory decision cases.

Court of last resort

SUPERIOR COURT (10 counties; 11 courts)   A

1 chief justice, 28 authorized associate justices; 10 full-time marital masters

CSP case types:
- Tort, contract, real property rights ($1,500/no maximum), miscellaneous civil.
- Exclusive marriage dissolution, paternity, support/custody jurisdiction.
- Exclusive felony, criminal appeals jurisdiction. Domestic violence.

Jury trials.

Court of general jurisdiction

PROBATE COURT (10 counties)*

10 judges (5 full-time, 5 part-time)

CSP case types:
- Guardianships, trusts, wills, estates, involuntary committments, and some equity matters
- Adoption, termination of parental rights.

No jury trials.

DISTRICT COURT (37 courts)*

20 authorized full-time judges (includes 1 administrative judge who also sits on the bench); 53 part-time judges

CSP case types:
- Tort, contract, real property rights ($0/$25,000), small claims ($5,000), miscellaneous civil.
- Misdemeanor, DWI/DUI, domestic violence.
- Traffic/other violation.
- Exclusive juvenile jurisdiction.
- Preliminary hearings.

Jury trials in three courts in two counties.

Courts of limited jurisdiction

* A Family Division Pilot Program was created by the Legislature in 1995 and operates in six district courts and two probate courts. The Family Division Pilot Program includes domestic violence, juvenile, marital matters, termination of parental rights, adoptions, and guardianships over minors in two counties. The municipal court merged with the District Court in May, 2000.

NEW JERSEY COURT STRUCTURE

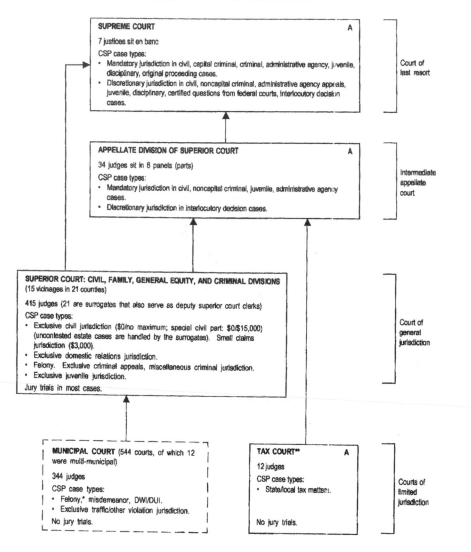

SUPREME COURT　　　　　　　　　　　　　　　　　　　　　　　　　A

7 justices sit en banc

CSP case types:
- Mandatory jurisdiction in civil, capital criminal, criminal, administrative agency, juvenile, disciplinary, original proceeding cases.
- Discretionary jurisdiction in civil, noncapital criminal, administrative agency appeals, juvenile, disciplinary, certified questions from federal courts, interlocutory decision cases.

Court of last resort

APPELLATE DIVISION OF SUPERIOR COURT　　　　　　　　　　　　A

34 judges sit in 8 panels (parts)

CSP case types:
- Mandatory jurisdiction in civil, noncapital criminal, juvenile, administrative agency cases.
- Discretionary jurisdiction in interlocutory decision cases.

Intermediate appellate court

SUPERIOR COURT: CIVIL, FAMILY, GENERAL EQUITY, AND CRIMINAL DIVISIONS
(15 vicinages in 21 counties)

415 judges (21 are surrogates that also serve as deputy superior court clerks)

CSP case types:
- Exclusive civil jurisdiction ($0/no maximum; special civil part: $0/$15,000) (uncontested estate cases are handled by the surrogates). Small claims jurisdiction ($3,000).
- Exclusive domestic relations jurisdiction.
- Felony. Exclusive criminal appeals, miscellaneous criminal jurisdiction.
- Exclusive juvenile jurisdiction.

Jury trials in most cases.

Court of general jurisdiction

MUNICIPAL COURT (544 courts, of which 12 were multi-municipal)

344 judges

CSP case types:
- Felony,* misdemeanor, DWI/DUI.
- Exclusive traffic/other violation jurisdiction.

No jury trials.

TAX COURT**　　　　　　　　A

12 judges

CSP case types:
- State/local tax matters.

No jury trials.

Courts of limited jurisdiction

* Felony cases are handled on first appearance in the Municipal Courts and then are transferred through the county Prosecutor's office to the Superior Court.

** Tax court is considered a limited jurisdiction court because of its specialized subject matter. Nevertheless, it receives appeals from administrative bodies and its cases are appealed to the intermediate appellate court. Tax court judges have the same general qualifications and terms of service as superior court judges and can be cross assigned.

NEW MEXICO COURT STRUCTURE.

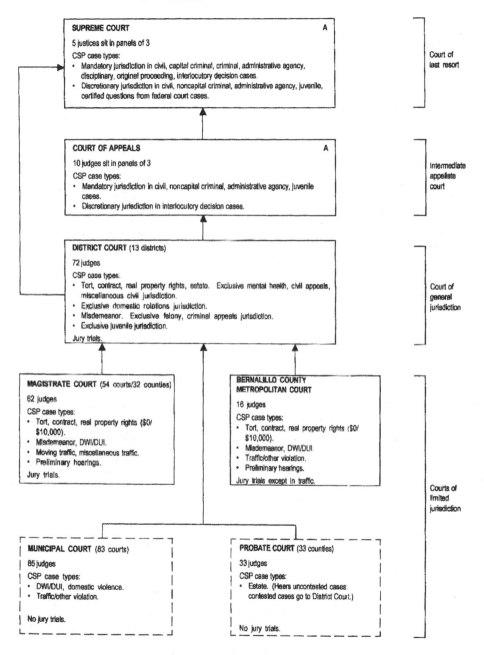

SUPREME COURT A

5 justices sit in panels of 3

CSP case types:
- Mandatory jurisdiction in civil, capital criminal, criminal, administrative agency, disciplinary, original proceeding, interlocutory decision cases.
- Discretionary jurisdiction in civil, noncapital criminal, administrative agency, juvenile, certified questions from federal court cases.

Court of last resort

COURT OF APPEALS A

10 judges sit in panels of 3

CSP case types:
- Mandatory jurisdiction in civil, noncapital criminal, administrative agency, juvenile cases.
- Discretionary jurisdiction in interlocutory decision cases.

Intermediate appellate court

DISTRICT COURT (13 districts)

72 judges

CSP case types:
- Tort, contract, real property rights, estate. Exclusive mental health, civil appeals, miscellaneous civil jurisdiction.
- Exclusive domestic relations jurisdiction.
- Misdemeanor. Exclusive felony, criminal appeals jurisdiction.
- Exclusive juvenile jurisdiction.

Jury trials.

Court of general jurisdiction

MAGISTRATE COURT (54 courts/32 counties)

62 judges

CSP case types:
- Tort, contract, real property rights ($0/ $10,000).
- Misdemeanor, DWI/DUI.
- Moving traffic, miscellaneous traffic.
- Preliminary hearings.

Jury trials.

BERNALILLO COUNTY METROPOLITAN COURT

16 judges

CSP case types:
- Tort, contract, real property rights ($0/ $10,000).
- Misdemeanor, DWI/DUI.
- Traffic/other violation.
- Preliminary hearings.

Jury trials except in traffic.

Courts of limited jurisdiction

MUNICIPAL COURT (83 courts)

85 judges

CSP case types:
- DWI/DUI, domestic violence.
- Traffic/other violation.

No jury trials.

PROBATE COURT (33 counties)

33 judges

CSP case types:
- Estate. (Hears uncontested cases; contested cases go to District Court.)

No jury trials.

NEW YORK COURT STRUCTURE

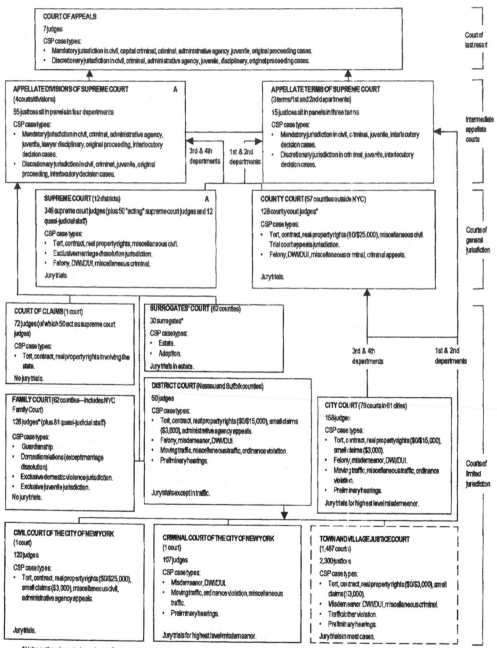

COURT OF APPEALS

7 judges

CSP case types:
- Mandatory jurisdiction in civil, capital criminal, criminal, administrative agency, juvenile, original proceeding cases.
- Discretionary jurisdiction in civil, criminal, administrative agency, juvenile, disciplinary, original proceeding cases.

Court of last resort

APPELLATE DIVISIONS OF SUPREME COURT   **A**

(4 courts/divisions)

55 justices sit in panels in four departments

CSP case types:
- Mandatory jurisdiction in civil, criminal, administrative agency, juvenile, lawyer disciplinary, original proceeding, interlocutory decision cases.
- Discretionary jurisdiction in civil, criminal, juvenile, original proceeding, interlocutory decision cases.

APPELLATE TERMS OF SUPREME COURT

(3 terms/1st and 2nd departments)

15 justices sit in panels in three terms

CSP case types:
- Mandatory jurisdiction in civil, criminal, juvenile, interlocutory decision cases.
- Discretionary jurisdiction in criminal, juvenile, interlocutory decision cases.

3rd & 4th departments   1st & 2nd departments

Intermediate appellate courts

SUPREME COURT (12 districts)   **A**

346 supreme court judges (plus 50 "acting" supreme court judges and 12 quasi-judicial staff)

CSP case types:
- Tort, contract, real property rights, miscellaneous civil.
- Exclusive marriage dissolution jurisdiction.
- Felony, DWI/DUI, miscellaneous criminal.

Jury trials.

COUNTY COURT (57 counties outside NYC)

128 county court judges*

CSP case types:
- Tort, contract, real property rights ($0/$25,000), miscellaneous civil. Trial court appeals jurisdiction.
- Felony, DWI/DUI, miscellaneous criminal, criminal appeals.

Jury trials.

Courts of general jurisdiction

COURT OF CLAIMS (1 court)

72 judges (of which 50 act as supreme court judges)

CSP case types:
- Tort, contract, real property rights involving the state.

No jury trials.

SURROGATES' COURT (62 counties)

30 surrogates*

CSP case types:
- Estate.
- Adoption.

Jury trials in estate.

3rd & 4th departments   1st & 2nd departments

FAMILY COURT (62 counties—includes NYC Family Court)

126 judges* (plus 81 quasi-judicial staff)

CSP case types:
- Guardianship.
- Domestic relations (except marriage dissolution).
- Exclusive domestic violence jurisdiction.
- Exclusive juvenile jurisdiction.

No jury trials.

DISTRICT COURT (Nassau and Suffolk counties)

50 judges

CSP case types:
- Tort, contract, real property rights ($0/$15,000), small claims ($3,000), administrative agency appeals.
- Felony, misdemeanor, DWI/DUI.
- Moving traffic, miscellaneous traffic, ordinance violation.
- Preliminary hearings.

Jury trials except in traffic.

CITY COURT (79 courts in 61 cities)

158 judges

CSP case types:
- Tort, contract, real property rights ($0/$15,000), small claims ($3,000).
- Felony, misdemeanor, DWI/DUI.
- Moving traffic, miscellaneous traffic, ordinance violation.
- Preliminary hearings.

Jury trials for highest level misdemeanor.

Courts of limited jurisdiction

CIVIL COURT OF THE CITY OF NEW YORK

(1 court)

120 judges

CSP case types:
- Tort, contract, real property rights ($0/$25,000), small claims ($3,000), miscellaneous civil, administrative agency appeals.

Jury trials.

CRIMINAL COURT OF THE CITY OF NEW YORK

(1 court)

107 judges

CSP case types:
- Misdemeanor, DWI/DUI.
- Moving traffic, ordinance violation, miscellaneous traffic.
- Preliminary hearings.

Jury trials for highest level misdemeanor.

TOWN AND VILLAGE JUSTICE COURT

(1,487 courts)

2,300 justices

CSP case types:
- Tort, contract, real property rights ($0/$3,000), small claims ($3,000).
- Misdemeanor, DWI/DUI, miscellaneous criminal.
- Traffic/other violation.
- Preliminary hearings.

Jury trials in most cases.

*Unless otherwise noted, numbers reflect statutory authorization. Many judges sit in more than one court so the number of judgeships indicated in this chart does not reflect the actual number of judges in the system. Fifty County Court judges also serve Surrogates' Court and six County Court judges also serve Family Court.

NORTH CAROLINA COURT STRUCTURE

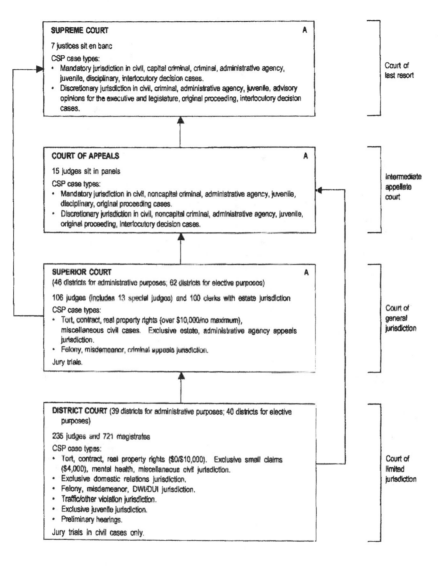

SUPREME COURT   A

7 justices sit en banc

CSP case types:
- Mandatory jurisdiction in civil, capital criminal, criminal, administrative agency, juvenile, disciplinary, interlocutory decision cases.
- Discretionary jurisdiction in civil, criminal, administrative agency, juvenile, advisory opinions for the executive and legislature, original proceeding, interlocutory decision cases.

Court of last resort

COURT OF APPEALS   A

15 judges sit in panels

CSP case types:
- Mandatory jurisdiction in civil, noncapital criminal, administrative agency, juvenile, disciplinary, original proceeding cases.
- Discretionary jurisdiction in civil, noncapital criminal, administrative agency, juvenile, original proceeding, interlocutory decision cases.

Intermediate appellate court

SUPERIOR COURT   A

(46 districts for administrative purposes; 62 districts for elective purposes)

106 judges (includes 13 special judges) and 100 clerks with estate jurisdiction

CSP case types:
- Tort, contract, real property rights (over $10,000/no maximum), miscellaneous civil cases. Exclusive estate, administrative agency appeals jurisdiction.
- Felony, misdemeanor, criminal appeals jurisdiction.

Jury trials.

Court of general jurisdiction

DISTRICT COURT (39 districts for administrative purposes; 40 districts for elective purposes)

235 judges and 721 magistrates

CSP case types:
- Tort, contract, real property rights ($0/$10,000). Exclusive small claims ($4,000), mental health, miscellaneous civil jurisdiction.
- Exclusive domestic relations jurisdiction.
- Felony, misdemeanor, DWI/DUI jurisdiction.
- Traffic/other violation jurisdiction.
- Exclusive juvenile jurisdiction.
- Preliminary hearings.

Jury trials in civil cases only.

Court of limited jurisdiction

NORTH DAKOTA COURT STRUCTURE

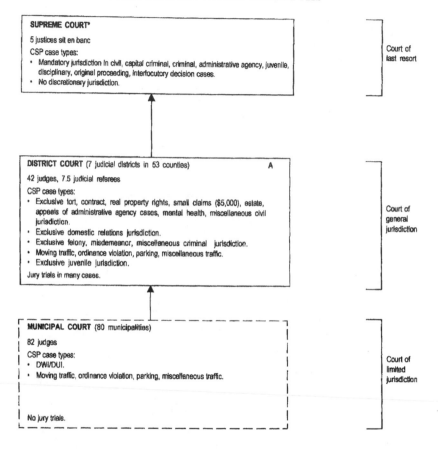

SUPREME COURT*

5 justices sit en banc

CSP case types:
- Mandatory jurisdiction in civil, capital criminal, criminal, administrative agency, juvenile, disciplinary, original proceeding, interlocutory decision cases.
- No discretionary jurisdiction.

Court of last resort

DISTRICT COURT (7 judicial districts in 53 counties)   **A**

42 judges, 7.5 judicial referees

CSP case types:
- Exclusive tort, contract, real property rights, small claims ($5,000), estate, appeals of administrative agency cases, mental health, miscellaneous civil jurisdiction.
- Exclusive domestic relations jurisdiction.
- Exclusive felony, misdemeanor, miscellaneous criminal jurisdiction.
- Moving traffic, ordinance violation, parking, miscellaneous traffic.
- Exclusive juvenile jurisdiction.

Jury trials in many cases.

Court of general jurisdiction

MUNICIPAL COURT (80 municipalities)

82 judges

CSP case types:
- DWI/DUI.
- Moving traffic, ordinance violation, parking, miscellaneous traffic.

No jury trials.

Court of limited jurisdiction

* A temporary court of appeals was established July 1, 1987, to exercise appellate and original jurisdiction as delegated by the supreme court. This court does not sit, has no assigned judges, and has heard no appeals. It is currently unfunded.

OHIO COURT STRUCTURE

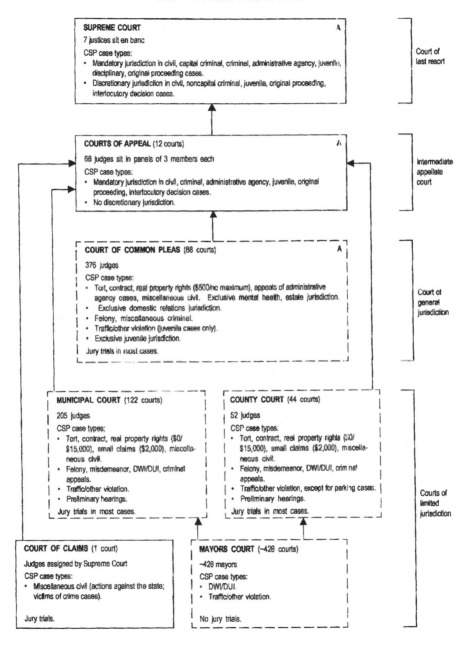

SUPREME COURT A

7 justices sit en banc

CSP case types:

- Mandatory jurisdiction in civil, capital criminal, criminal, administrative agency, juvenile, disciplinary, original proceeding cases.
- Discretionary jurisdiction in civil, noncapital criminal, juvenile, original proceeding, interlocutory decision cases.

Court of last resort

COURTS OF APPEAL (12 courts) A

68 judges sit in panels of 3 members each

CSP case types:

- Mandatory jurisdiction in civil, criminal, administrative agency, juvenile, original proceeding, interlocutory decision cases.
- No discretionary jurisdiction.

Intermediate appellate court

COURT OF COMMON PLEAS (88 courts) A

376 judges

CSP case types:

- Tort, contract, real property rights ($500/no maximum), appeals of administrative agency cases, miscellaneous civil. Exclusive mental health, estate jurisdiction.
- Exclusive domestic relations jurisdiction.
- Felony, miscellaneous criminal.
- Traffic/other violation (juvenile cases only).
- Exclusive juvenile jurisdiction.

Jury trials in most cases.

Court of general jurisdiction

MUNICIPAL COURT (122 courts)

205 judges

CSP case types:

- Tort, contract, real property rights ($0/$15,000), small claims ($2,000), miscellaneous civil.
- Felony, misdemeanor, DWI/DUI, criminal appeals.
- Traffic/other violation.
- Preliminary hearings.

Jury trials in most cases.

COUNTY COURT (44 courts)

52 judges

CSP case types:

- Tort, contract, real property rights ($0/$15,000), small claims ($2,000), miscellaneous civil.
- Felony, misdemeanor, DWI/DUI, criminal appeals.
- Traffic/other violation, except for parking cases.
- Preliminary hearings.

Jury trials in most cases.

Courts of limited jurisdiction

COURT OF CLAIMS (1 court)

Judges assigned by Supreme Court

CSP case types:

- Miscellaneous civil (actions against the state; victims of crime cases).

Jury trials.

MAYORS COURT (~428 courts)

~428 mayors

CSP case types:

- DWI/DUI.
- Traffic/other violation.

No jury trials.

OKLAHOMA COURT STRUCTURE

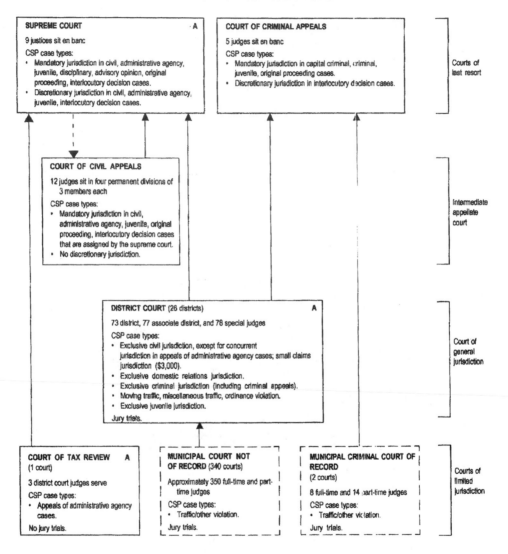

SUPREME COURT · A

9 justices sit en banc

CSP case types:
- Mandatory jurisdiction in civil, administrative agency, juvenile, disciplinary, advisory opinion, original proceeding, interlocutory decision cases.
- Discretionary jurisdiction in civil, administrative agency, juvenile, interlocutory decision cases.

COURT OF CRIMINAL APPEALS

5 judges sit en banc

CSP case types:
- Mandatory jurisdiction in capital criminal, criminal, juvenile, original proceeding cases.
- Discretionary jurisdiction in interlocutory decision cases.

Courts of last resort

COURT OF CIVIL APPEALS

12 judges sit in four permanent divisions of 3 members each

CSP case types:
- Mandatory jurisdiction in civil, administrative agency, juvenile, original proceeding, interlocutory decision cases that are assigned by the supreme court.
- No discretionary jurisdiction.

Intermediate appellate court

DISTRICT COURT (26 districts) A

73 district, 77 associate district, and 78 special judges

CSP case types:
- Exclusive civil jurisdiction, except for concurrent jurisdiction in appeals of administrative agency cases; small claims jurisdiction ($3,000).
- Exclusive domestic relations jurisdiction.
- Exclusive criminal jurisdiction (including criminal appeals).
- Moving traffic, miscellaneous traffic, ordinance violation.
- Exclusive juvenile jurisdiction.

Jury trials.

Court of general jurisdiction

COURT OF TAX REVIEW A
(1 court)

3 district court judges serve

CSP case types:
- Appeals of administrative agency cases.

No jury trials.

MUNICIPAL COURT NOT OF RECORD (340 courts)

Approximately 350 full-time and part-time judges

CSP case types:
- Traffic/other violation.

Jury trials.

MUNICIPAL CRIMINAL COURT OF RECORD
(2 courts)

8 full-time and 14 part-time judges

CSP case types:
- Traffic/other violation.

Jury trials.

Courts of limited jurisdiction

- - Indicates assignment of cases.

Note: Oklahoma has a workers' compensation court, which hears complaints that are handled exclusively by administrative agencies in other states.

OREGON COURT STRUCTURE

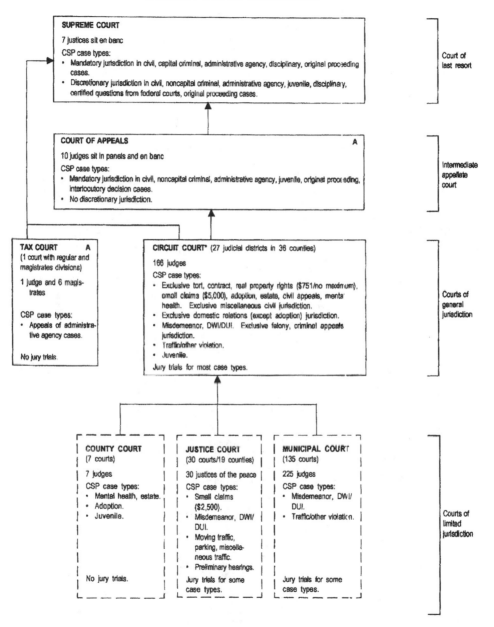

SUPREME COURT

7 justices sit en banc

CSP case types:
- Mandatory jurisdiction in civil, capital criminal, administrative agency, disciplinary, original proceeding cases.
- Discretionary jurisdiction in civil, noncapital criminal, administrative agency, juvenile, disciplinary, certified questions from federal courts, original proceeding cases.

Court of last resort

COURT OF APPEALS   A

10 judges sit in panels and en banc

CSP case types:
- Mandatory jurisdiction in civil, noncapital criminal, administrative agency, juvenile, original proceeding, interlocutory decision cases.
- No discretionary jurisdiction.

Intermediate appellate court

TAX COURT   A
(1 court with regular and magistrates divisions)

1 judge and 6 magistrates

CSP case types:
- Appeals of administrative agency cases.

No jury trials.

CIRCUIT COURT* (27 judicial districts in 36 counties)

166 judges

CSP case types:
- Exclusive tort, contract, real property rights ($751/no maximum), small claims ($5,000), adoption, estate, civil appeals, mental health. Exclusive miscellaneous civil jurisdiction.
- Exclusive domestic relations (except adoption) jurisdiction.
- Misdemeanor, DWI/DUI. Exclusive felony, criminal appeals jurisdiction.
- Traffic/other violation.
- Juvenile.

Jury trials for most case types.

Courts of general jurisdiction

COUNTY COURT
(7 courts)

7 judges

CSP case types:
- Mental health, estate.
- Adoption.
- Juvenile.

No jury trials.

JUSTICE COURT
(30 courts/19 counties)

30 justices of the peace

CSP case types:
- Small claims ($2,500).
- Misdemeanor, DWI/ DUI.
- Moving traffic, parking, miscellaneous traffic.
- Preliminary hearings.

Jury trials for some case types.

MUNICIPAL COURT
(135 courts)

225 judges

CSP case types:
- Misdemeanor, DWI/ DUI.
- Traffic/other violation.

Jury trials for some case types.

Courts of limited jurisdiction

* Effective January 15, 1998, all District Courts were eliminated and District judges became Circuit judges.

PENNSYLVANIA COURT STRUCTURE

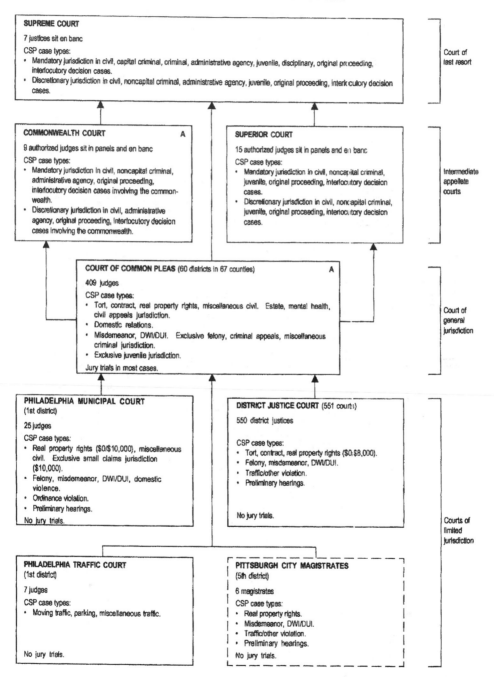

SUPREME COURT

7 justices sit en banc

CSP case types:
- Mandatory jurisdiction in civil, capital criminal, criminal, administrative agency, juvenile, disciplinary, original proceeding, interlocutory decision cases.
- Discretionary jurisdiction in civil, noncapital criminal, administrative agency, juvenile, original proceeding, interlocutory decision cases.

Court of last resort

COMMONWEALTH COURT   **A**

9 authorized judges sit in panels and en banc

CSP case types:
- Mandatory jurisdiction in civil, noncapital criminal, administrative agency, original proceeding, interlocutory decision cases involving the commonwealth.
- Discretionary jurisdiction in civil, administrative agency, original proceeding, interlocutory decision cases involving the commonwealth.

SUPERIOR COURT

15 authorized judges sit in panels and en banc

CSP case types:
- Mandatory jurisdiction in civil, noncapital criminal, juvenile, original proceeding, interlocutory decision cases.
- Discretionary jurisdiction in civil, noncapital criminal, juvenile, original proceeding, interlocutory decision cases.

Intermediate appellate courts

COURT OF COMMON PLEAS (60 districts in 67 counties)   **A**

409 judges

CSP case types:
- Tort, contract, real property rights, miscellaneous civil. Estate, mental health, civil appeals jurisdiction.
- Domestic relations.
- Misdemeanor, DWI/DUI. Exclusive felony, criminal appeals, miscellaneous criminal jurisdiction.
- Exclusive juvenile jurisdiction.

Jury trials in most cases.

Court of general jurisdiction

PHILADELPHIA MUNICIPAL COURT
(1st district)

25 judges

CSP case types:
- Real property rights ($0/$10,000), miscellaneous civil. Exclusive small claims jurisdiction ($10,000).
- Felony, misdemeanor, DWI/DUI, domestic violence.
- Ordinance violation.
- Preliminary hearings.

No jury trials.

DISTRICT JUSTICE COURT (551 courts)

550 district justices

CSP case types:
- Tort, contract, real property rights ($0/$8,000).
- Felony, misdemeanor, DWI/DUI.
- Traffic/other violation.
- Preliminary hearings.

No jury trials.

Courts of limited jurisdiction

PHILADELPHIA TRAFFIC COURT
(1st district)

7 judges

CSP case types:
- Moving traffic, parking, miscellaneous traffic.

No jury trials.

PITTSBURGH CITY MAGISTRATES
(5th district)

6 magistrates

CSP case types:
- Real property rights.
- Misdemeanor, DWI/DUI.
- Traffic/other violation.
- Preliminary hearings.

No jury trials.

RHODE ISLAND COURT STRUCTURE

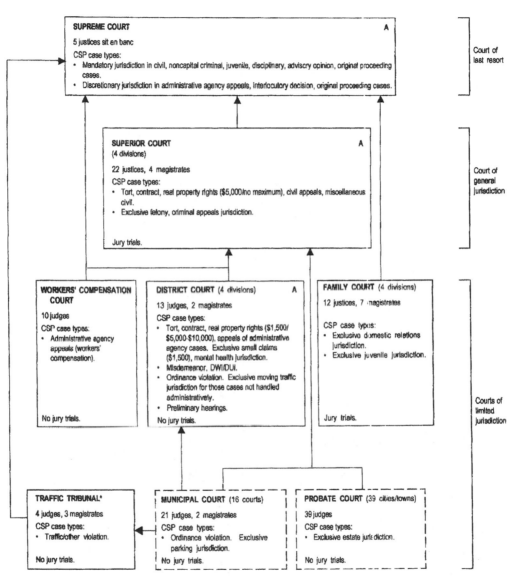

SUPREME COURT A

5 justices sit en banc

CSP case types:
- Mandatory jurisdiction in civil, noncapital criminal, juvenile, disciplinary, advisory opinion, original proceeding cases.
- Discretionary jurisdiction in administrative agency appeals, interlocutory decision, original proceeding cases.

Court of last resort

SUPERIOR COURT A
(4 divisions)

22 justices, 4 magistrates

CSP case types:
- Tort, contract, real property rights ($5,000/no maximum), civil appeals, miscellaneous civil.
- Exclusive felony, criminal appeals jurisdiction.

Jury trials.

Court of general jurisdiction

WORKERS' COMPENSATION COURT

10 judges

CSP case types:
- Administrative agency appeals (workers' compensation).

No jury trials.

DISTRICT COURT (4 divisions) A

13 judges, 2 magistrates

CSP case types:
- Tort, contract, real property rights ($1,500/ $5,000-$10,000), appeals of administrative agency cases. Exclusive small claims ($1,500), mental health jurisdiction.
- Misdemeanor, DWI/DUI.
- Ordinance violation. Exclusive moving traffic jurisdiction for those cases not handled administratively.
- Preliminary hearings.

No jury trials.

FAMILY COURT (4 divisions)

12 justices, 7 magistrates

CSP case types:
- Exclusive domestic relations jurisdiction.
- Exclusive juvenile jurisdiction.

Jury trials.

Courts of limited jurisdiction

TRAFFIC TRIBUNAL*

4 judges, 3 magistrates

CSP case types:
- Traffic/other violation.

No jury trials.

MUNICIPAL COURT (16 courts)

21 judges, 2 magistrates

CSP case types:
- Ordinance violation. Exclusive parking jurisdiction.

No jury trials.

PROBATE COURT (39 cities/towns)

39 judges

CSP case types:
- Exclusive estate jurisdiction.

No jury trials.

* This court was formerly known as the Rhode Island Administrative Adjudication Court.

SOUTH CAROLINA COURT STRUCTURE

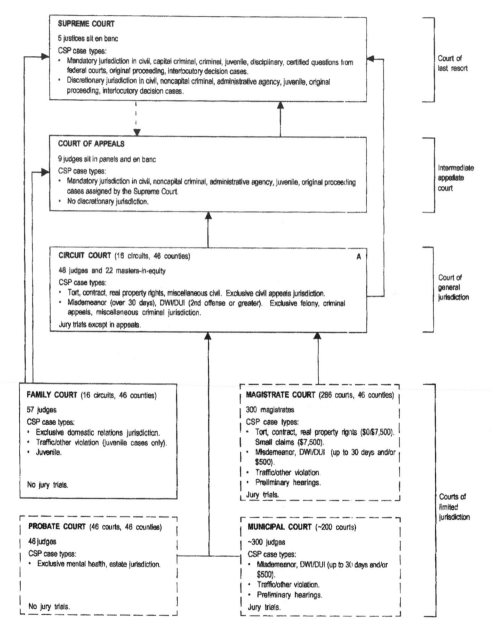

SUPREME COURT

5 justices sit en banc

CSP case types:
- Mandatory jurisdiction in civil, capital criminal, criminal, juvenile, disciplinary, certified questions from federal courts, original proceeding, interlocutory decision cases.
- Discretionary jurisdiction in civil, noncapital criminal, administrative agency, juvenile, original proceeding, interlocutory decision cases.

Court of last resort

COURT OF APPEALS

9 judges sit in panels and en banc

CSP case types:
- Mandatory jurisdiction in civil, noncapital criminal, administrative agency, juvenile, original proceeding cases assigned by the Supreme Court.
- No discretionary jurisdiction.

Intermediate appellate court

CIRCUIT COURT (16 circuits, 46 counties)   A

48 judges and 22 masters-in-equity

CSP case types:
- Tort, contract, real property rights, miscellaneous civil. Exclusive civil appeals jurisdiction.
- Misdemeanor (over 30 days), DWI/DUI (2nd offense or greater). Exclusive felony, criminal appeals, miscellaneous criminal jurisdiction.

Jury trials except in appeals.

Court of general jurisdiction

FAMILY COURT (16 circuits, 46 counties)

57 judges

CSP case types:
- Exclusive domestic relations jurisdiction.
- Traffic/other violation (juvenile cases only).
- Juvenile.

No jury trials.

MAGISTRATE COURT (286 courts, 46 counties)

300 magistrates

CSP case types:
- Tort, contract, real property rights ($0/$7,500). Small claims ($7,500).
- Misdemeanor, DWI/DUI (up to 30 days and/or $500).
- Traffic/other violation.
- Preliminary hearings.

Jury trials.

PROBATE COURT (46 courts, 46 counties)

46 judges

CSP case types:
- Exclusive mental health, estate jurisdiction.

No jury trials.

MUNICIPAL COURT (~200 courts)

~300 judges

CSP case types:
- Misdemeanor, DWI/DUI (up to 30 days and/or $500).
- Traffic/other violation.
- Preliminary hearings.

Jury trials.

Courts of limited jurisdiction

— —   Indicates assignment of cases.

SOUTH DAKOTA COURT STRUCTURE

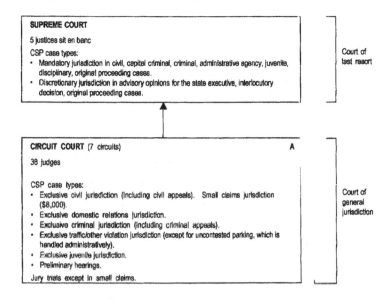

SUPREME COURT

5 justices sit en banc

CSP case types:
- Mandatory jurisdiction in civil, capital criminal, criminal, administrative agency, juvenile, disciplinary, original proceeding cases.
- Discretionary jurisdiction in advisory opinions for the state executive, interlocutory decision, original proceeding cases.

Court of last resort

CIRCUIT COURT (7 circuits)   **A**

38 judges

CSP case types:
- Exclusive civil jurisdiction (including civil appeals). Small claims jurisdiction ($8,000).
- Exclusive domestic relations jurisdiction.
- Exclusive criminal jurisdiction (including criminal appeals).
- Exclusive traffic/other violation jurisdiction (except for uncontested parking, which is handled administratively).
- Exclusive juvenile jurisdiction.
- Preliminary hearings.

Jury trials except in small claims.

Court of general jurisdiction

TENNESSEE COURT STRUCTURE

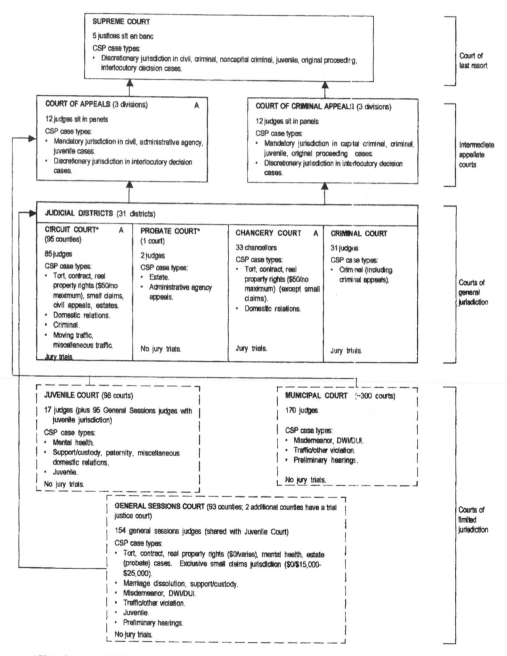

SUPREME COURT

5 justices sit en banc

CSP case types:
- Discretionary jurisdiction in civil, criminal, noncapital criminal, juvenile, original proceeding, interlocutory decision cases.

Court of last resort

COURT OF APPEALS (3 divisions)   A

12 judges sit in panels

CSP case types:
- Mandatory jurisdiction in civil, administrative agency, juvenile cases.
- Discretionary jurisdiction in interlocutory decision cases.

COURT OF CRIMINAL APPEALS (3 divisions)

12 judges sit in panels

CSP case types:
- Mandatory jurisdiction in capital criminal, criminal, juvenile, original proceeding cases.
- Discretionary jurisdiction in interlocutory decision cases.

Intermediate appellate courts

JUDICIAL DISTRICTS (31 districts)

CIRCUIT COURT*   A
(95 counties)

85 judges

CSP case types:
- Tort, contract, real property rights ($50/no maximum), small claims, civil appeals, estates.
- Domestic relations.
- Criminal.
- Moving traffic, miscellaneous traffic.

Jury trials.

PROBATE COURT*
(1 court)

2 judges

CSP case types:
- Estate.
- Administrative agency appeals.

No jury trials.

CHANCERY COURT   A

33 chancellors

CSP case types:
- Tort, contract, real property rights ($50/no maximum) (except small claims).
- Domestic relations.

Jury trials.

CRIMINAL COURT

31 judges

CSP case types:
- Criminal (including criminal appeals).

Jury trials.

Courts of general jurisdiction

JUVENILE COURT (98 courts)

17 judges (plus 95 General Sessions judges with juvenile jurisdiction)

CSP case types:
- Mental health.
- Support/custody, paternity, miscellaneous domestic relations.
- Juvenile.

No jury trials.

MUNICIPAL COURT (~300 courts)

170 judges

CSP case types:
- Misdemeanor, DWI/DUI.
- Traffic/other violation.
- Preliminary hearings.

No jury trials.

GENERAL SESSIONS COURT (93 counties; 2 additional counties have a trial justice court)

154 general sessions judges (shared with Juvenile Court)

CSP case types:
- Tort, contract, real property rights ($0/varies), mental health, estate (probate) cases. Exclusive small claims jurisdiction ($0/$15,000–$25,000).
- Marriage dissolution, support/custody.
- Misdemeanor, DWI/DUI.
- Traffic/other violation.
- Juvenile.
- Preliminary hearings.

No jury trials.

Courts of limited jurisdiction

* Effective September 1, 1998 Davidson County Probate Court became a Circuit Court with Probate jurisdiction.

TEXAS COURT STRUCTURE

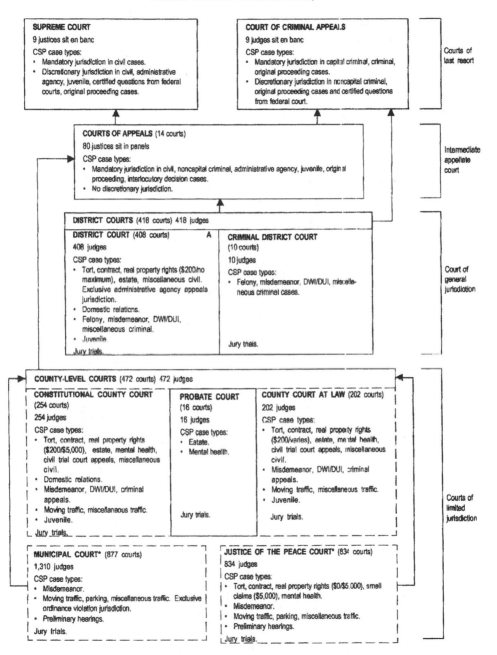

SUPREME COURT

9 justices sit en banc

CSP case types:
- Mandatory jurisdiction in civil cases.
- Discretionary jurisdiction in civil, administrative agency, juvenile, certified questions from federal courts, original proceeding cases.

COURT OF CRIMINAL APPEALS

9 judges sit en banc

CSP case types:
- Mandatory jurisdiction in capital criminal, criminal, original proceeding cases.
- Discretionary jurisdiction in noncapital criminal, original proceeding cases and certified questions from federal court.

Courts of last resort

COURTS OF APPEALS (14 courts)

80 justices sit in panels

CSP case types:
- Mandatory jurisdiction in civil, noncapital criminal, administrative agency, juvenile, original proceeding, interlocutory decision cases.
- No discretionary jurisdiction.

Intermediate appellate court

DISTRICT COURTS (418 courts) 418 judges

DISTRICT COURT (408 courts)   A

408 judges

CSP case types:
- Tort, contract, real property rights ($200/no maximum), estate, miscellaneous civil. Exclusive administrative agency appeals jurisdiction.
- Domestic relations.
- Felony, misdemeanor, DWI/DUI, miscellaneous criminal.
- Juvenile.

Jury trials.

CRIMINAL DISTRICT COURT (10 courts)

10 judges

CSP case types:
- Felony, misdemeanor, DWI/DUI, miscellaneous criminal cases.

Jury trials.

Court of general jurisdiction

COUNTY-LEVEL COURTS (472 courts) 472 judges

CONSTITUTIONAL COUNTY COURT (254 courts)

254 judges

CSP case types:
- Tort, contract, real property rights ($200/$5,000), estate, mental health, civil trial court appeals, miscellaneous civil.
- Domestic relations.
- Misdemeanor, DWI/DUI, criminal appeals.
- Moving traffic, miscellaneous traffic.
- Juvenile.

Jury trials.

PROBATE COURT (16 courts)

16 judges

CSP case types:
- Estate.
- Mental health.

Jury trials.

COUNTY COURT AT LAW (202 courts)

202 judges

CSP case types:
- Tort, contract, real property rights ($200/varies), estate, mental health, civil trial court appeals, miscellaneous civil.
- Misdemeanor, DWI/DUI, criminal appeals.
- Moving traffic, miscellaneous traffic.
- Juvenile.

Jury trials.

Courts of limited jurisdiction

MUNICIPAL COURT* (877 courts)

1,310 judges

CSP case types:
- Misdemeanor.
- Moving traffic, parking, miscellaneous traffic. Exclusive ordinance violation jurisdiction.
- Preliminary hearings.

Jury trials.

JUSTICE OF THE PEACE COURT* (834 courts)

834 judges

CSP case types:
- Tort, contract, real property rights ($0/$5,000), small claims ($5,000), mental health.
- Misdemeanor.
- Moving traffic, parking, miscellaneous traffic.
- Preliminary hearings.

Jury trials.

* Some municipal and justice of the peace courts may appeal to the district court.

UTAH COURT STRUCTURE

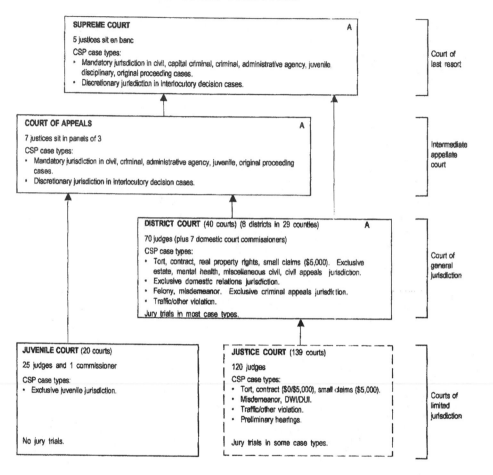

SUPREME COURT   A

5 justices sit en banc

CSP case types:
- Mandatory jurisdiction in civil, capital criminal, criminal, administrative agency, juvenile disciplinary, original proceeding cases.
- Discretionary jurisdiction in interlocutory decision cases.

Court of last resort

COURT OF APPEALS   A

7 justices sit in panels of 3

CSP case types:
- Mandatory jurisdiction in civil, criminal, administrative agency, juvenile, original proceeding cases.
- Discretionary jurisdiction in interlocutory decision cases.

Intermediate appellate court

DISTRICT COURT (40 courts) (8 districts in 29 counties)   A

70 judges (plus 7 domestic court commissioners)

CSP case types:
- Tort, contract, real property rights, small claims ($5,000). Exclusive estate, mental health, miscellaneous civil, civil appeals jurisdiction.
- Exclusive domestic relations jurisdiction.
- Felony, misdemeanor. Exclusive criminal appeals jurisdiction.
- Traffic/other violation.

Jury trials in most case types.

Court of general jurisdiction

JUVENILE COURT (20 courts)

25 judges and 1 commissioner

CSP case types:
- Exclusive juvenile jurisdiction.

No jury trials.

JUSTICE COURT (139 courts)

120 judges

CSP case types:
- Tort, contract ($0/$5,000), small claims ($5,000).
- Misdemeanor, DWI/DUI.
- Traffic/other violation.
- Preliminary hearings.

Jury trials in some case types.

Courts of limited jurisdiction

VERMONT COURT STRUCTURE.

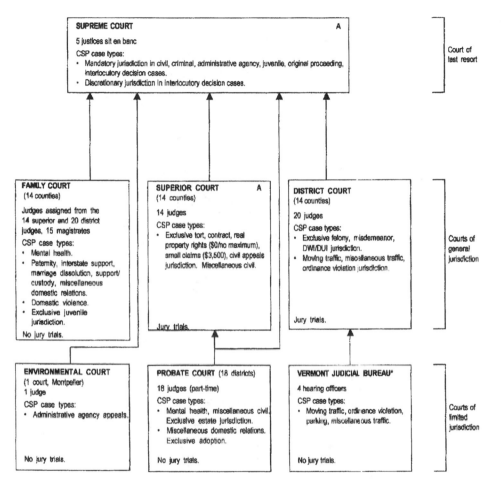

SUPREME COURT A

5 justices sit en banc

CSP case types:
- Mandatory jurisdiction in civil, criminal, administrative agency, juvenile, original proceeding, interlocutory decision cases.
- Discretionary jurisdiction in interlocutory decision cases.

Court of last resort

FAMILY COURT
(14 counties)

Judges assigned from the 14 superior and 20 district judges, 15 magistrates

CSP case types:
- Mental health.
- Paternity, interstate support, marriage dissolution, support/ custody, miscellaneous domestic relations.
- Domestic violence.
- Exclusive juvenile jurisdiction.

No jury trials.

SUPERIOR COURT A
(14 counties)

14 judges

CSP case types:
- Exclusive tort, contract, real property rights ($0/no maximum), small claims ($3,500), civil appeals jurisdiction. Miscellaneous civil.

Jury trials.

DISTRICT COURT
(14 counties)

20 judges

CSP case types:
- Exclusive felony, misdemeanor, DWI/DUI jurisdiction.
- Moving traffic, miscellaneous traffic, ordinance violation jurisdiction.

Jury trials.

Courts of general jurisdiction

ENVIRONMENTAL COURT
(1 court, Montpelier)
1 judge

CSP case types:
- Administrative agency appeals.

No jury trials.

PROBATE COURT (18 districts)

18 judges (part-time)

CSP case types:
- Mental health, miscellaneous civil. Exclusive estate jurisdiction.
- Miscellaneous domestic relations. Exclusive adoption.

No jury trials.

VERMONT JUDICIAL BUREAU*

4 hearing officers

CSP case types:
- Moving traffic, ordinance violation, parking, miscellaneous traffic.

No jury trials.

Courts of limited jurisdiction

* Renamed VERMONT JUDICIAL BUREAU as of 7/1/98, this court was formerly known as the Vermont Traffic and Municipal Ordinance Bureau.

Note: An additional 28 assistant judges participate in findings of fact in Superior and Family Court cases. Some assistant judges, after special training, may hear small claims cases and traffic complaints, conduct criminal arraignments, and decide child support, parentage, and uncontested divorce proceedings. These assistant judges (who need not be attorneys) are elected to four-year terms by voters in Vermont's 14 counties.

VIRGINIA COURT STRUCTURE.

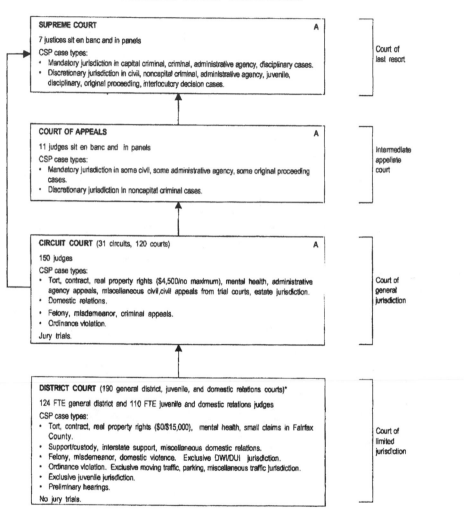

SUPREME COURT   **A**

7 justices sit en banc and in panels

CSP case types:

- Mandatory jurisdiction in capital criminal, criminal, administrative agency, disciplinary cases.
- Discretionary jurisdiction in civil, noncapital criminal, administrative agency, juvenile, disciplinary, original proceeding, interlocutory decision cases.

Court of last resort

COURT OF APPEALS   **A**

11 judges sit en banc and in panels

CSP case types:

- Mandatory jurisdiction in some civil, some administrative agency, some original proceeding cases.
- Discretionary jurisdiction in noncapital criminal cases.

Intermediate appellate court

CIRCUIT COURT (31 circuits, 120 courts)   **A**

150 judges

CSP case types:

- Tort, contract, real property rights ($4,500/no maximum), mental health, administrative agency appeals, miscellaneous civil, civil appeals from trial courts, estate jurisdiction.
- Domestic relations.
- Felony, misdemeanor, criminal appeals.
- Ordinance violation.

Jury trials.

Court of general jurisdiction

DISTRICT COURT (190 general district, juvenile, and domestic relations courts)*

124 FTE general district and 110 FTE juvenile and domestic relations judges

CSP case types:

- Tort, contract, real property rights ($0/$15,000), mental health, small claims in Fairfax County.
- Support/custody, interstate support, miscellaneous domestic relations.
- Felony, misdemeanor, domestic violence. Exclusive DWI/DUI jurisdiction.
- Ordinance violation. Exclusive moving traffic, parking, miscellaneous traffic jurisdiction.
- Exclusive juvenile jurisdiction.
- Preliminary hearings.

No jury trials.

Court of limited jurisdiction

* The district court is referred to as the juvenile and domestic relations court when hearing juvenile and domestic relations cases and as the general district court for the balance of the cases.

WASHINGTON COURT STRUCTURE

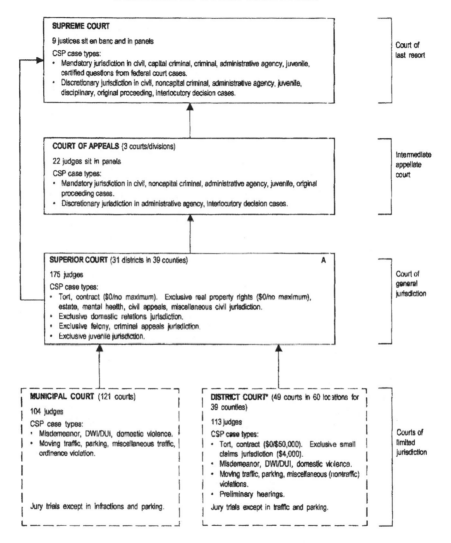

SUPREME COURT

9 justices sit en banc and in panels

CSP case types:
- Mandatory jurisdiction in civil, capital criminal, criminal, administrative agency, juvenile, certified questions from federal court cases.
- Discretionary jurisdiction in civil, noncapital criminal, administrative agency, juvenile, disciplinary, original proceeding, interlocutory decision cases.

Court of last resort

COURT OF APPEALS (3 courts/divisions)

22 judges sit in panels

CSP case types:
- Mandatory jurisdiction in civil, noncapital criminal, administrative agency, juvenile, original proceeding cases.
- Discretionary jurisdiction in administrative agency, interlocutory decision cases.

Intermediate appellate court

SUPERIOR COURT (31 districts in 39 counties)   A

175 judges

CSP case types:
- Tort, contract ($0/no maximum). Exclusive real property rights ($0/no maximum), estate, mental health, civil appeals, miscellaneous civil jurisdiction.
- Exclusive domestic relations jurisdiction.
- Exclusive felony, criminal appeals jurisdiction.
- Exclusive juvenile jurisdiction.

Court of general jurisdiction

MUNICIPAL COURT (121 courts)

104 judges

CSP case types:
- Misdemeanor, DWI/DUI, domestic violence.
- Moving traffic, parking, miscellaneous traffic, ordinance violation.

Jury trials except in infractions and parking.

DISTRICT COURT* (49 courts in 60 locations for 39 counties)

113 judges

CSP case types:
- Tort, contract ($0/$50,000). Exclusive small claims jurisdiction ($4,000).
- Misdemeanor, DWI/DUI, domestic violence.
- Moving traffic, parking, miscellaneous (nontraffic) violations.
- Preliminary hearings.

Jury trials except in traffic and parking.

Courts of limited jurisdiction

* District court provides services to municipalities that do not have a municipal court.

Appendix K

WEST VIRGINIA COURT STRUCTURE

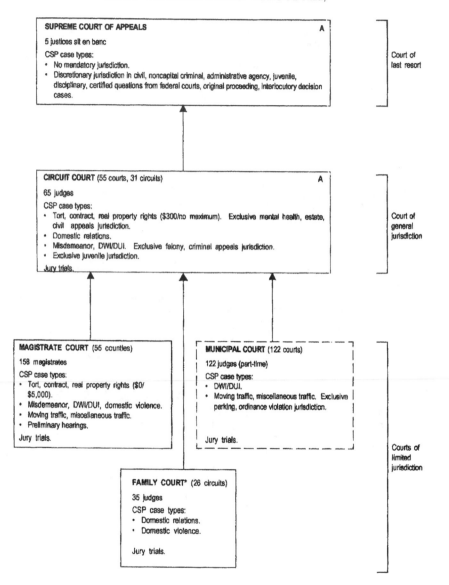

SUPREME COURT OF APPEALS   **A**

5 justices sit en banc

CSP case types:
- No mandatory jurisdiction.
- Discretionary jurisdiction in civil, noncapital criminal, administrative agency, juvenile, disciplinary, certified questions from federal courts, original proceeding, interlocutory decision cases.

Court of last resort

CIRCUIT COURT (55 courts, 31 circuits)   **A**

65 judges

CSP case types:
- Tort, contract, real property rights ($300/no maximum). Exclusive mental health, estate, civil appeals jurisdiction.
- Domestic relations.
- Misdemeanor, DWI/DUI. Exclusive felony, criminal appeals jurisdiction.
- Exclusive juvenile jurisdiction.

Jury trials.

Court of general jurisdiction

MAGISTRATE COURT (55 counties)

158 magistrates

CSP case types:
- Tort, contract, real property rights ($0/$5,000).
- Misdemeanor, DWI/DUI, domestic violence.
- Moving traffic, miscellaneous traffic.
- Preliminary hearings.

Jury trials.

MUNICIPAL COURT (122 courts)

122 judges (part-time)

CSP case types:
- DWI/DUI.
- Moving traffic, miscellaneous traffic. Exclusive parking, ordinance violation jurisdiction.

Jury trials.

FAMILY COURT* (26 circuits)

35 judges

CSP case types:
- Domestic relations.
- Domestic violence.

Jury trials.

Courts of limited jurisdiction

*The Family Court was created in 2002.

WISCONSIN COURT STRUCTURE

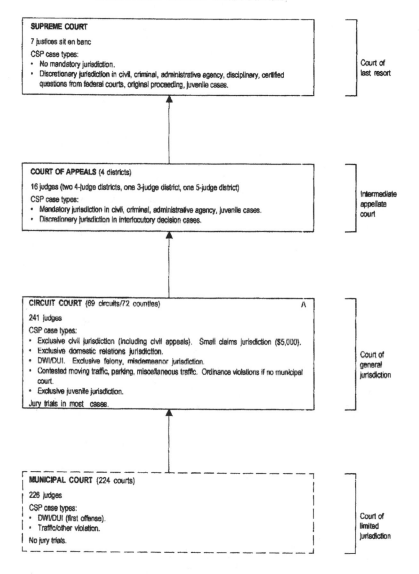

SUPREME COURT

7 justices sit en banc

CSP case types:
- No mandatory jurisdiction.
- Discretionary jurisdiction in civil, criminal, administrative agency, disciplinary, certified questions from federal courts, original proceeding, juvenile cases.

Court of last resort

COURT OF APPEALS (4 districts)

16 judges (two 4-judge districts, one 3-judge district, one 5-judge district)

CSP case types:
- Mandatory jurisdiction in civil, criminal, administrative agency, juvenile cases.
- Discretionary jurisdiction in interlocutory decision cases.

Intermediate appellate court

CIRCUIT COURT (69 circuits/72 counties)   A

241 judges

CSP case types:
- Exclusive civil jurisdiction (including civil appeals). Small claims jurisdiction ($5,000).
- Exclusive domestic relations jurisdiction.
- DWI/DUI. Exclusive felony, misdemeanor jurisdiction.
- Contested moving traffic, parking, miscellaneous traffic. Ordinance violations if no municipal court.
- Exclusive juvenile jurisdiction.

Jury trials in most cases.

Court of general jurisdiction

MUNICIPAL COURT (224 courts)

226 judges

CSP case types:
- DWI/DUI (first offense).
- Traffic/other violation.

No jury trials.

Court of limited jurisdiction

WYOMING COURT STRUCTURE

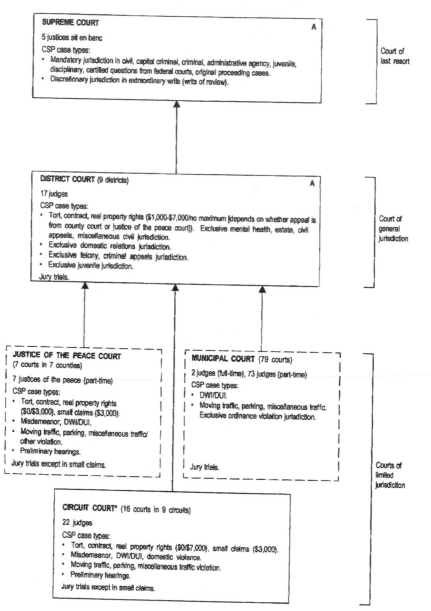

SUPREME COURT   A

5 justices sit en banc

CSP case types:

- Mandatory jurisdiction in civil, capital criminal, criminal, administrative agency, juvenile, disciplinary, certified questions from federal courts, original proceeding cases.
- Discretionary jurisdiction in extraordinary writs (writs of review).

Court of last resort

DISTRICT COURT (9 districts)   A

17 judges

CSP case types:

- Tort, contract, real property rights ($1,000-$7,000/no maximum [depends on whether appeal is from county court or justice of the peace court]). Exclusive mental health, estate, civil appeals, miscellaneous civil jurisdiction.
- Exclusive domestic relations jurisdiction.
- Exclusive felony, criminal appeals jurisdiction.
- Exclusive juvenile jurisdiction.

Jury trials.

Court of general jurisdiction

JUSTICE OF THE PEACE COURT
(7 courts in 7 counties)

7 justices of the peace (part-time)

CSP case types:

- Tort, contract, real property rights ($0/$3,000), small claims ($3,000).
- Misdemeanor, DWI/DUI.
- Moving traffic, parking, miscellaneous traffic/ other violation.
- Preliminary hearings.

Jury trials except in small claims.

MUNICIPAL COURT (79 courts)

2 judges (full-time), 73 judges (part-time)

CSP case types:

- DWI/DUI.
- Moving traffic, parking, miscellaneous traffic. Exclusive ordinance violation jurisdiction.

Jury trials.

Courts of limited jurisdiction

CIRCUIT COURT* (16 courts in 9 circuits)

22 judges

CSP case types:

- Tort, contract, real property rights ($0/$7,000), small claims ($3,000).
- Misdemeanor, DWI/DUI, domestic violence.
- Moving traffic, parking, miscellaneous traffic violation.
- Preliminary hearings.

Jury trials except in small claims.

* County Courts were renamed Circuit Courts.

L

2003 CHANGES IN ESTATE AND GIFT TAX RATES

ESTATE TAX EXCLUSION AMOUNTS INCREASED

In 2003, the Internal Revenue Service increased tax exclusion amounts on a sliding scale through 2011. Currently, an estate tax return for a U.S. citizen needs to be filed only if the gross estate exceeds the applicable exclusion amount for the year of death, as listed below.

Year	Exclusion Amount
2003	$1,000,000
2004 and 2005	$1,500,000
2006, 2007, 2008	$2,000,000
2009	$3,500,000
2010	No estate tax
2011	$1,000,000

ANNUAL EXCLUSION FOR GIFTS INCREASED

The annual exclusion for gifts made to spouses who are not U.S. citizens increased to $112,000.

MAXIMUM ESTATE AND GIFT TAX RATES REDUCED

For estates of decedents dying, and gifts made, after 2002, the maximum rate for the estate tax and gift tax is as follows:

Year	Maximum Tax Rate
2003	49%
2004	48
2005	47
2006	46
2007, 2008, 2009	45

CREDIT FOR STATE DEATH TAXES REDUCED

For estates of decedents dying in 2003, the credit allowed for state death taxes is limited to 50 percent of the amount that would otherwise be allowed. For estates of decedents dying in 2004, the credit will be limited to 25 percent. For estates of decedents dying after 2004, the state death tax credit will be replaced with a deduction for state death taxes.

abatement A proportional diminution or reduction of monetary inheritances, when there are not sufficient funds to pay them in full.

ademption The act by which the testator makes a gift during his or her lifetime of a legacy specified in his or her will.

administrator A male person or institution appointed by the court, usually when there is no will, to act on behalf of the deceased person in connection with the administration of a decedent's estate. The female equivalent is called an *administratrix*. Also called a personal representative or PA.

administrator with will annexed (or administrator CTA) An administrator appointed by the court to act on behalf of the estate of a deceased person who left a will, in the event no nominated executor is willing or able to act.

administration unnecessary Small estate where the value of the assets are below limits requiring a probate. There is no probate of any kind.

affidavit A written statement or affirmation made under penalty of perjury, and which requires notarization.

ancillary administration An administration of a decedent's property located in a state other than the state of the decedent's domicile.

annuity A sum of money payable yearly, at other regular intervals, or as a lump sum on a designated date in the future.

appreciated property Property, such a real estate or stock, that has increased in value.

assets All money and real and personal property owned by an individual or organization.

attorney of record The attorney handling probate of the estate on behalf of the deceased.

bequest To give or leave assets to another individual or an organization by means of a will.

beneficiary An individual or corporation that receives the benefits of a transaction, such as the beneficiary of a life insurance policy, a trust, or the terms of a will.

charitable gift annuity Typically an agreement in which an individual or organization transfers cash or other assets to a charitable organization in exchange for its promise to pay that individual or organization an annuity for life or for a stipulated period.

charitable trust A trust having a charitable organization as its beneficiary.

claimant The individual who administers a small estate.

codicil An addition to a will. The codicil may modify, add to, subtract from, qualify, alter, or revoke provisions in the will. The codicil is a separate document, signed with the same legal formalities as the will. It can be changed, revoked, or cancelled at any time.

community property Real or personal property that is owned in common by husband and wife as a kind of marital partnership. A joint checking account is the simplest example. Either spouse has management and control of community real and personal property; however, both spouses must join in a transfer of ownership; or in a lease for more than one year of community real property; or in a gift of community personal property. All property acquired during marriage from earnings, and the earnings themselves, are community property. Property acquired by gift or inheritance is separate property, not community property.

conservator The individual, institution, or corporation that legally provides care and management of an individual, property, or both for an adult who is unable to provide for his or her personal needs, or who is substantially unable to manage his or her financial affairs. Limited conservatorships may be established for developmentally disabled adults.

contingent beneficiary One to whom distribution of assets is dependent on the occurrence of an event.

corporate fiduciary An institution that acts for the benefit of an individual or other legal entity. One example is a bank acting as a trustee for an individual, or managing the retirement accounts of an individual.

cost basis The original value of an asset, such as a stock, before its appreciation or depreciation.

credit estate tax A state tax assessed against the assets of someone who has died. It applies only to estates that are required to pay federal estate taxes. The estate does not pay double taxes. Instead, by paying a credit estate tax, it "rebates" part of the federal estate tax back to the state.

creditor The individual or organization to whom a monetary debt is due.

decedent An individual who has died and has left property to be administered.

declaration A written statement that becomes a legal document, made under penalty of perjury.

devisees and legatees Individuals named by a decedent in his or her will. A bequest or *devise* generally refers to real property; a *legacy* refers to money or personal property.

disclaimer A refusal to accept a designated gift made in a prescribed manner and at a prescribed time.

distributee An individual who inherits; an heir.

domicile The specific location of an individual's permanent residence, which determines, for many purposes, the laws that will govern his or her affairs. An individual may have many residences, but he or she can only have one domicile. The *domiciliary proceeding* is that held in the jurisdiction of the decedent's domicile.

donee An individual or organization that receives a gift from another.

donor An individual or organization that makes a gift to another.

durable power of attorney A written legal document that empowers an individual to designate another individual to act on his or her behalf, even in the event that individual becomes disabled or incapacitated.

escheat The term that describes the reversion of property to the state in the event an individual dies leaving no valid will and no legally identified heirs surviving him or her.

estate taxes, federal Death taxes imposed by the federal government on the transfer of assets from a decedent to another individual or to an organization in the event of death.

entire estate Usually refers to the transfer of all the decedent's property to the surviving spouse.

executor A male individual or corporation appointed by the terms of a decedent's will to manage disposition of the decedent's property after his or her death. A female is referred to as an *executrix*. Also called a *personal representative*.

federal estate tax A federal death tax assessed against the assets of a person who has died, if the value of those assets exceeds certain prescribed dollar limits (see Appendix I).

ex parte A judicial proceeding granted without notice, and not held in open court.

fiduciary Relating to assigned financial responsibility; also, an individual or institution charged with a high degree of care who acts on behalf of another. Executors and trustees are fiduciaries.

foreign will The will of any decedent domiciled outside the state in which the disposition of the estate is being handled.

Gift Tax Annual Exclusion The federal law that enables a donor to exclude an amount of gifts from taxation each year, if the gifts are a) of a present interest, and b) to a specific individual. A *present interest gift* is one that the donee has an immediate unrestricted right of use, benefit, and enjoyment. The federal amount is currently $11,000 per donor per donee per year.

gift and inheritance exemptions The federal government allows each donor or beneficiary an exemption, the amount of which depends on the donee's relationship to the donor. In some states, gift and inheritance taxes are now unified, so that individual exemptions are only available one time. Use of assets during the lifetime of the donor eliminates their availability for inheritance tax purposes.

grantor The individual or corporation that makes a grant (transfer) of property to another individual, such as the grantor of a trust or the grantor of a deed of property.

gross estate The total property and other assets held by an individual as defined for federal and/or state estate tax purposes.

guardian The individual or corporation that legally maintains care and management of the person, property, or both of a minor child, or one who has been incapacitated.

heir The individual who inherits property under state law.

Homestead Exemption The body of state laws that enables the head of a family to keep that family's primary residence safe from creditors, or exempts a portion of that home's assessed value from state or county taxes.

inheritance taxes Taxes imposed at rates determined by the relationship to the decedent, on the individual who receives property according to the terms of the will or a judgment.

interest Any right or ownership in property.

intestate Describes an individual who dies leaving no will.

***inter vivos* trust** A living trust; literally, a trust created "between the living." The grantor or trustor is still alive. An *inter vivos* trust can be revocable or irrevocable.

irrevocable trust A trust the terms and provisions of which cannot be changed, modified, altered, amended, or revoked.

issue Progeny, offspring, lineal descendents. A testator or trustor can define issue to include or exclude adopted children. The word *descendents* is now commonly used to describe issue.

inventory A detailed accounting required by the court to settle most estates, to include all articles of property with their estimated value.

joint tenancy A form of property ownership by two or more individuals, often designated as "joint tenants with right of survivorship." Joint tenants always own equal parts of joint tenancy property. When a joint tenant dies, his or her interest in the property automatically goes to the surviving joint tenant(s).

letters: testamentary or administration Court documents obtained by personal representatives that confirm their authority to settle a decedent's estate.

life estate An interest in property, the term of which is measured by the life of its owner.

life insurance trust A trust that has the proceeds of an individual's life insurance policy as its principal.

life tenant The individual who receives the benefits from real or personal property during his or her lifetime only; the benefits cease with his or her death and cannot be passed on to others.

living will A legal document directing that the maker's or signer's life is not to be artificially supported in the event of a terminal illness or accident.

marital deduction A deduction allowing for the unlimited transfer of any and all property from one spouse to the other, generally free of estate and gift taxes.

minor An individual under the age of legal competence.

nonprobate assets Some states that recognize community property allow half of the value, or all of the value, of community property to be deducted from the probate estate when one spouse dies. For example, with join tenancy property, the house of residence is considered "outside of the probate" and not part of the probated assets.

notice Information about certain facts. For example, the personal representative is usually responsible for informing—by serving notices on—all parties interested in opening the estate of the deceased for probate.

order A written command or direction by a judge or court clerk. An order may outlive a decision of the court, direct or forbid an action, or be the final decision of the court.

personal property All property other than land and its fixtures.

personal representative A common term for an executor or executrix, an administrator or administrix.

power of appointment The actual power of legal authority given by the trust or will of one individual, the *donor* of the power, to a second individual, the *donee,* of the power, which enables the second individual to designate the manner of disposing of the property. A power of appointment may be general or special, as defined here:

- *General power* enables the donee to designate himself or herself, his or her creditors, the creditors of the estate, or any other person, as owner of the subject property.
- *Special power* limits the donee as to the individuals to whom he or she can designate as owners of the property over which he or she has power of appointment. Limitation of appointment can be very specific—e.g., to a group consisting only of the donee's children—but can never be the donee, his or her estate, creditors, or the creditors of the estate, because this would defeat the purpose of the special power—namely, to keep the appointive property from being taxed in the estate of the donee at his or her death.

power of attorney A written legal document that gives an individual the authority to act on behalf of another.

pour-over will A will that provides for the transfer, after or during the probate court proceedings, of all or part of the net assets of a decedent's probate estate from the executor's control to the control of a trustee who is in charge of a trust that was in existence immediately before the death of the deceased person (*inter vivos* trust).

pretermitted heir One who would normally be beneficiary of the decedent, but who is not mentioned in the will.

probate The legal process of establishing the validity or proof of a deceased person's last will and testament. Commonly used to mean the entire process and procedure for settling an estate.

probate administration The legal process whereby a probate court supervises the marshalling of a deceased persons debts and taxes, and orders the property to be distributed according to the decedent's will, or in its absence, to the deceased person's heirs. The probate court has jurisdiction over the personal representative and the deceased person's assets.

quasi-community property In California only, that property defined in Probate Code §201.5 as property acquired by a decedent while living outside California, which, if acquired in California, would have been community property. For federal estate tax purposes, quasi-community property is treated like separate property.

real property Land and/or property permanently affixed to land.

remainder interest An ownership interest in property that will become a present interest after the present owner or life tenant has received all the property benefits to which he or she is entitled.

residue The remaining part of a decedent's estate after the payments of debts and legacies. Also called *residuary estate.*

resident agent An individual living in a state who is authorized to accept legal documents on behalf of another.

residuary beneficiary One to whom all or part of the residue is distributed.

residuary estate That portion of an estate that remains after all bequests have been made and all claims have been satisfied. Also called *residue.*

reversionary interest An ownership interest in property that returns to the original owner when the intervening interest expires.

revocable trust A trust the terms and provisions of which can be changed, modified, altered, amended, or revoked.

right of representation A method of distribution, sometimes referred to as *per stirpes,* whereby the share of distribution of a deceased beneficiary is divided equally among his or her children.

separate property A category of property between husband and wife that is not community property or quasi-community property, but that is owned separately and solely by the husband or wife.

settlor Another term for grantor or the trustor of a trust; i.e., the individual who "settles" the assets into a trust.

small estate administration A simplified process for probating estates that are less than the specified dollar limit set by state laws.

statutory Established by legislative law.

summary administration A simple way of distributing assets. It usually needs a notice of administration to be given to all interested parties and an inventory filed with the court.

supervised Court intervention and required approval of all activity and actions.

tenancy by the entirety A form of spousal ownership in which the property is equally shared and automatically transferred to the surviving spouse. While both spouses are living, ownership of the property can only be altered by divorce or mutual agreement.

tenancy in common A form of holding title to real or personal property by two or more persons. Because there is no right of survivorship, the legal relationships and results are very different from joint tenancy. Tenants in common need not hold equal interests, and on the death of a tenant in common, his or her interests will pass by will or according to the laws of intestate succession.

testamentary trust A trust that comes into being only as a result of the death of a person whose will provides for the creation of the trust after his or her death; hence, the term *testamentary*. Once in existence, this trust is irrevocable.

testate Describes an individual who dies leaving a will.

testator The individual who signs the will that disposes of his or her property. A female signer is called a *testatrix*, but common practice uses "testator" to refer to either gender.

Totten trust A form of irrevocable trust, usually a bank account, which allows distribution to the beneficiary upon the death of the trustee, without the need for probate on the asset. Example: Jim Smith as trustee for Gloria Smith.

trust A legal entity established either during a trustor's lifetime (*inter vivos*) or at his or her death (testamentary). The trust is governed by the terms set forth in the trust documents. A trust must have a trustee, a beneficiary, and a *corpus*, or property subject to the trust.

trustee The individual, institution, or other organization that, in a trust, maintains bare legal title to the assets and has the power given in the trust to carry out the wishes of the person or persons who created the trust. The trustee has a fiduciary obligation to the trust's beneficiaries, enforceable in court if not carried out. The trustee is subject to strict regulation. Although he or she has legal title for convenience, the beneficial or equitable title is in fact owned by the beneficiaries. When there is more than one trustee, the trustees are called cotrustees.

trustor The individual or individuals who establish a trust. There can be more than one trustor.

Uniform Gifts to Minors Act A law that permits an individual ("donor") to register stock, bank accounts, or insurance in the name of another adult ("custodian") for the benefit of one who at the time is a minor ("beneficiary"), without preparing a formal trust document. In effect, the trust document has been written into the law. In so doing, the donor makes an irrevocable gift of the property to the minor, but the custodian holds, invests, reinvests, and applies the property for the benefit of the minor until his or her majority, at which time the property is turned over to the minor. This is a simple, inexpensive way to make small gifts to a minor.

unified credit A federal tax credit that offsets gift tax and estate tax liability. For gift tax purposes, the unified credit remains at $345,000 through 2009, which is equivalent to an applicable exclusion amount of $1 million. For estate tax purposes, the unified credit is gradually being increased from $345,000 in 2003 to $1,455,800 in 2009. This is the equivalent to an applicable exclusion amount of $1.5 million in 2004 and 2005, to $3.5 million in 2009. This tax expires completely in 2010. In 2011, it reverts to $1 million.

unsupervised Without court intervention or approval for any actions or activity.

will A document prepared and executed by a person with the formality required by the laws of the state of his or her domicile at the time. The will is intended to govern and direct the disposition of his or her estate and settlement of his or her legal affairs at the time of death, and has no legal effect until his or her death. If the document is entirely in the person's own handwriting, it is called a *holographic will*. If a will is typed, it is called a *witnessed* will because the signing of it generally requires two or more witnesses to testify later, if necessary, that the execution was not procured by fraud, duress, or misrepresentation.

will contest The challenge of a will by a person who believes the will is unfair or that one or more of its provisions does not accurately reflect how the deceased person wanted his or her property distributed.

witness An individual who is present at an occurrence or at the signing of a document such as a will.

Share the message!

Bulk discounts
Discounts start at only 10 copies and range from 30% to 55% off
retail price based on quantity.

Custom publishing
Private label a cover with your organization's name and logo.
Or, tailor information to your needs with a custom pamphlet
that highlights specific chapters.

Ancillaries
Workshop outlines, videos, and other products are available on
select titles.

Dynamic speakers
Engaging authors are available to share their expertise and insight
at your event.

**Call Dearborn Trade Special Sales at
1-800-621-9621, ext. 4444,
or e-mail trade@dearborn.com**